The Limits of a Catholic Spirit

The Limits of a Catholic Spirit

JOHN WESLEY, METHODISM, AND CATHOLICISM

⤴

Kelly Diehl Yates

Foreword by Howard A. Snyder

☙PICKWICK *Publications* · Eugene, Oregon

THE LIMITS OF A CATHOLIC SPIRIT
John Wesley, Methodism, and Catholicism

Pickwick Publications
An Imprint of Wipf and Stock Publishers
199 W. 8th Ave., Suite 3
Eugene, OR 97401

www.wipfandstock.com

PAPERBACK ISBN: 978-1-7252-6947-7
HARDCOVER ISBN: 978-1-7252-6948-4
EBOOK ISBN: 978-1-7252-6949-1

Cataloguing-in-Publication data:

Names: Yates, Kelly Diehl, author. | Snyder, Howard A., foreword.
Title: The limits of a catholic spirit : John Wesley, Methodism, and Catholicism / Kelly Diehl Yates.
Description: Eugene, OR : Pickwick Publications, 2021 | Includes bibliographical references and index.
Identifiers: ISBN 978-1-7252-6947-7 (paperback) | ISBN 978-1-7252-6948-4 (hardcover) | ISBN 978-1-7252-6949-1 (ebook)
Subjects: LCSH: Wesley, John, 1703–1791. | Methodist Church. | Catholic Church.
Classification: BX8495.W5 .Y31 2021 (print) | BX8495.W5 .Y31 (ebook)

For Chris, with all my love

Contents

Foreword

I AM PLEASED TO recommend *The Limits of a Catholic Spirit: John Wesley, Methodism, and Catholicism*, by Kelly Diehl Yates. Based on thorough research, this comprehensive study shows how John Wesley during a turbulent time of virulent anti-Catholicism in Great Britain sought to promote *Catholic Spirit*, as Wesley titled it in a notable sermon on the topic. Dr. Yates shows however that the issues are complex; that in important ways there were "limits" to Wesley's Catholic spirit.

In the eighteenth century, negative attitudes toward Roman Catholics were strong even among Wesley's own Methodist people, most of whom were still members of the Church of England. While Wesley wanted to promote *Catholic Spirit* among his followers, Yates shows from his own writings that Wesley himself was in key respects anti-Catholic in some of his opinions and sentiments.

Certainly Wesley never foresaw any sort of union or open communion between Catholics and Protestants. Yates explores the complexity of Wesley's ideas, which necessarily involved not just faith and religious practice but also politics, strong sentiments regarding the Jesuits, and Wesley's extensive personal experiences in Ireland.

Like many others, Wesley had his own concerns about the threat posed by "popery," "papism," or "Romanism." One of the sharp ironies of the story is that Wesley's unique role as head of the Methodist movement, his stress on good works, and his emphasis on confession in Methodist band meetings, led critics to charge Wesley himself with "papism" and "Jesuitism." In his own spiritual journey, Wesley had himself of course benefited from (and often cited) Catholic writers from earlier generations.

Wesley's central theme was love for God and for all people. This was holiness, Christian perfection. Yates helpfully shows how in Wesley's own long life and writings, this focus on love inevitably clashed with Wesley's

own anti-Catholicism—a reality which Wesley himself sought to over-
come in himself and his Methodist people. Wesley strove to embody the
love of God toward all, including Roman Catholics, while also explaining
in some detail the points where he specifically disagreed with official Roman Catholic teachings, for example on the primacy of the pope and the
veneration of saints and images.

Yates fully surveys all that Wesley wrote on Roman Catholicism and
related topics over the sixty-some years of his active ministry. She nar-
rates as well Wesley's actions and his relationships with Roman Catholics,
especially in Ireland. Her book provides an important chapter in our understanding of John Wesley today by exploring a topic that until now has
received no truly in-depth treatment in Wesley studies.

— Howard A. Snyder, author, *The Radical Wesley and Patterns for
Church Renewal*; International Representative, Manchester Wesley
Research Centre

Acknowledgments

THIS BOOK IS A revision of my PhD thesis, which was completed through the University of Manchester and carried out at Nazarene Theological College.

First and foremost, I would like to express my appreciation to Geordan Hammond, whose excellent supervision has greatly contributed to this thesis. Next I would like to thank Peter Nockles, whose expertise has guided my writing. This research was made possible in part by a postgraduate assistantship from Manchester Wesley Research Centre, and for this I would like to thank the board, including Howard Snyder, visiting director. Additionally, this work has been enhanced by conversations with Henry Rack, who answered endless questions about Wesley and Jacobitism over tea and biscuits. Likewise, Randy Maddox has answered all my emails and provided key Wesley letters. This work has benefited from Timothy Crutcher who introduced me to rigorous academic study, and Brint Montgomery, who taught me to write philosophically, held me accountable to my studies, and gave me the "PhD lecture" when I started. I am indebted to the editors at Pickwick Publications.

To the following I owe a debt of gratitude:

Stephen Gunter, in whose class I first decided to pursue a PhD.

Thomas Noble and Kent Brower who offered insight, especially when I was in Kansas City.

Carla Sunberg, who encouraged me to apply and stick with it.

Hal Cauthron, who was the first to see a teacher within me.

Judith Schwanz, who encouraged me to apply for the PhD.

Rhonda Crutcher, who encouraged me.

Lori Cable, who offered friendship and a listening ear.

Hunter Cummings, who proofread the entire thesis and offered encouragement.

Andrew Pottenger, who took pictures of Wesley letters and sent them to me.

Joel Houston, for reading the entire thesis and providing helpful comments.

Isaac Hopper, Steve Johnson, Tammie Grimm, who encouraged me.

Julianne, Lindy, Seth, Richard, Gift, Nabil, Samantha, Mathieu, and Jacob, I could not have done this without you.

Daniel Chesney, Emma Carley, and Annette Gunter, who performed magic with Interlibrary Loans.

Katie King and Mark Winslow, who provided office space.

Helen Stocker, librarian at Nazarene Theological College library, who never tired of sending me scans.

Gareth Lloyd and the staff at the John Rylands Library, Manchester.

Robin Roddie at the Methodist Archives in Belfast.

The staff at the National Archives, London.

My husband Chris, who always sees more in me than I do in myself.

My daughters Brianna (who proofread) and Skyler, who put up with more information about Wesley than they ever wanted to know.

My parents, Steven and Paula Diehl, and my in-laws, Danny and Sandra Yates who provided encouragement.

Abbreviations

Names

CW   Charles Wesley

GW   George Whitefield

JW   John Wesley

Books

JWJ   John Wesley's published *Journal* in *Works.*

MJCW   *The Manuscript Journal of the Reverend Charles Wesley, M.A.* Edited by S. T. Kimbrough Jr. and Kenneth C. G. Newport. 2 vols. Nashville: Kingswood, 2007.

ODNB   *Oxford Dictionary of National Biography.* Edited by H. C. G. Matthew and Brian Harrison. 60 vols. Online edition. Oxford: Oxford University Press, 2004.

Telford   *The Letters of the Rev. John Wesley, A.M.* Edited by John Telford. 8 vols. London: Epworth, 1931.

Works   *The Works of John Wesley.* Edited by Frank Baker et al. Bicentennial Ed. Oxford: Clarendon, 1975–83.

Works (Jackson)   *The Works of John Wesley.* Edited by Thomas Jackson. 14 vols. Kansas City: Beacon Hill, 1978.

Journals

AM   *The Arminian Magazine, For the Years 1778–91. Consisting of Extracts and Original Treatises on Redemption.* Edited by John Wesley.

PWHS	*Proceedings of the Wesley Historical Society.*
WTJ	*Wesleyan Theological Journal.*

Archives

MARC	Methodist Archives and Research Centre, The John Rylands Library, Manchester.
TNA	The National Archives of the United Kingdom, London.

Other

Acts of Parliament	(for example) I Will & Mary, c. 18
"Forty-five"	The Second Jacobite Rebellion of 1745–1746
PA	Protestant Association

1

Introduction

IN HIS STUDY OF anti-Catholicism in eighteenth-century England, Colin Haydon (1993) demonstrated that "Early Methodism showed a powerful dislike of Popery"; therefore, it can be misleading to view John Wesley (1703–1791) as "foreshadowing ecumenical ideas, brilliantly combining Protestant and Catholic traditions in his writings."[1] David Chapman (2004) rightly warned: "Regrettable as Wesley's anti-Catholicism now appears in the light of the ecumenical movement, it would be anachronistic to judge him by modern standards."[2] However, some scholarship has portrayed Wesley as an ecumenical pioneer with his sermon *Catholic Spirit* (1748) and his *Letter to a Roman Catholic* (1749) exemplified as nearly magical twin documents that could usher Methodists and Catholics into a utopian ecumenical relationship.[3] Yet while lauding Wesley for his ecumenical spirit, most have overlooked the fact that three years after

---

1. Haydon, *Anti-Catholicism*, 63, and 17. In connection with the second quotation, Haydon referenced Burrows, "Wesley the Catholic," 54–66.

2. Chapman, *In Search*, 42.

3. Baker, *John Wesley*, 124. This book will use the date 1748 for the writing of a *Catholic Spirit* based upon Baker's statement that it was when Wesley first preached the sermon rather than the 1750 date commonly used as the date it was first printed in *Sermons on Several Occasions*, vol. 3. For other printings, see JW, *Catholick Spirit: A Sermon on 2 Kings x. 15*. London: Cock, 1755; Bristol: Pine, 1770; London: New Chapel, 1789. The sermon is reprinted in *Works*, 2:81–95. When Wesley's sermon is named, it will be capitalized and italicized. When the idea of catholic spirit is referenced, it will be in lower case with no quotations. JW, *Letter to a Roman Catholic*; *Works* (Jackson), 10:80–86. For examples of *Catholic Spirit* and *Letter to a Roman Catholic* as twin ecumenical documents, see Outler, *John Wesley*, 493; Baker, *John Wesley*, 126; and Tyson, *The Way*, 185–87.

writing *Letter to a Roman Catholic,* Wesley published *A Short Method of Converting all the Roman Catholicks in the Kingdom of Ireland: Humbly Proposed to the Bishops and Clergy of this Kingdom* (1752) with little evidence of the eirenical approach of the *Letter.*[4]

Henry Rack proposed that "Roman Catholicism [pertaining to Wesley] needs more study."[5] This book is written on the basis that a historical investigation of Wesley and Catholicism can examine the limits to which John Wesley, as an evangelical Protestant in a society in which anti-Catholicism was prevalent, was able to put into practice his self-professed ideal of a catholic spirit.

This book argues that although he expressed principles for religious tolerance towards British Protestants in his sermon, *Catholic Spirit,* Wesley never expected these principles to bring about unity between Protestants and Catholics in theology or politics. Furthermore, this study seeks to bridge the gap in Wesley studies concerning Wesley and Catholicism, as a book-length historical study of Wesley and Catholicism has yet to be written, especially regarding Jacobitism, his time in Ireland, Jesuitism, and his reaction to the Catholic Relief Act of 1778.

From the first accusation of monasticism at Oxford, to the Gordon Riots of 1780, allegations and events forced Wesley to confront what many Georgian Britons called the evils of Popery. "Wesley may have yearned for peace, but he often found himself embroiled in controversy."[6] He once observed: "When I say, 'I have no time to write largely in controversy,' I mean this. Every hour I have is employed more [than in writing in controversy] to the glory of God."[7] "This may be one of the reasons he wrote much of his corpus in pragmatic response to his opponents, even though he claimed he hated writing 'controversially.'"[8] Moreover, it cannot be denied that Wesley wrote far more about the dangers of "Popery" than about the hope of Protestants and Catholics living in harmony.[9]

4. For example: Schwenk, *Catholic Spirit,* 3; Crutcher, *John Wesley,* 168–69; and Burrows, "Wesley the Catholic," 54–66.

5. Rack, *Reasonable Enthusiast,* 558.

6. Yates, "'Perhaps He Cannot Know,'" 331.

7. JW to Samuel Furley, December 9, 1760, *Works,* 27:224.

8. Yates, "'Perhaps He Cannot Know,'" 331–32.

9. For example: *A Short Method of Converting all the Roman Catholicks in the Kingdom of Ireland. Humbly Proposed to the Bishops and Clergy of this Kingdom;* and *The Advantage of the Members of the Church of England over the Members of the Church of Rome.*

Wesley's contemporaries described his mindset towards Catholicism in various ways. Expressing concern for her brother's possible "papism," his sister, Emilia (1692–1771) reproached him for "Romish errors," imploring him to set aside his beliefs in "auricular confession and bodily austerities."[10] Furthermore, Bishop George Lavington (1684–1762) assumed that Wesley's alleged "enthusiasm" led to "papism" and "Jesuitism."[11] Wesley wrote to Thomas Church (1707–1756), a Church of England clergyman who had accused him of "abandoning the true church for Rome," saying: "Some of you have said, that there is no *true church* but yours; yea, that there are no *true Christians* out of it . . . They are exceeding great mistakes [in the Church of Rome], yet in as great mistakes have holy men lived and died."[12] Mark Massa suggested that this phrase in the letter to Church was the first literary step Wesley made on his way to composing *Catholic Spirit*.[13] However, he had already taken steps in that direction in the preface to his first published *Journal*, and in *The Character of a Methodist* (1742).[14]

In *Character of a Methodist*, Wesley indicated the importance of Christian love: "a Methodist is one who has 'the love of God shed abroad in his heart by the Holy Ghost given unto him.'"[15] Further, Wesley said: "this commandment is written in his [the Methodist's] heart, that 'he who loveth God, loves his brother also.' And he accordingly "loves his neighbour as himself;" he loves every man as his own soul."[16] The Methodists wanted to do the will of God, including doing good "unto neighbours, and strangers, friends, and enemies."[17] It was loving God and loving others, including enemies that were "the *principles* and *practices* of our sect; these are the *marks* of a true Methodist."[18] He desired that the Methodists have no division. He quoted 2 Kgs 10:15, the verse he used for the text of *Catholic Spirit*: "'Is thy heart right, as my heart is with thine?' I ask

---

10. Emilia (Wesley) Harper to JW, June 17, 1741, MARC DDwf 6/11, *Works*, 26:63.

11. [Lavington], *Enthusiasm*, 8, 31–33.

12. JW, *An Answer to Mr. Church*, 6.

13. Massa, "The Catholic Wesley," 40.

14. See *JWJ* [Preface], October [19], 1732, *Works*, 18:127–28; and JW, *The Character of a Methodist*, *Works*, 9:32–46.

15. JW, *The Character of a Methodist*, *Works*, 9:35.

16. JW, *The Character of a Methodist*, *Works*, 9:37.

17. JW, *The Character of a Methodist*, *Works*, 9:41.

18. JW, *The Character of a Methodist*, *Works*, 9:41.

no farther question. 'If it be, give my thy hand.'"[19] Wesley worked hard to convince others, especially those who accused him of Dissent, that "from real Christians, or whatsoever denomination they be, we earnestly desire not to be distinguished at all. Nor from any who sincerely follow after what they know they have not attained."[20] Wesley expanded the principles outlined in *Character of a Methodist* when he wrote *Catholic Spirit* six years later.

Albert Outler reported that Wesley preached on the text used in *Catholic Spirit*, 2 Kgs 10:15, thrice: November 23, 1740, September 8, 1749, and November 3, 1749, although it is not certain the sermon preached was *Catholic Spirit* on each occasion.[21] He quoted or referred to 2 Kgs 10:15 at least eight other times in his publications.[22] After discussing loving one's neighbor in the sermon, Wesley argued that "there is a peculiar love which we owe to those who love God."[23] Peculiar, as defined by Samuel Johnson means, "not common to other things."[24] This "peculiar love" Wesley set out to define in the remainder of the sermon.

He believed that what prevented Christians from practicing "catholic love" and having an "external union" was "difference of opinions or modes of worship."[25] Wesley explored what it meant for one Christian's heart to be "right" with another Christian's heart.[26] In *Catholic Spirit*, Wesley said he would not "impose" his, that is the Church of England's, "mode of worship" on any other Christian. He believed that his mode was "primitive and apostolical;" and continued by asserting: "but my belief is no rule for another."[27] Further, he said in a letter to Baptist pastor Gilbert

---

19. JW, *The Character of a Methodist,Works*, 9:42. Wesley used variants of these two phrases in the following: *An Earnest Appeal to Men of Reason and Religion* (1743), *Works*, 11:73; *Farther Appeal to Men of Reason and Religion, Part II* (1745), *Works*, 11:237; *A Word to Methodist* (1748), *Works*, 9:243; "On Laying the Foundation of the New Chapel" (1777), *Works*, 3:592; "Hymn 486," in *A Collection of Hymns for the People Called Methodist* (1780), *Works*, 7:673; and *Thoughts upon a Late Phenomenon* (1788), *Works*, 9:537.

20. JW, *The Character of a Methodist, Works*, 9:42.

21. Outler, "Introduction to Sermon 39," *Works*, 2:80; see also Baker, *John Wesley*, 124.

22. See *Works*, 3:592; 7:673; 9:42, 243, 537; 11:73, 237; and 21:440.

23. JW, *Catholic Spirit, Works*, 2:81.

24. Johnson, *Dictionary*, s.v. "Peculiar."

25. JW, *Catholic Spirit, Works*, 2:82.

26. JW, *Catholic Spirit, Works*, 2:86.

27. JW, *Catholic Spirit, Works*, 2:86.

Boyce in 1750: "I do not conceive that unity in the outward modes of worship is *so* necessary among the children of God that they cannot be the children of God without it–although I once thought it was." In the same letter to Boyce, Wesley said that baptism was not necessary to salvation, "If it were, every Quaker must be damned, which I can in no wise believe."[28] Believing in Jesus Christ was the center of importance. Love had to be shown by works. If Christians could express: "thy heart is right, as my heart is with thy heart," then the two "right hearts" did not need the same opinions or modes of worship to "love alike."[29]

In the final words of *Catholic Spirit*, Wesley emphasized that a Christian steadfast in his or her religious principles embraces all people.[30] Thus, a person with the foundation of a catholic spirit could truly love others, especially other Christians. He described a person who has a catholic spirit near the end of the sermon:

> But while he is steadily fixed in his religious principles, in what he believes to be the truth as it is in Jesus; while he firmly adheres to that worship of God which he judges to be most acceptable in his sight; and while he is united by the tenderest and closest ties to one particular congregation; his heart is enlarged toward all mankind, those he knows and those he does not; he embraces with strong and cordial affection neighbours and strangers, friends and enemies. This is catholic or universal love. And he that has this is of a catholic spirit. For love alone gives the title to this character–catholic love is a catholic spirit.[31]

The methodology used in this research requires examination and analysis of Wesley's corpus. Attention is paid to Wesley's *Journals* and *Diaries*, and *Letters*, together with *Sermons*, pamphlets, essays, and Conference *Minutes*, with an occasional glance at *Hymns*. Charles Wesley's *Manuscript Journal*, *Letters*, and hymns are also examined. Letters written to and from other Methodists are analyzed as well. Unpublished letters and manuscripts held in the John Rylands Library, Manchester are also utilized. Eighteenth-century newspapers and periodicals offer important perspectives on the Methodist movement. Publications of

28. JW to Gilbert Boyce, May 22, 1750, *Works*, 26:425.
29. JW, *Catholic Spirit*, *Works*, 2:82.
30. JW, *Catholic Spirit*, *Works*, 2:94.
31. JW, *Catholic Spirit*, *Works*, 2:94.

Wesley's contemporaries, especially those who opposed the Methodists, also provide vital information concerning Wesley and Catholicism.

If Wesley did not intend *Catholic Spirit* to apply to relations between Protestants and Catholics, to whom did he aim the sermon? Did Wesley have a vision for all Protestants to be united? There are conflicting views on this. A clue is to be found in *Catholic Spirit*: "although a difference in opinions or modes of worship may prevent an entire external union, yet need it prevent our union in affection?"[32] Heitzenrater indicated that in 1748 Wesley "continued to envision a union of the various branches of the revival."[33] For instance, the Wesleys sought to work with George Whitefield (1714–1770) and the Countess of Huntingdon at a conference in August 1749, just months after Wesley wrote *Catholic Spirit*.[34] This came ten years after the publication of Wesley's sermon *Free Grace*, which deepened the disagreement between Wesley and Whitefield over predestination.[35] However, the fragile alliance between Wesley's societies and Whitefield's followers experienced further turmoil over the 1770 *Minutes* controversy, which will be discussed in chapter 5 of this book.[36]

Additionally, Wesley defined "toleration" as "sufferance, permission, allowance."[37] "Allowance" implies power. In relation to toleration, or allowance of Catholics to have political freedom in Britain, the Protestant government held the power. The King in Parliament was the only authority that could grant toleration. In promoting toleration among Protestants, Wesley was simply practicing what the Act of Toleration allowed.

In addition to writing *Catholic Spirit*, Wesley wrote *Letter to a Roman Catholic* from Dublin early in 1749 while on his third journey across Ireland.[38] It is significant that Wesley wrote *Catholic Spirit* and *Letter to a Roman Catholic* after controversies between the Methodists and Catholics. Although it seems that this letter offers friendship to Catholics, Wesley's continued attempt to convert Catholics after writing

32. JW, *Catholic Spirit*, *Works*, 2:82.

33. Heitzenrater, *Wesley and the People*, 191.

34. Heitzenrater, *Wesley and the People*, 191.

35. JW, *Free Grace*; see also *Works*, 3:54–63; and Hammond, "Whitefield, Wesley, and Revival Leadership," 104–13.

36. For the *Minutes* controversy see Coppedge, *John Wesley in Theological Debate*, 191–254; Gunter, *Limits*, 251–66; and Rack, *Reasonable Enthusiast*, 450–70.

37. JW, *The Complete English Dictionary*, s.v. "Toleration."

38. JW, *Letter to a Roman Catholic*, *Works* (Jackson), 10:81–85; Baker, *John Wesley*, 126.

it strongly suggests that his purpose was to convince Catholics to stop rioting and listen to Methodist preaching in order to experience evangelical conversion. In the *Letter*, he indicated doctrines on which Catholics and Protestants agree, avoiding points of contention.[39] Yet in 1753, Wesley wrote *Advantage of the Members of the Church of England over the Members of the Church of Rome* in which he outlined the Catholic doctrines that he viewed as mistaken. This book contends that *Catholic Spirit* and *Letter to a Roman Catholic* (1749) should be considered alongside Wesley's critical writings about Catholicism.[40] These critical writings will be introduced below in order of their publication. Each document will be discussed in detail later in the book.

Wesley's first attempt at outlining his perspective on Catholicism can be found in a 1735 letter to an unknown Catholic priest.[41] It is significant that he inserted this letter in his *Journal* after writing that he had been accused of being a Jesuit, and that he had been "(fundamentally) a Papist and knew it not" for ten years because he had preached "that *we are justified by works* or (to express the same thing a little more decently) by faith *and* works."[42] He called this letter his "serious judgment concerning the Church of Rome."[43] He outlined his contentions with the Catholic Church: the supremacy of the Bishop of Rome, and that they add to "those things written in the Book of Life."[44] Written at the beginning of Wesley's ministry, these issues remained his disagreements with Catholicism throughout his life.

One can perceive the themes that run through Wesley's writings on Catholicism by turning next to *A Word to a Protestant* (1746), in which Wesley wrote about the reasons he thought the Protestant Reformation had to take place: "The making void Christian faith, by holding that man may *merit* heaven by his own works, the overthrowing the love of God by *idolatry*; and the (overthrowing) the love of our neighbour by persecution."[45] Wesley wrote *A Word* during the "Forty-five" to clarify that Methodists were true Protestants.

---

39. JW, *Letter to a Roman Catholic*, *Works* (Jackson), 10:81–82.

40. JW, *Letter to a Roman Catholic*, *Works* (Jackson), 10:80–86.

41. Letter to a Roman Catholic priest, reprinted in *JWJ*, August 27, 1739, but probably written in 1735; see *Works*, 19:90–92 and 25:428–30.

42. *JWJ*, August 20, 1739, *Works*, 19:89.

43. *JWJ*, August 20, 1739, *Works*, 19:90.

44. *JWJ*, August 20, 1739, *Works*, 19:91–92.

45. *Works* (Jackson), 11:189; and Schwenk, *Catholic Spirit*, 78.

Wesley wrote *Catholic Spirit* and *Letter to a Roman Catholic* between the publication of *A Word to a Protestant* and *A Short Method of Converting all the Roman Catholicks in the Kingdom of Ireland. Humbly Proposed to the Bishops and Clergy of this Kingdom* (1752).[46] It was in this period that Methodists took their message to Ireland and encountered violent opposition from Catholics. Yet, this work has often been neglected when discussing Wesley in Ireland. The method Wesley proposed for conversion of Catholics was for the Church of Ireland clergy to live like the Apostles, for in Wesley's opinion the clergy did not live in accordance with the Scriptures.[47]

The Advantage of the Members of the Church of England over the Those of the Church of Rome (1753) was written by Wesley following continued opposition from Catholics in Ireland.[48] The advantages were first, that the "Church of England contends *for* the word of God and the Church of Rome *against* it."[49] Next, like his former documents on Catholicism, Wesley argued that the Church of England had the advantage because it taught that the Pope is not the successor of Peter, "because the primitive church knew of no such thing as a universal head." Further, the members of the Church of England were given liberty to learn of faith from the written word of God, if they gave themselves "to the guidance of the holy spirit."[50]

Three years after writing *Advantage*, Wesley published *A Roman Catechism: with a Reply Hereto* (1756).[51] This work was not original to Wesley as he abridged John Williams's (1633x6–1709) *A Catechism Truly Representing the Doctrines and Practices of the Church of Rome: With an Answer Thereunto* (1686).[52] Wesley changed little of Williams's work. He published *A Roman Catechism* to make clear his disagreements with Catholicism.

Later, the Catholic Bishop of Debra, Richard Challoner (1691–1781), printed an attack on Wesley and the Methodists called *Caveat against the Methodists* (1760). Wesley replied in a letter to the editor of *Lloyd's*

---

46. *Works* (Jackson), 10:129–32.

47. *Short Method, Works* (Jackson), 10:130.

48. *Works* (Jackson), 10:133–39.

49. *Short Method, Works* (Jackson), 10:135.

50. *Short Method, Works* (Jackson), 10:139.

51. *Works* (Jackson), 10:86–128.

52. (1633x6–1709) is the date given by the *ODNB*.

Evening Post.[53] Wesley identified *Caveat* as an attack on all Protestants, not just the Methodists, and "yet I am no more concerned to refute him than any other Protestant in England and still the less, as those arguments are refuted over and over in books which are still common among us."[54] He did not say to which books he referred, but it is probable that one of them was Williams's *Catechism* which he had recently abridged.

Wesley's final critical writings on Catholicism were written in the years 1779 to 1782, and all relate to Parliament's passing of the first act for Catholic relief.[55] These documents will be examined in chapter 6 of this book. Wesley published *Popery Calmly Considered* (1779), another abridgement of Williams's *Catechism*, shortly after the Catholic Relief Act of 1778 passed.[56] In *Popery*, Wesley highlighted the doctrines of the Catholic Church that he thought were most dangerous, for he believed that if Catholics were given political power, Protestants would suffer. His next publication concerning Catholicism was "Letter to the Printer of the *Public Advertiser*" (1780).[57] Wesley wrote this in reply to *An Appeal of the Protestant Association to the People of Great Britain* (1779). The Protestant Association had been formed in reaction to the Catholic Relief Act. In this letter, Wesley insisted he would have nothing to do with persecution, but he believed that "Catholics were increasing daily," and that this was a threat to Great Britain. These two documents attracted opposition to Wesley. One of the main critiques of this "Letter" was by Arthur O'Leary (1729–1802), an Irish Catholic priest. In response to O'Leary's reply, Wesley wrote "On Popery, Two Letters to the Editors of the *Freeman's Journal*," which he reprinted in the *Arminian Magazine* (1781).[58] In these letters, Wesley reiterated what he had said in *Popery Calmly Considered* and in "Letter to the Printer of the *Public Advertiser*:" giving "papists" political power would be dangerous to Great Britain.

---

53. Challoner, *Caveat against the Methodists.* For Wesley's reply, see November 22, 1760, *Works*, 27:215–16.

54. JW to *Lloyd's Evening Post*, November 22, 1760, *Works*, 27:217.

55. 18 George III c. 60.

56. *Works* (Jackson), 10:140–49.

57 See *General Evening Post* 7192, February 5–8, 1780; *London Chronicle* 3616, February 5–8, 1780; *Morning Chronicle and London Advertiser* 3344, February 5, 1780; *Whitehall Evening Post* 5279, February 5–8, 1780; *London Evening Post* 9022, February 3–5, 1780; and *AM* 4 (April 1781), 239–42. The broadsheet survives, see MARC MAW.G.339 [a]. For a reprint, see *Works* (Jackson), 10:159–61.

58. *AM* 4 (June 1781), 295–300; *Works* (Jackson), 10:162–73.

Wesley used "Romanist" exclusively with no reference to "Papist" or "Catholic" in his letter to a Catholic priest in 1735.[59] However, in *Letter to a Roman Catholic* (1749), he never used the word "Romanist," nor did he use the words "Popery" or "Papist."[60] Nonetheless, in *A Short Method of Converting all the Roman Catholics in the Kingdom of Ireland*, Wesley freely used the words "Papist" and "Popery."[61] He returned to using "Romanist," and used "Romish Church" and "Church of Rome" when writing *The Advantage of the Church of England over Those of the Church of Rome*. "Papist" and "Popery" are absent from *Advantage*.[62] In, "Letter to the Printer of the *Public Advertiser*," Wesley used "Romish" and "Roman Catholic," never "Papist" or "Popery," but *Popery Calmly Considered* referred to "Papists."[63] He did use the word "Popery" in *Catholic Spirit*, which is one of the reasons it will be argued that he did not intend *Catholic Spirit* to apply to Catholics.[64]

The Protestant Association organized a march in June 1780 to present the London petition they had gathered for the repeal of the Act. The gathering of this mob ultimately led to the Gordon Riots. Due to Wesley's advocacy for the repeal of the Act, he was accused of influencing the riots.[65] Among many responses to the allegations which will be discussed in chapter 5, Wesley published "A Disavowal of Persecuting Papists" (1782).[66]

In sum, these critical writings demonstrate that Wesley held a negative view of Catholicism all his life. They illustrate that *Letter to a Roman Catholic*, due to its eirenic nature, is indeed an exception in Wesley's writings on Catholicism. Furthermore, these documents provide evidence that Wesley never intended *Catholic Spirit* to bring about unity between Catholics and Protestants. Each of these publications will be examined in detail in this book.

59. *JWJ, Works*, 19:90–92.

60. *Works* (Jackson), 10:80–85.

61. *Works* (Jackson), 10:129–33.

62. *Works* (Jackson), 10:133–45.

63. *Works* (Jackson), 10:159–61; and 10:140–58.

64. JW, *Catholic Spirit, Works*, 2:86.

65. For the allegations that JW influenced the Gordon Riots, see Husenbeth, *Life of Milner,* 21; Romilly, *Memoirs of Romilly,* 1:84; Barnard, *Life of Challoner,* 135; and John Whittingham to JW, *Morning Chronicle and London Advertiser* 3500, August 5, 1780.

66. *Works* (Jackson), 10:173–74.

Wesley's life nearly spanned the entire eighteenth century. At the time of his birth, France was a threat to European Protestantism, and Jacobitism threatened the Protestant monarchy in Great Britain. The latter came close to home, as his parents disagreed about Jacobitism. Yet Wesley lived to see Jacobitism diminished and Jesuitism dissolved. Even though he saw Catholicism's power reduced over the course of his life, this concern about the political influence of Catholicism on Britain did not diminish. From the writing of his letter to a Catholic priest in 1735 to the publication of *Popery Calmly Considered* in 1779, his views remained steadfast.[67] This quotation from "Letter to the Printer of the *Public Advertiser*" demonstrates his concern: "Therefore, they [Catholics] ought not to be tolerated by any Government, Protestant, Mahometan, or Pagan."[68] His entire life, he strongly believed Catholicism was a real threat not only to the well-being of his beloved Great Britain, but to other countries as well.

The purpose of the Methodist movement, according to Wesley, was "to reform the nation, more particularly the church, and to spread Christian holiness over the land."[69] Upon reading *Letter to a Roman Catholic*, one might perceive that Wesley thought it possible for Methodists to work with Catholics for the spreading of Christian holiness across the land. However, Wesley's answer was clear: the only way anyone can spread Christian holiness is to first experience the New Birth. Catholics could experience the New Birth, yet were they still Catholics once they experienced it? This answer is not clear in Wesley's writings, and chapter 4 will wrestle with this issue. Nonetheless, Wesley's letter to his nephew Samuel, Charles Wesley's son, who had converted to Catholicism, provides a vital clue concerning Wesley's attitude towards the Catholic Church:

> Whether of this church or that I care not; you may be saved in either, or damned in either: but I fear you are not born again, and except you be born again you cannot see the kingdom of God. You believe the Church of Rome is right. What then? If you are not born of God, *you* are of *no Church*. Whether [Robert] Bellarmine [1542–1621] or [Martin] Luther [1483–1546] be right, you are certainly wrong, if you are not born of the Spirit,

67. Letter to a Roman Catholic priest, *Works*, 19:90–92; and JW, *Popery Calmly Considered*, *Works* (Jackson), 10:140–49.

68. *Works* (Jackson), 10:160.

69. *The Large Minutes A and B*, *Works*, 10:845.

if you are not renewed in the spirit of your mind in the likeness
of Him that created you.[70]

It can be safely inferred then, that he regarded the New Birth or evangelical conversion, as the only way to "see the kingdom of God." In some
churches, it was easier than others to encounter the Spirit which leads
to conviction of sin which in turn may lead to the New Birth. It was not
that Wesley thought that no one could experience the New Birth in a
Catholic Church, but that it would be more difficult than if they were in
a Protestant one.

This book demonstrates that in spite of the argument of *Letter to a
Roman Catholic* where Wesley appealed to Catholics to love Methodists,
his purpose in writing that plea was not to bring Methodists and
Catholics to a working relationship. It should be emphasized that Wesley
never encouraged physical persecution of Catholics.[71] However, perhaps
he believed that some Catholics were able to show love. For instance,
Charles Wesley (1707–1788) mentioned friendly Catholics in Ireland,
but John Wesley thought most of them were so beguiled by their priests
and bishops that they would always choose the authority of the church
over compassion.[72]

The rise of mass publishing in the eighteenth century provided op-
portunities for political and religious pamphlet wars about the "evils of
Popery."[73] Many anti-Methodist publications emerged during Wesley's
lifetime. Anti-Methodist literature has proved to be a helpful tool in study-
ing Wesley. Four major works have been produced in the past sixty years:
Albert M. Lyles, *Methodism Mocked* (1960), Donald Henry Kirkham's
PhD dissertation, "Pamphlet Opposition to the Rise of Methodism"
(1973); W. Stephen Gunter, *The Limits of Love Divine* (1989); and most
recently, Brett C. McInelly, *Textual Warfare and the Making of Methodism*
(2014).[74] Whereas Kirkham, McInelly, and Gunter offered broad analyzes
on published works, Lyles focused on satirical anti-Methodist publications. McInelly offered a thorough study of anti-Methodist documents.

---

70. JW to Samuel Wesley [his nephew], August 19, 1784, in Telford, 7:231.

71. Macquiban, "Wesley's Practice of Intra-faith Love," 199.

72. JW, "Letter to the Printer of the *Public Advertiser*," *Works* (Jackson), 10:161.

73. For instance, Sherlock, *A Preservative against Popery*.

74. Lyles, *Methodism Mocked*; Kirkham, "Pamphlet Opposition;" Gunter, *Limits*;
and McInelly, *Textual Warfare*.

W. Stephen Gunter indicated that "a vital factor that has clouded the picture we have of early Methodism is an unwillingness to admit that Wesley was responsible for many of the conflicts in which Methodism was engaged. This is a posture which Wesley's admirers copied from him."[75] This study will offer an alternative to hagiographical approaches. This book agrees with Gunter's view that difficulties can arise in interpreting Wesley's writings because "the reader of the Wesley corpus looks in vain for a single instance in which John Wesley accepted any significant responsibility for the many controversies in which Methodism became embroiled."[76] Additionally, J. C. D. Clark provided guidance concerning historical studies of early Methodism:

> A proper historical appraisal of Methodism would therefore need to give balanced attention to the writings of Methodism's supporters and its critics, but this is almost never done. Opposition to Methodism has seldom been reconstructed from original sources, and so has often been parodied: the self-interest of corrupt churchmen, snobbery, a fear of leveling tendencies, or (inconsistently) a fear of Jacobite associations.[77]

While Clark may be overstating his case, because some studies have been written on anti-Methodist writings, it still bears consideration.

The psychological need among Wesley's spiritual descendants for him to be saintly has a long history.[78] This perspective is waning, but has not entirely disappeared.[79] Some of his earliest biographers admired Wesley for what they perceived as his anti-Catholicism, for they believed that Methodists had a responsibility to counteract Popery. John Hampson (1791), along with Henry Moore and Thomas Coke (1792), and John Whitehead (1793) divulged their anti-Catholicism. Hampson remarked: "but the good Catholics will hardly thank him for the association; though many of our readers will perhaps join him in supposing, that to allow Popery to be better than infidelity, is to say all that can be said upon it."[80]

75. Gunter, *Limits*, 12.

76. Gunter, *Limits*, 12.

77. Clark, "The Eighteenth-Century Context," 13.

78. For instance, Moore, *The Life of the Rev. John Wesley*; Watson, *Life of John Wesley*; Tyerman, *The Life and Times of the Rev. John Wesley*; and Halévy, *The Birth of Methodism*.

79. For the caution against this, see Gunter, *Limits*, 9; and Wynkoop, "John Wesley–Mentor or Guru?," 5–14.

80. Hampson, *Memoirs*, 1:185, 419.

While much of Whitehead's biography is copied from Wesley's *Journals*, Whitehead's occasional comments provided insight into Whitehead's views of Catholics. For example, he commented that "There was never a more indecent abuse of words, than in the Church of Rome assuming the title of Catholic Church."[81]

The Methodists stood out against Catholic emancipation even though the British Parliament began offering toleration to Catholics in a 1778 Act, with another Catholic Relief Act passed in 1791 focused on toleration of worship and one in 1829 granting civil rights to Catholics.[82] There was also a Catholic Relief Act for Scotland in 1793. The Methodist leadership at the time of the 1829 Act, other than Jabez Bunting (1779–1858) and Matthew Tobias (1770–1845), did not support the Act.[83]

In the nineteenth century, a debate arose concerning Wesley's catholic spirit after Robert Southey (1820) accused Wesleyan Methodism of sectarianism.[84] Southey argued that as Methodism "gained ground in among the educated classes" it "substituted a sectarian in the place of a catholic spirit."[85] Southey observed:

> In its [Methodism's] insolent language, all unawakened persons, that is to say, all except themselves, or such graduated professors in other evangelical sects as they are pleased to admit *ad eundem*, are contemptuously styled unbelievers. Wesley could not communicate to his followers his own catholic charity; indeed, the doctrine which he held forth was not always consistent with his own better feelings.[86]

There is some truth in Southey's statement, for Wesley did style every person who had not experienced the New Birth an "unbeliever."[87]

Appalled at Southey's critique, Henry Moore (1824) and Richard Watson (1831) sought to deny that Wesley was sectarian. For instance, Moore wrote:

81. Whitehead, *Life of Wesley*, 238.

82. 18 Geo. III, c. 60; 31 Geo. III, c. 32; and 10 Geo. IV, c. 7.

83. See Hempton, "The Methodist Crusade in Ireland," 41; Colley, *Britons*, 333; and Selén, *Oxford Movement*, 47.

84. Southey, *Rise and Progress*, 319; and Nockles, "Reactions to Robert Southey's Life," 61–80.

85. Southey, *Rise and Progress*, 2:319.

86. Southey, *Rise and Progress*, 2:318.

87. See JW's sermons, "Scripture Way of Salvation," "Original Sin," and "The New Birth," *Works*, 2:153–201.

The cordial and intimate friendship and union of ministerial labours, which for so many years subsisted between Mr. Wesley and Mr. Grimshaw, furnish high evidence of that catholic spirit, which Mr. Wesley so incessantly cultivated and preserved. Mr Grimshaw did not agree with every point of doctrine with Mr. Wesley; but he had so much of *'the wisdom from above,'* that he was *'easy to be convinced'* of any truth, and easy to be *'persuaded'* in any good way.[88]

Moore also stated, "though of a truly catholic spirit he was firm to his own principles . . . He knew God had given us a standard of truth; and that nothing was indifferent which was found therein." Moore referred directly to Wesley's work with other denominations to refute Southey. Moore, however, was clearly anti-Catholic as he called "Popery" the "Christianity of the world," meaning that Catholics were "worldly" and not true Christians.[89]

Moreover, Watson, in reply to Southey, reported that "one fundamental principle of Wesleyan Methodism is anti-sectarianism and a *Catholic Spirit*."[90] Watson quoted a large section of *Catholic Spirit*, interpreting it to mean that Wesley had an "ardent wish for unity among those of different denominations and opinions who love the Lord Jesus," and that "no man ever set a better example for Christian charity."[91] Furthermore, Watson argued that the followers of Wesley would be "an inexcusable class of Christians were they to indulge in that selfish sectarianism with which he was so often unjustly charged."[92] Unfortunately, Watson did not mention Wesley's attitude towards Catholicism.

Some of Wesley's nineteenth-century biographers perceived that Wesley was anti-Catholic. Thomas Jackson (1842) claimed that John and Charles Wesley believed not only that the Catholic Church was an enemy to liberty, but that the Wesley brothers laboured faithfully to "counteract the sorceries of Rome."[93] According to Jackson, one of the reasons Methodism existed was to counteract Catholicism. His comments

88. Moore, *Life of Wesley*, 2:213–14.
89. Moore, *Life of Wesley*, 2:210, 213, 233.
90. Watson, *Life*, 318.
91. Watson, *Life*, 112–13.
92. Watson, *Life*, 112–13.
93. Jackson, *Life of CW*, 1:10.

should be read in the light of the Methodist backlash towards the Oxford Movement of the mid-nineteenth century.[94]

Luke Tyerman (1871), the Victorian Methodist historian, referring to Wesley's publication of *Popery Calmly Considered* (1779), maintained that "Wesley had been called a papist times without number; but now, in a time of danger, he proved himself one of Popery's most trenchant opponents," and cautioned his readers: "John Wesley's successors will be recreant to his Protestant principles unless they do their duty as he did his."[95] This duty, Tyerman believed, was to counteract "Popery."[96]

If most of Wesley's nineteenth-century biographers proclaimed an anti-Catholic Wesley, most of his twentieth and twenty-first century biographers tried to portray him as an ecumenical figure. George Croft Cell (1935) called *Catholic Spirit* "one of the noblest sermons ever preached."[97] He posed the question, "Is there a principle of agreement within Wesley to Catholic Christianity?" answering "yes." Wesley "restored the neglected doctrine of holiness to its merited position in the Protestant understanding of Christianity, —a defect frequently attacked by Catholic critics and too much ignored by early Protestant apologists."[98] Maxim Piette (1937), approaching Methodism as a Catholic, observed of the Methodists:

> Their founder, John Wesley, has been compared to St. Benedict as regards to his liturgical sense and piety; to St. Dominic for his apostolic zeal; to St. Francis of Assisi for his love of Christ and detachment from the world; to St. Ignatius of Loyola for his genius as an organizer; to his contemporary, St. Alphonsus di Liguori for those terrifying appeals to the judgments of God as the beginning of conversion.[99]

While there may be some truth in this statement, Piette goes too far in his attempt to portray Wesley as a man who bridged the gap between Protestantism and Catholicism.

There were additional writers of the twentieth century who took up the task of exploring Wesley and Catholicism. John Todd (1958), a

94. Selén, *Oxford Movement*, 43–52. For the Oxford Movement, see Nockles, *Oxford Movement*.

95. Tyerman, *Life and Times*, 3:316; and JW, *Popery Calmly Considered, Works* (Jackson), 10:140–49.

96. Tyerman, *Life and Times*, 3:316.

97. Cell, *Rediscovery*, 360.

98. Cell, *Rediscovery*, 358–59.

99. Piette, *John Wesley*, 480.

Catholic layperson, reached his goal of writing an examination of the doctrines of Wesley, to see how they relate to the Catholic Church.[100] His study also gave a helpful analysis of the inner development of Wesley's life. Nonetheless, Todd was careful to explain that he was not writing a "full-scale historical appreciation of John Wesley."[101]

David Butler (1995) made a vital contribution to the topic of Wesley and Catholicism, aiming "to show Wesley 'warts and all' in his relationships with Roman Catholics."[102] Although he mentioned accusations against Wesley for "Popery," and discussed some anti-Methodist documents, Butler's study falls short of a thorough historical investigation because he did not address anti-Methodist literature or archival sources in sufficient depth. Additionally, Daniel Luby in his 1984 PhD dissertation, "The Perceptibility of Grace in the Theology of John Wesley: A Roman Catholic Consideration," analyzed Wesley's views on grace and their similarities to a Catholic view but did not address specific historical contexts.[103]

Regarding the sermon *Catholic Spirit*, Herbert McGonigle (2002) noted in his helpful study: "there was a great need to call fellow-believers back to the catholic spirit and that was the sermon's intention."[104] McGonigle provided several historical illustrations as to how Wesley practiced a catholic spirit, even though he was accused otherwise. He argued that "while John Wesley took a vigorous stand against Roman Catholic doctrines such as transubstantiation, purgatory, indulgences, papal infallibility, and all forms of Mariolatry, yet he was willing to recognize that some Catholic writers were helpful in promoting practical Christianity."[105] This book concurs with this view, as will be demonstrated.

David Chapman (2004) was correct when he stated: "the fact that scholars from all ecclesial traditions have reached contrasting conclusions about Wesley's attitude to Roman Catholicism demonstrates how difficult it is to get to the heart of his ecclesiology and its theological presuppositions."[106] Chapman's study traced Methodist relationships

---

100. Todd, *John Wesley*, 10–11.

101. Todd, *John Wesley*, 12.

102. Butler, *Methodists and Papists*, xiii.

103. Luby, "The Perceptibility of Grace." Randy Maddox covers *Catholic Spirit* briefly in "Opinion, Religion, and 'Catholic Spirit,'" 63–88.

104. McGonigle, "Exemplar," 52.

105. McGonigle, "Exemplar," 67.

106. Chapman, *In Search*, 11.

with Catholics from Wesley's time to the writing of the book. He only has one chapter on Wesley's specific views of Catholics, as most the book is about Methodism after Wesley.[107] In his study, Jonathan Dean (2014) placed *Letter to a Roman Catholic* in the same chapter as *Catholic Spirit*, but was careful to say that Wesley did publish anti-Catholic works like *Popery Calmly Considered* (1779).[108]

D. Stephen Long (2017) argued that Wesley's sermon *Catholic Spirit* "perhaps never was, 'catholic.'"[109] Long suggested that *Catholic Spirit* worked to identify the "minimal doctrinal commitments necessary for Methodists to remain connected to the Christian tradition."[110] Long asserted that the sermon was intended for Anglicans and Dissenters within the Methodist movement. He wanted Dissenters to know that they could be Methodist without changing their modes of worship, and for Anglicans to accept this.[111] This book agrees with Long that *Catholic Spirit* was aimed at Protestants and not Catholics. In the same edited volume, Ted Campbell's chapter correctly pronounces that the Church of England "made a particular claim to catholicity in the age in which the Wesleyan movement emerged."[112] Campbell rightly enunciated that Wesley challenged the "inherited notion of territorial catholicity," and that *Catholic Spirit* clarified Wesley's view that "unity in the faith depended on a relatively small core of essential or fundamental doctrines."[113] Neither Long nor Campbell stated that Wesley intended *Catholic Spirit* to apply to Catholics, although Campbell pointed out that *Letter to a Roman Catholic* indicated shared doctrines between Protestants and Catholics.[114]

David N. Field (2017) indicated that Wesley's interaction with Catholics did not have the depth of his attempt at cooperation with Calvinists. Field rightly acknowledged that Wesley's "positive encounters with Catholicism were largely through their writings rather than personal meetings." He also emphasized that Wesley rejected much Catholic theology and opposed the repeal of the penal laws.[115]

---

107. Chapman, *In Search*, 3–6.

108. Dean, *Heart Strangely Warmed*, 215.

109. Long, "Non-Catholicity," 51.

110. Long, "Non-Catholicity," 51.

111. Long, "Non-Catholicity," 61.

112. Campbell, "Negotiating Wesleyan Catholicity," 2.

113. Campbell, "Negotiating Wesleyan Catholicity," 4.

114. Campbell, "Negotiating Wesleyan Catholicity," 4.

115. Field, *Bid Our Jarring*, 43, 44–45.

This main body of this book falls into five parts. Chapter 2 considers that anti-Catholicism in eighteenth-century Great Britain was the outcome of many features of the English Protestant Reformation, and these are examined in detail. In addition to exploring how the anti-Catholicism of eighteenth-century Britain shaped Wesley, several attempts at religious toleration are analyzed including those advocated by Nonjurors, Latitudinarians, and empiricists. Additionally, Wesley's ancestry and diverse theological upbringing are analyzed.

Chapter 3 examines events that took place before Wesley wrote *Catholic Spirit*, including the opposition Wesley and the Methodists faced at Oxford for alleged Jacobitism. Furthermore, the popular mood generated by the "Forty-five" led Wesley and other Methodists to be accused of Jacobitism. Finally, several preachers were conscripted into the army during the "Forty-five." This chapter will argue that these events may have indeed influenced the writing of a *Catholic Spirit*, but it also explores Wesley's reactions when accused of Jacobitism. After examining the evidence, this chapter will demonstrate that Wesley was not a Jacobite. It seems that Methodist suffering during the "Forty-five" may have also reinforced Wesley's anti-Catholicism. Likewise, this chapter illustrates that for Wesley, Catholicism was never just a religion. It was a political force.

Chapter 4 considers that Wesley wrote *Catholic Spirit* after experiencing opposition on his second journey to Ireland in late 1748. Further, this chapter contends that *Letter to a Roman Catholic*, written a few months later, was aimed at Catholics to influence them to stop rioting against the Methodists. Furthermore, Wesley wrote *Letter to a Roman Catholic* to convince Catholics to listen to Methodist preaching and allow Wesley and the Methodists to preach evangelical conversion to them. Wesley believed that the New Birth was required before a person could practice a catholic spirit.

Chapter 5 examines Wesley's critique of the Moravians for their "Jesuit ways," and explores the accusations Wesley's opponents aimed at him for alleged Jesuitism and Popery. Several Anglican bishops and Calvinists alleged he practiced Jesuitism, including trickery, magic, and tyranny. Furthermore, many accused him of Jesuitism for his publication of *A Calm Address to Our American Colonies* (1775). The chapter analyzes whether Wesley practiced a catholic spirit when accused of Jesuitism.

Chapter 6 studies the events surrounding the Gordon Riots of 1780 and Wesley's alleged involvement. The Protestant Association started a petition campaign to repeal the Catholic Relief Act of 1778 and presented the petitions to the House of Commons. When the Members of Parliament did not immediately address the crowd's wishes that they repeal the Act, riots broke out in London. Wesley was accused of influencing the riots. Wesley's writings in response to the Catholic Relief Act of 1778 are explored, and the allegations that he associated with the Protestant Association are analyzed. Wesley's supposed involvement in the Gordon Riots and their aftermath are considered.

Chapter 7 considers Wesley's use of Catholic devotional material. An overview of Wesley as publisher is given, and the Catholic devotional authors he used are described. Wesley's disagreements with Catholic devotional authors are given. Finally, the chapter explores the positive influences the Catholic devotional authors have on Wesley. Chapter 8 provides a summary of the book and forms a conclusion.

This book covers only the lifetime of Wesley, and does not delve into nineteenth-century issues concerning Methodists and Catholics except to tie matters briefly to eighteenth-century actions or writings. Although there are a few references to the Methodists in America, the focus is on British and Irish Methodism from 1725 to 1791. Additionally, presenting an authentic Wesley as the primary sources portray him is more important to this book than allowing him to remain an exemplar of a catholic spirit. Further, this study is not a comparison of Catholic and Methodist theology, nor is it a survey of Catholic and Methodist intersections. Instead it provides analyses of the sources for Wesley's sermon *Catholic Spirit*, his writings on Catholicism, and how his ideal of catholic spirit was applied within four case studies related to Catholicism over the span of his lifetime.

2

Foundations of a *Catholic Spirit*

THE ENGLISH PROTESTANT REFORMATION produced a culture of anti-Catholicism.[1] Due to schism in the Church of England over the course of the seventeenth century, leading philosophers and theologians sought to develop ways in which differences in Christian theology and practice could be tolerated both inside and outside of the Established Church. These methods would be reflected in the Act of Toleration of 1688–1689.[2] However, this Act did not lift penal laws against Catholics, and "anti-Popery" remained a defining feature of the Church of England. This chapter intends to explore on the one hand, sources for Wesley's sermon, *Catholic Spirit*, and on the other hand, how some of the sources influenced his anti-Catholicism.

In order to understand Wesley's views of Catholicism, one must first understand the anti-Catholic society in which he lived. The first section of this chapter provides an overview of John Foxe's (1516/17–1587) *Actes and Monuments*. This includes an evaluation of Wesley's abridgement of Foxe. The second section considers the Oath of Allegiance, the Nonjurors, and anti-Catholicism. Next, the chapter looks directly at Nonconformist Richard Baxter's influence upon Wesley. In the fourth section, Wesley's ancestry is examined. Primitive Christianity and the latitudinarians is analyzed in the fifth section. In the sixth section, the influence of British "Empiricism" upon Wesley's *Catholic Spirit* and his anti-Catholicism is

---

1. See Haydon, *Anti-Catholicism*; Haydon, "Parliament and Popery," 49–63; Hempton, *Religion and Political Culture*; Norman, *Roman Catholicism in England*; Bossy, *English Catholic Community*; and Butler, *Methodists and Papists*, 1–19.

2. 1 Will & Mary, c. 18.

examined. The influence of George Whitefield and Howel Harris is considered, and finally, an overview of *Catholic Spirit* is given.

Foxe's *Actes and Monuments*

The influence of Foxe's *Actes and Monuments of These Latter and Perillous Days, Touching Matters of the Church*, more popularly known as the *Book of Martyrs*, cannot be underestimated when considering early anti-Catholicism in England.[3] Written five years after the death of Mary I in 1563, it traced the martyrdom of Christians from the time of Nero to the time of its writing. Foxe provided names, dates, and details of the death of every individual man and woman executed under Mary so that this tragic portion of history would never die in the collective memory of the English people.[4] Not only did Foxe recount the deaths of English martyrs, in the second edition, published in 1570, he described the persecution Catholics had inflicted upon the Protestants throughout Europe in the sixteenth century.[5] Although self-exiled and penniless during the reign of Mary, Foxe achieved celebrity status after returning to England following her death. His celebrity status was due to the wild popularity of his book, which went through four editions in his lifetime.[6] Foxe not only wrote *Actes and Monuments*, but several other pieces including *Papas Confutatas*, an outright attack on Catholicism which accused the Pope of being the Antichrist and listing (what he considered) all of the errors of the Catholic Church.[7]

It has been argued that Foxe's *Actes and Monuments* was placed into every church by order of Elizabeth I. Leslie M. Oliver argued against this, especially since John Day (1522–1584), Foxe's printer had only produced two copies by November 27, 1570.[8] Nevertheless, Evenden and Freeman

---

3. John Foxe, *Actes and Monuments of These Latter and Perillous Days, Touching Matters of the Church*, about 1800 pages, is the first edition of the book. By the second edition Foxe changed the title to *The Ecclesiasticall History, Conteyning the Actes and Monuments of the Martyrs* and added about five hundred pages.

4. The number of Marian martyrs is still debated; see "A Five-Minute Introduction," *The Unabridged Acts and Monuments Online or TAMO*.

5. Foxe, *Unabridged Acts and Monuments Online or TAMO* (1576 ed). For studies on Foxe, see King, *Foxe's* Book of Martyrs; and Greenberg, "Reflective Foxe."

6. Freeman, "Foxe, John (1516/17–1587)," *ODNB*.

7. Foxe, *Pope Confuted*.

8. See Evenden, *Patents, Patronage*. The first edition of *Actes and Monuments* was

asserted that the book did have influence and honour as it was promoted by Archbishop Matthew Parker and officially presented to Elizabeth I. They stressed that Elizabeth's Privy Council wrote to the Archbishops of York and Canterbury on November 27, 1570 with a request that *Actes and Monuments* be put into every church, but the evidence suggests that it probably was not placed into every church at that time. However, by 1583 it is most likely the book was prominently displayed in every cathedral along with the Bible, the Thirty-Nine Articles, and the Book of Common Prayer.[9] This type of public display would have demonstrated to common people the importance of the book, especially since it was strategically positioned alongside the most treasured and sacred volumes in the Established Church. The enormous proportions of it: two thousand pages, and the detail of the original woodcuts would have attracted attention, as they were some of most elaborate illustrations that had ever been put to print.[10] The second edition of the book was the largest printing project to date to have been undertaken in England.[11]

The eighteenth century offered no diminishment of the value of Foxe's text in English print culture, as the book was reprinted and abridged at least fifty times from 1732 to 1800, and Devorah Greenberg proclaimed that surviving Foxe texts may be just a scratch on the eighteenth-century surface of what might have been printed.[12] Wesley himself participated in this cultural phenomenon as he included an abridged version of *Actes*

---

printed by John Day at his shop on Aldersgate Street. The debate surrounding whether Foxe's Acts and Monuments was placed in every church is discussed in Evenden and Freeman, "Print, Profit, and Propaganda," 1288–1307. Evenden and Freeman assert that only one copy of the letter between the Privy Council and the Archbishops of November 27, 1570 exists in the Borthwick Institute, Institution Act Book II, part III, f.85v, (p. 1290), picture of the letter on p. 1291. See also Oliver, "The Seventh Edition of John Foxe's Acts and Monuments," 245–47.

9. Evenden and Freeman, "Print, Profit, Propaganda," 1303.

10. Greenberg noted the erotic nature of the illustrations would also have attracted attention as they may have been the only pictures of such that many of the viewers had ever seen; Greenberg, "Eighteenth-century 'Foxe.'"

11. King, *Early Modern Print Culture*, xli.

12. Greenberg, "Eighteenth-century 'Foxe.'" For instance: Foxe, *The Book of Martyrs: Containing an Account of the Sufferings and Death of the Protestants in the Reign of Queen Mary the First Illustrated.* London: John Hart and John Lewis, 1732; *The Book of Martyrs of the History of the Church from the Beginning of Christianity.* 2 vols. London: John Lewis, 1747–1748; London: John Fuller, 1760–1761; *The Book of Martyrs*, revised by the Revd Mr. [Martin] Madan. London, 1776; and London, 1784.

and Monuments as volumes II, III, and IV of his fifty-volume *A Christian Library* in 1750.[13]

Greenberg argued Wesley's abridgement of *Foxe's Book of Martyrs* showed he was not anti-Catholic.[14] Wesley's introductory comments on the abridgement stated nothing about anti-Catholicism, only the reasons for his condensations: leaving out the "secular" history and the examinations of the martyrs, which contained nothing instructive.[15] He hoped that his readers would learn from "these worthies, to be, not almost only, but altogether, Christians! To reckon all things but dung and dross for the excellency of the experimental knowledge of Jesus Christ!"[16]

Greenberg observed that Wesley rarely used the words "Pope" or "papacy" in his abridgment. Further, instead of portraying the Catholics as malevolent monsters assaulting the Protestant "true Church" as Foxe did, Wesley's designation of "two churches" is more like Augustine's use of "two cities."[17] Wesley's Foxe was among several editions of the text that did not "participate in a narrowly, anti-Catholic and/or anti-papist campaign," and Wesley's 1750 abridgement was possibly printed as an ecclesiastical history rather than a pure martyrology.[18] In his *Journal* Wesley reported, "I set upon cleansing Augeas's stable upon purging that huge work, Mr. Foxe's *Actes and Monuments*, from all the trash which that honest injudicious writer has heaped together and mingled with those most venerable records which are worthy to be had in everlasting remembrance."[19] Augeas' stable referred to a story in Greek mythology where Eurystheus ordered Hercules to clean some stables. The livestock produced much waste, and the stables had not been cleaned in thirty years. Since this reference to Augeas was used to describe something filthy, it suggests that Wesley thought there was much to be cleaned out of Foxe's text. Greenberg claimed it was much of the material on the papacy, including the process of Mary's return of England to Catholicism, and finally, the stories of the "common English folk" who were martyred. She concluded that Wesley's abridgement was a promotion of Christian

13. JW, *Christian Library*, 2–4.

14. Greenberg, "In a Tradition," 227–28.

15. JW, *Christian Library*, 2:209–10.

16. JW, *Christian Library*, 2:210.

17. Greenberg, "In a Tradition," 233.

18. Greenberg, "Eighteenth-Century 'Foxe.'"

19. *JWJ*, December 17, 1750, *Works*, 20:373.

tolerance.[20] However, a careful examination of the text, especially in *The Life of John Foxe as Written by his Son*, reveals serious criticism of the Catholic Church.[21] This *Life of John Foxe* contains a description of the "reformed religion" flourishing in England and of "Papists" being in decline.[22]

By comparing Wesley's version of Foxe to two contemporary abridgements, Wesley's purpose comes into focus. For instance, a version that appeared in 1732 stated in the introduction:

> May God give a blessing to the undertaking; and grant that these dreadful accounts of popish tyranny, may not only prove a means of preserving our Church from falling into such gross errors and enormities, but also teach us, and all Christians, to set a greater value upon that Religion, which, by the blessing of God is established in this Kingdom, whose doctrine and constitution is so exactly agreeable to that of Primitive Christians.[23]

This version obviously had the objective of safeguarding the Church of England from "popish tyranny" and retelling the story of the lives of the martyrs. Wesley's abridgement did not include such an introduction.

Another abridgment, appearing in 1746 as a *Select History of the Lives and Sufferings of the Principle English Protestant Martyrs*, emphasized in the title that the book was "designed as cheap and useful for the Protestant families of all denominations."[24] This was a shorter version than even Wesley printed, with just over three hundred pages. The preface stated the version was useful because of the daring attempt of enemies to ruin the happy constitution and the Established religion.[25] The date reveals that this was printed not long after the "Forty-five." Most likely the purpose of this printing was to remind the public of the perceived possible danger to peace if the Jacobites gained power. Although Wesley valued Foxe's work enough to place it his *A Christian Library*, his abridgment suggests that he was not interested in using Foxe's work to warn against the dangers of Catholicism as much as he was in highlighting the actions of the martyrs. Perhaps Wesley wished to provide

20. Greenberg, "Eighteenth-Century 'Foxe.'"

21. JW, *Christian Library*, 2:214.

22. JW, *Christian Library*, 2:232.

23. Foxe, *The Book of Martyrs* (1732).

24. Foxe, *A Select History* (1746).

25. Foxe, *A Select History* (1746), preface.

encouragement to Methodists under persecution. However, the evidence does not indicate as Greenburg asserts, that Wesley's version promoted toleration.

The Oath of Allegiance, the Nonjurors, and Anti-Catholicism

Elizabeth I died without heir, and James VI of Scotland and I of England (1566–1625) ascended to the throne upon her death. One of the most significant events in James's rule was the Gunpowder Treason Plot on November 5, 1605. Guy Fawkes (1570–1606) and others, all Catholics, attempted to blow up the House of Lords while the King was present. They were caught and executed; afterward anti-Catholicism exploded.[26] This day came to be annually celebrated as a holiday with parades, fireworks, and burnings of effigies of the Pope and Fawkes. Samuel (1766–1837), the son of Charles Wesley mentioned that his uncle John gave him and his brother, Charles (1757–1834), money with which to celebrate on November 5.[27]

When James I died, his son Charles I (1600–1649) ascended to the throne. Charles I was beheaded in 1649. Oliver Cromwell (1599–1658) ruled as Lord Protector, succeeded by his son Richard (1626–1717), but in 1660, the throne was restored to Charles II (1630–1685), Charles I's son. Due to political anxiety that surrounded the Restoration of the monarchy, many laws were passed to ensure the authority of the Established Church. The Corporation Act of 1661 required all municipal officials to receive communion in the Church of England, and excluded Nonconformists from public office if they did not take communion in the Church.[28] Parliament passed the Act of Uniformity of 1662, which required all clergy to use the rites in the Book of Common Prayer.[29] Around 2000 clergy were ejected from the Church of England because they refused to use it, including John Wesley's great-grandfather and two grandfathers. The Five Mile Act of 1665 further enforced the Act of Uniformity, as it forbade Nonconformist ministers from coming within five miles of the

26. See James I et al., *The Gunpowder-Treason*.

27. Samuel Wesley to [Thomas Jackson] (1835) in Wesley, *Letters of Samuel Wesley*, 480.

28. Corporation Act (1661), 13 Car. 2 st. 2 c. 1

29. Act of Uniformity (1662), 14 Car. 2 c. 4.

town in which they had served as clergy.[30] The Conventicle Act of 1670 forbade unauthorized worship of more than five people not of the same household.[31]

The memory of the Gunpowder Treason Plot had invoked trepidation of Catholic rule. Seven peers wrote to William of Orange (1650–1702) on June 30, 1688, vowing to support William if he invaded England. William had married James II's sister, Mary (1662–1694). This plot succeeded and William III and Mary II ruled side by side, requiring all Church of England clergy to take the Oath of Allegiance and Supremacy:

> I do sincerely promise and swear, that I will be faithful, and bear true Allegiance to their Majesties, King William and Queen Mary.
> *So help me God.*
> I do swear, That I do from my Heart abhor, detest and abjure, as impious and heretical, this damnable Doctrine and Position, That Princes excommunicated or deprived by the Pope, or any Authority of the See of Rome, may be deposed or murdered by their Subjects, or any other whatsoever. And I do declare, That no Foreign Prince, Person, Prelate, State or Potentate hath or ought to have, any Jurisdiction, Power, Superiority, Pre-eminence, or Authority Ecclesiastical or Spiritual, within this Realm.
> *So help me God.*[32]

There were many Church of England clergy who refused to take this oath because they believed that they were still bound by their previous oath to King James II and his heirs and successors. This group became known as the Nonjurors.[33] A Nonjuror from Manchester, Thomas Deacon (1697–1753), would become a major influence on Wesley at Oxford. This group of Nonjurors with whom Susanna Wesley was associated, were labelled "Jacobites" for their support of James II.[34] The reign of William

30. Five Mile Act (1665), 17 Car. 2 c. 2.

31. Conventicle Act (1670), 22 Car. 2 c. 1

32. See "King James' Parliament" in *The History and Proceedings of the House of Commons*, 2:258.

33. Ollard, "The Nonjurors," in Ollard and Crosse, *A Dictionary of English Church History*, 410–15. Cornwall asserts that High Churchmen and Nonjurors were of the same theological beliefs, but one could believe in High Church practices and stay within the Established Church; Cornwall, *Visible and Apostolic*, 42. The Nonjurors refused to change their loyalty from James II to William and Mary; this is what caused their separation from the Church of England.

34. This book will assume the definition of Jacobite as those who supported the

and Mary also saw the passing of the Act of Toleration in 1689, which allowed limited freedom of worship for all Trinitarian Christians, except Catholics.[35]

Eighteenth-century British anti-Catholicism was displayed in many ways. Parades, parties, and effigy-burnings of the Pope and devil together, especially on holidays such as the Fifth of November embedded anti-Catholicism into popular culture. The extreme to which the Britons would go to avoid Catholicism showed itself in the rules of dynastic succession that were fractured so the perceived wickedness of Catholicism could be avoided: in 1689 with the crowning of William and Mary, and in 1714 with the Hanoverian succession.

Linda Colley proclaimed that the centrality of Protestantism to British religion in the eighteenth century is so evident that it has been easy to neglect, asserting that most British historians writing about this century have emphasized the divisions within Protestantism rather than the chasm between Catholic and Protestant.[36] There is no denying that eighteenth-century Britain was laden with conflict between Catholic and Protestant, sometimes the strain was slight; other times the tension erupted into violence, such as in the 1715 and 1745–1746 Jacobite Risings and the 1780 Gordon Riots.[37] Colley argued that throughout the eighteenth century a shared Protestantism, with all the associated values of cultural prejudice, remained the most important element in the formation of a British identity.[38] David Hempton specified that eighteenth-century Britons were divided over matters of religion: orthodox and heterodox churchmen, Dissenters, Evangelicals, and High churchmen, and they were not united in their Protestantism. Hempton continued, "even within a single denomination such as Methodism, a vigorous Protestantism and anti-Catholicism was not sufficient to maintain internal discipline nor to override other religious issues that many saw to be more important to their daily lives."[39] Colley closed her first chapter with a bold statement: "Protestantism was the foundation that made the

---

exiled Stuarts after the Glorious Revolution of 1688–1689. Cornwall, *Visible and Apostolic*, 17, is careful to indicate that not all Nonjurors were Jacobite.

35. An Act for Exempting their Majesty's Protestant Subjects Dissenting from the Church of England from the Penalties of Certain Laws, 1 Will & Mary c. 18.

36. Colley, *Britons*, 18–19.

37. Haydon, *Anti-Catholicism*, 2.

38. Colley, *Britons*, 53–54.

39. Hempton, *Religion and Political Culture*, 174.

invention of Great Britain possible."[40] While this book agrees with Colley that conflict between Catholicism and Protestantism certainly took place in eighteenth-century Britain, Hempton's view must also be considered. Protestantism was not a united force because the Established Church had reluctantly allowed for Nonconformity, and not every Protestant agreed with the practice of anti-Catholicism.

Richard Baxter

The phrase *Catholic Spirit* did not originate with John Wesley. It is uncertain who first used the phrase in England, but Richard Baxter (1615–1691), ejected minister and colleague of Wesley's maternal grandfather Samuel Annesley (c. 1620–1696), used the phrase as early as 1660 in *Of Catholick Unity*, and *The True Catholick and the Catholick Church Described*. These essays used the phrase "Catholick Spirit" to apply to Protestant Christians desirous of peace and unity among different denominations, which was also the way Wesley later used the term.[41]

In *The Saints' Everlasting Rest*, which Wesley included in *A Christian Library*, Baxter emphasized the unity of Christians:

> For brethren here to live together in unity [Psalm 133:1], how good and how pleasant a thing is it! . . . O then, what a blessed a society will be in the family of heaven, and those peaceful inhabitants of the new Jerusalem! Where there is no division, nor disaffection, nor strangeness, nor deceitful friendship, never an angry thought, or look, never an unkind expression, but all one in Christ who is one with the Father, and live in the love of love himself.[42]

When Wesley wrote his sermon *Justification by Faith* in 1738 and published it in 1746, he may have used Baxter's sermon, *Aphorisms of Justification* as a source.[43]

---

40. Colley, *Britons*, 54.

41. Keeble, "Baxter Richard (1615–1691)," *ODNB*.

42. See Baxter, "Saints' Everlasting," in JW, *Christian Library*, 37:7–257; and Baxter, "Saints Everlasting," 432.

43. Cunningham, "'Justification by Faith,'" 56. For JW's sermon, "Justification by Faith," see *Works*, 1:53–64; for JW's abridgement of *Mr. Richard Baxter's Aphorisms of Justification* (1745), see *Works*, 12:45–53. Ward, *Protestant Evangelical Awakening*, 346, speaks of Baxter's "middle way" between Arminianism and Calvinism.

In Baxter's popular work, *The Reformed Pastor*, he lamented that it was rare to meet people with a "Catholick Spirit," for those who did not have a "Catholick Spirit" elevated their sect over the universal Church. He grieved over the misuse of the word "Catholick:" "The Papists have so long abused the name of the Catholick Church, that in opposition to them, many either put it out of their creed, or only retain the name, while they understand not, or consider not the nature of the thing, and behave not as members of that body."[44] Baxter insisted "in all our work we should be as peaceable as we can" and that ministers should study "day and night" to figure out ways to unite the church.[45] To pastors he exhorted, "keep close to the ancient simplicity of the Christian faith, the foundation and center of catholick unity."[46] If this was not enough, he besought pastors to "learn to distinguish between certainties and uncertainties; between necessaries and unnecessaries: between catholick truths and private opinions; and lay the stress upon the former instead of the latter."[47]

In *A True Catholick*, Baxter described his purpose: "to speak of the unity and concord of the catholick church."[48] He explained that every member of the church should have special love towards each other: "all members have an inward inclination to hold communion with fellow members, so far as they discern them to be members indeed."[49] Likewise, Wesley's plea to his listeners in *Catholic Spirit* insisted that they "first, love me. And that not only as thou lovest all mankind; not only as thou lovest thine enemies or the enemies of God, those that hate thee."[50] Wesley used first-person language, but he was simply beseeching his listeners to love each other: "love me (but in an higher degree than thou dost the bulk of mankind) with the love that is 'longsuffering and kind;' that is patient if I am ignorant or out of the way."[51]

Paul Chang-Ha Lim noted that in *A True Catholick*, Baxter's "catholicity and anti-Popery converge, and it was for the purity and unity of

44. Baxter, *Reformed Pastor*, 193.

45. Baxter, *Reformed Pastor*, 192.

46. Baxter, *Reformed Pastor*, 200.

47. Baxter, *Reformed Pastor*, 202.

48. Baxter, *True Catholick*, in *Practical Works*, 16:285. Albert Outler indicated this connection between *True Catholick* and *Catholic Spirit*, *Works*, 2:344n.

49. Baxter, *Practical Works*, 16:298.

50. JW, *Catholic Spirit*, *Works*, 2:90.

51. JW, *Catholic Spirit*, *Works*, 2:90.

this church that he devoted a considerable part of his literary output."[52] Baxter's work, in part, was to prove that the Catholic Church was no longer the true catholic church. According to Lim:

> Baxter focused on the alleged Roman usurpation of Christ's headship of the church. The Church of England, however, had maintained its fidelity to the faith and honoured Christ as its head, thus making it a 'truly Catholike church.' Thus Baxter denounced the Church of Rome for having narrowed the ecclesial boundaries and for having demonized the vast majority of Christians who did not pledge allegiance to the Pope.[53]

Baxter's and later Wesley's criticisms of the Catholic Church narrowed "ecclesial boundaries" as well. *A True Catholick*, however, was an articulate call to Protestant unity, written two years before the Great Ejection.[54]

Wesley's Ancestry

Bartholomew Westley (1596–1680) and John White (d. 1644), Wesley's great-grandfathers, were Puritans active during the Commonwealth.[55] Both Bartholomew and his son, John (1635/36–1671), were priests who were ejected on St. Bartholomew's Day August 24, 1662.[56] John Westley had to leave his home in Allington due to the Five Mile Act, and in 1661 he stood before Bishop of Bristol, Gilbert Ironsides (1588–1671), for charges of unwillingness to use the Book of Common Prayer.[57] Although he eventually swore allegiance to Charles II at the Restoration, he would not accept the Act of Uniformity, so he was ejected from his parish in Winterbourne in 1662.[58] Wesley showed his interest in the transcription of his grandfather's interview with Ironsides by publishing it in his 1765 *Journal*.[59] Samuel Wesley, Sr. (bap. 1662, d. 1735), John's father, was born the year his father was ejected, and was given a strong education

---

52. Lim, *In Pursuit of Purity*, 143.

53. Lim, *In Pursuit of Purity*, 143.

54. Jenkinson, *Culture and Politics*, 78.

55. Monk, *Puritan Heritage*, 8–9.

56. Monk, *Puritan Heritage*, 8–9.

57. Spurr, "Ironside, Gilbert (1588–1671)," *ODNB*.

58. Monk, *Puritan Heritage*, 9. The transcript of his trial before the bishop is found in Clarke, *Memoirs*, 24–30.

59. *JWJ*, May 25, 1765, *Works*, 21:513–18.

in dissenting academies. However, he forsook his nonconforming family tradition and communicated with the Church of England before he went up to Oxford.[60]

Samuel Annesley, John Wesley's mother, Susanna's (1669–1742) father, likewise ejected, became known as the "patriarch of Dissent" in London until he died in 1696.[61] Susanna may have taught John to value this grandfather's work, as he printed some of his grandfather's sermons in *A Christian Library*.[62] After Annesley was ejected, he organized a parish of Nonconformists in Spitalfields (London). It was while he was leading this congregation that his youngest daughter and approximately twenty-fifth child Susanna was born.[63] Among Annesley's friends were Richard Baxter and Daniel Defoe (c. 1660–1731), and many other leading Nonconformists.[64]

Susanna and Samuel were married in the parish church at Marylebone (London) in 1688. He was appointed to Epworth parish in 1695, moving there in 1697. Into this religious world entered John Wesley, born in 1703 at Epworth. Susanna's influence on her son's spiritual upbringing is evidenced through many surviving letters between them. Susanna communicated with the Church of England, but her tie to the Nonjuring cause is evidenced through her actions and letters. For instance, she refused to say "amen" to the prayer of her husband for William III in 1702.[65] Geordan Hammond asserted that it was the death of James II and VII (1633–1701) in exile that led to this difference of opinion, rather than the death of Mary II. Hammond stated: "Susanna's belief in divine hereditary monarchy led her to oppose the removal of a ruling monarch and sympathize with the Nonjuring clergy who were dismissed from their cures."[66] She struggled with her decision, especially

---

60. Clarke, *Memoirs*, 50–51; for the life of Samuel Wesley, see Tyerman, *The Life and Times of the Rev. Samuel Wesley*.

61. For Samuel Annesley, see Newton, "Samuel Annesley (1620–1696)," 29–46; and Baker, "Wesley's Puritan Ancestry," 183–84.

62. JW, *Christian Library*, 38:297–354; and Collins, *John Wesley*, 14.

63. See Wallace's "Introduction," in Susanna Wesley, *Complete Writings*, 5.

64. For Samuel Annesley, see *The Character of the Late Dr. Samuel Annesley*. The preface to this elegy was written by "D. F.," most likely Daniel DeFoe; see Wallace's "Introduction," in Susanna Wesley, *Complete Writings*, 5.

65. Walmsley, "John Wesley's Parents," 50–57; and Hammond, *JW in America*, 16–17.

66. Hammond, *JW in America*, 16.

since Samuel left the family home for a time because he was angry with her for not saying "amen" to his prayer, but remained firm.

She wrote to her friend Lady Yarborough for advice, and asked her to refer her case to a Nonjuror bishop, George Hickes (1642–1715), confessing, "I'm almost ashamed to own what extreme disturbance this accident has given me, yet I value not the world."[67] Hickes, an Oxford educated churchman, was deprived in 1690 for refusing to take the oaths of allegiance to William and Mary.[68] She penned a letter to Hickes, explaining the situation and beseeching him for spiritual guidance. Hickes wrote back, and told her to fulfil the rights of her own conscience, but shortly after he wrote, King William died (March 8, 1702), and both Samuel and Susanna agreed on Anne's (1665-1714) right to the throne.[69] Samuel returned home, and their reunion brought a son whom they named John.

Primitive Christianity and Latitudinarianism

Wesley inherited his father's High Church views, which included an emphasis on primitive Christianity. One of the tenets of primitive Christianity was the promotion of Christian unity: what Wesley would label *Catholic Spirit*. Ted A. Campbell wrote of Wesley's emphasis on Christian antiquity: "John Wesley was born into an age in which Christian antiquity, far from being a subject of merely historical interest, had been a focal point for theological, ecclesiastical, and moral discourse for more than a century."[70] Christian antiquity was the focus of *Primitive Christianity* by William Cave (1637–1713), an influential book in Wesley's life.[71] Primitive Christians, according to Cave, were those who lived before the Council of Nicaea.[72] During the three centuries after Christ, Christians were "careful not to offend either God or men, but to keep and maintain

67. Susanna Wesley to Lady Yarbrough, March 15, 1702, Susanna Wesley, *Complete Writings*, 36.

68. Gregory and Stevenson, *The Routledge Companion to the Eighteenth Century*, 343. For an example of his writing, see Hickes, *A Discourse to Prove*.

69. Susanna Wesley to George Hickes, July 13, 1702, Susanna Wesley, *Complete Writings*, 39.

70. Campbell, *Christian Antiquity*, 21.

71. Cave, *Primitive Christianity*; and Hammond, *JW in America*, 22–23. Wesley recommended Cave as reading for the Methodist preachers at the 1746 Conference, *Works*, 10:180.

72. Cave, *Primitive Christianity*, 2:98.

peace with both."[73] These primitive Christians "abhorred all divisions as a plague and firebrand."[74] Cave described Eusebius (c. 261-c. 341) as writing that nations under paganism had wars, but Christianity brought peace.[75]

Two other influences on Wesley concerning the primitive Church were Anthony Horneck (1641–1697) and Claude Fleury (1640–1723). Horneck was a German-born Anglican who wrote to expose the neglect of the Established Church's attention to the primitive Church. He was appointed as chaplain to William III in 1693.[76] His rules for religious societies most likely influenced John and Charles Wesley in their organization of the Oxford Methodists, as Wesley read Horneck while at Oxford.[77] In his book, *The Happy Ascetick*, Horneck wrote of the Church of England as his hope for reviving primitive Christianity.[78]

Claude Fleury's *Manners of the Antient Christians* (1682) was required reading at Kingswood School.[79] Wesley read it at least twice according to his *Journal*, and published it in 1749.[80] This work was similar to Cave, but Fleury was Catholic, and focused on the lives of Christians from the first to the seventh century.[81] Another group that may have influenced Wesley's *Catholic Spirit* arose during the time of Charles II, the Latitudinarians, for they too, stressed primitive Christianity.

Towards the end of the sermon, Wesley explained what a catholic spirit was not. A catholic spirit was not speculative or practical Latitudinarianism. Speculative Latitudinarianism means indifference to all opinions or unsettledness of thought. Practical Latitudinarianism had to do with indifference to public worship. Wesley advocated that public worship was important, but that it was acceptable for people to worship in different ways. The fact that Wesley needed to argue that he was not

73. Cave, *Primitive Christianity*, 2:109.

74. Cave, *Primitive Christianity*, 2:103.

75. Cave, *Primitive Christianity*, 2:101.

76. See Ward, "Horneck, Anthony (1641–1697)," *ODNB*.

77. Heitzenrater, "Oxford Methodists," appendix.

78. Horneck, *The Happy Ascetic*, dedicatory; and Campbell, *Christian Antiquity*, 20.

79. Fleury, *The Manners of the Antient Christians*; and JW, "A Short Account of the School in Kingswood, near Bristol," in *Works* (Jackson), 13:283–84.

80. April 27, 1736; September 13, 1736; July 28, 1737; October 23, 1737; MSS *Journal*, *Works*, 18:379–80, 530, 567.

81. Campbell, *Christian Antiquity*, 19.

advocating for speculative or practical Latitudinarianism indicated that he understood that his advocacy for tolerance might have reminded his listeners of the Latitudinarian movement. The term "Latitudinarian" was used in a derogatory way towards a group of clergy in the Church of England around 1662.[82] They were accused of making religion "too reasonable," that their doctrine of salvation was Pelagian, and that they were lax in their opinions of liturgy and church government. They were criticized by Catholics, Calvinists, and High Church Anglicans, and labelled as being unorthodox.[83]

By the time of the writing of *Catholic Spirit*, almost a hundred years later, Latitudinarianism had come to mean "one who fancies all religions are saving," as defined by Wesley in his *English Dictionary* of 1753.[84] In 1755, Samuel Johnson (1696–1772) defined a Latitudinarian as "one who departs from orthodoxy."[85] Whereas Wesley defined it as universalism, Johnson defined it as heresy. It would be difficult to deny that the sermon *Catholic Spirit* had a Latitudinarian spirit, yet it was not a type of spirit that allowed for unsettledness of thought or indifference to public worship as Wesley may have interpreted the Latitudinarians as promoting.

British Empiricism

Wesley, in his pragmatism, most likely drew from another major source for his method in *Catholic Spirit*: the British Empiricists. The British Empiricists attempted to keep Britain from another revolution, seeing one of their most vital tasks as working out how Christians of differing beliefs and practices could coexist. Francis Bacon (1561–1626), Thomas Hobbes (1588–1679), John Locke (1632–1704), and later George Berkeley (1685–1753) and David Hume (1711–1776) adopted this task, providing slightly different solutions.[86] It is in John Locke's *An Essay Concerning Human Understanding* (1689) and *Letter Concerning Toleration* (1689) that we locate the nearest connection to Wesley's sermon *Catholic Spirit*.

82. See Griffin, *Latitudinarianism*.

83. Griffin, *Latitudinarianism*, 8–9.

84. [JW], *Complete English Dictionary*, s.v. "Latitudinarianism"; and Johnson, *Dictionary*, s.v. "Latitudinarian."

85. Griffin, *Latitudinarianism*, 10.

86. For an overview of British Empiricism, see Priest, *The British Empiricists*, 1–10; for Locke and toleration, see Marshall, *John Locke*.

Wesley drew indirectly from Locke regarding the limits of human understanding, which included acknowledgment that one's own opinions could be incorrect, or that doubting one's opinions may lead to admitting that another person's or church's opinions could possibly be correct. Together, these themes could lead to what Locke called 'toleration': which may be seen as a synonym for Wesley's 'Catholic Spirit.'[87]

Wesley read Locke's *An Essay Concerning Human Understanding* in 1725, only weeks after he was ordained deacon at Christ Church.[88] He wrote an evaluation of it in 1781, saying that Locke's work contained "many excellent truths."[89] However, appraising Locke's influence may proceed further than Wesley reading Locke himself, for he also read Peter Browne's (d. 1735) assessment of Locke.[90] While Wesley used precepts from Locke, he was not aspiring for a purely epistemological approach to tolerance. This is not an effort to demonstrate that Wesley had Locke's works in view while penning *Catholic Spirit*. This book accepts that, in philosophical terms, as Henry Rack has argued, Wesley was an "empiricist disciple of Locke even though with some important limitations."[91] Timothy Crutcher rightly argues that Wesley was influenced by Aristotle; however, this does not necessitate denying that Locke influenced Wesley.[92] Rather, this book argues that *Catholic Spirit* evokes the intrinsic nature of the toleration that was articulately expressed in Locke's work: the hope that Christians could coexist without violence.[93]

Of individual Christian groups before 1777, Wesley stated that their peculiarities could often be described only as opinions. In 1745, he began *A Farther Appeal to Men of Reason and Religion* Part II with, "it is not my present design to touch on any particular *opinions*, whether they are right or wrong; nor on any of those smaller points of practice which are

---

87. Yates, "'Perhaps He Cannot Know,'" 333.

88. Heitzenrater, "Oxford Methodists," appendix.

89. Wesley, *Remarks upon Mr. Locke's Essay, Works* (Jackson), 13:455–64.

90. Brown, *The Procedure, Extent, and Limits*.

91. Rack, *Reasonable Enthusiast*, 33; and Yates, "'Perhaps He Cannot Know,'" 332–33. See also Rack, "A Man of Reason, " 2–17. Brantley, *Locke, Wesley*, 23–102; aligned Wesley directly with Locke. Rack disagreed with Brantley arguing that Brantley conveniently avoided Wesley's appeal to spiritual senses which was not Lockean, in Rack, "Methodism and Romanticism," 64–65.

92. Crutcher, *Crucible of Life*, 16; and Yates, "'Perhaps He Cannot Know,'" 334.

93. Yates, "'Perhaps He Cannot Know,'" 334.

variously held by men of different persuasions."[94] "In this case, then, he distinguishes the opinions from the argument, so as to minimize their importance."[95]

Wesley defined "opinion" in a letter he wrote fifteen years after publishing *Catholic Spirit*. Answering John Newton's (1725–1807) request that he clarify the difference between essential and "opinion," Wesley answered, "Whatever is 'compatible with a love to Christ and a work of grace,' I term an opinion."[96] Specifically regarding his theological disputes with Calvinists, he designated "Particular Election" and "Final Perseverance" as opinions, which, he explained, was the reason he had not expelled preachers from his connexion who had Calvinist leanings. Nonetheless, some preachers he should have expelled for behavior had left on their own accord, and they "*pretended* 'they did not hold our doctrine.'"[97] These preachers considered "Particular Election" and "Final Perseverance" as essential, but Wesley did not.

Unfortunately, Wesley did not give his definition of "essential" in this letter to Newton. However, in a letter to William Legge (1731–1801) in April 1764, Wesley said that the "essentials" are belief in original sin, justification by faith, and holiness of heart and life.[98] Further, Wesley's *Letter to a Roman Catholic* comprises a list of beliefs shared by both Protestants and Catholics which Ted Campbell has suggested could be viewed as defining Wesley's "essentials," these include: one God, incarnation and atonement, crucifixion and resurrection, the work of the Holy Spirit, forgiveness of sin, and heaven and hell. From this, Campbell concludes that Wesley would label any religious statements other than these essentials as opinions.[99]

Randy Maddox, on the other hand, in an attempt to clarify Wesley's use of the word "opinion," contrasted it with his use of the word "doctrine." In this reading, "doctrines," according to Wesley, were "authoritative Christian teachings of religion in their own right."[100] These included Scripture, the Church Fathers, the Thirty-Nine Articles, and the *Homilies*.

94. JW, *A Farther Appeal to Men of Reason and Religion*, Part II, *Works*, 11:203.

95. Yates, "'Perhaps He Cannot Know,'" 336.

96. John Wesley to John Newton, May 14, 1765, *Works*, 27:426.

97. John Wesley to John Newton, May 14, 1765, *Works*, 27:426.

98. JW to William Legge, 2nd Earl of Dartmouth, April 19, 1764, *Works*, 27:360. See also Rivers, *Reason, Grace, and Sentiment*, 227.

99. Campbell, "The Shape of Wesleyan Thought," 27–48.

100. Maddox, "Opinion, Religion," 64–65.

"Opinions," in contrast, were an individual's personal understanding or interpretation of those doctrines. Maddox observed that, "such a distinction between opinions and doctrines was essentially a theological expression of the emerging 'Enlightenment' conviction of a disjunction between one's knowledge or ideas (opinions) and their objects (doctrines)."[101] Maddox traced this specific conviction to Locke's *An Essay Concerning Human Understanding*.[102] The central proposition of this conviction "was not that some ideas were less certain than others, but that all human ideas and judgements were fallible," and that therefore, they must forever remain open since further evidence might cause them to change.[103] Wesley articulated it this way: "although every man necessarily believes that every particular opinion he holds is true (for to believe any opinion is not true is the same thing as not to hold it), yet no man can be assured that all his opinions taken together can be true."[104] Locke expounded on "opinions" in a similar way in *A Letter Concerning Toleration*:

> We must, therefore, seek another cause of those evils that are charged upon religion. And if, we consider right, we shall find it to consist wholly in the subject that I am treating of. It is not the diversity of opinions (which cannot be avoided), but the refusal of toleration to those that are of different opinions (which might have been granted), that has produced all the bustles and wars that have been in the Christian world upon account of religion.[105]

Richard Challoner (1691–1781), vicar apostolic of the London district, wrote that Wesley and his followers, along with other Protestants, were not part of the true church of God.[106] Challoner's assumption was that salvation is only guaranteed to those who belong to the true church of God, which he defined as the Catholic Church. It had been this sort of

---

101. Maddox, "Opinion, Religion," 65. The 'Enlightenment' is no longer a useful term of historical explanation according to Clark, *English Society*, 9. That is why there are quotation marks when the term is used.

102. Locke, *An Essay Concerning Human Understanding*, 134.

103. Maddox, "Opinion, Religion," 65.

104. JW, *Catholic Spirit*, *Works*, 2:83–84.

105. Locke, *A Letter Concerning Toleration*, 55.

106. Challoner, *A Caveat Against the Methodists*, 17–18. This went through six editions according to Beckerlegge, *John Wesley's Writings*, 19. For more on Challoner, see Barnard, *Life of Challoner*; and Duffy, *Challoner and His Church*.

thinking that Wesley had sought to counter in *Catholic Spirit*. This is one of the many disagreements Wesley had with the Catholic Church.

Wesley had commented on Challoner's earlier publication, *The Grounds of the Old Religion*, in his *Journal* during 1743, criticizing Challoner's claim that "the Scripture is not the sole rule of faith; at least if not interpreted by private judgment, because private judgment has no place in matters of religion." Wesley responded: "Why, at this moment you are appealing to *my* private judgment; and you cannot possibly avoid it. The foundation of *your* as well as *my*, religion must necessarily rest here." He continued: "First you (as well as I) must judge for yourself whether you are implicitly to follow the church or no. And also which is the true church. Else it is not possible to move one step forward."[107] "This assertion of the importance of private judgement is indicative of the value Wesley attributed to liberty of conscience."[108] Wesley also said, "and how shall we choose among such variety? No man can choose for or prescribe to another. But everyone must follow the dictates his own conscience in simplicity and godly sincerity."[109]

Wesley used the phrases liberty of conscience and liberty of thought, or thinking, interchangeably. Most eighteenth-century Anglicans believed that liberty of conscience comprised at the very least two components: the preservation of an Established Church and freedom of worship, secured by law, for Protestant Nonconformists (excluding Unitarians).[110] Put simply, liberty of conscience was a principle that allowed people freedom to choose their own religion (provided that it was Protestant and Trinitarian) and freedom to worship God according to their own conscience, though Jews and Catholics were not granted the same rights as Protestants. With religious liberty, Wesley argued for natural right, such as in his *Thoughts upon Liberty* where he asserted that religious liberty was the right to choose our own religion, "to worship God according to our own conscience, according to the best light we have."[111] However, it was Wesley's view that Catholics did not allow for liberty of conscience; therefore, they could not be tolerated.[112] "Though Wesley was utterly

107. *JWJ*, March 25, 1743, *Works*, 19:320.

108. Yates, "'Perhaps He Cannot Know,'" 340.

109. JW, *Catholic Spirit*, *Works*, 2:85.

110. English, "Rights of Conscience," 352.

111. JW, *Thoughts upon Liberty*, *Works* (Jackson), 11:37–38. See also Weber, *Politics*, 322.

112. JW, "Letter to the Printer of the *Public Advertiser*," *Works* (Jackson), 10:161.

opposed to physical persecution and recognized Catholics could be saved despite their wrong 'opinions,' he shared traditional English prejudices against them as disloyal and persecuting, so he opposed granting them full civil rights."[113] The Reformation allowed for liberty of conscience. Wesley believed that the Catholic Church did not.

Locke said Catholics could not be "granted full toleration because their church is so constituted that all who enter it *ipso facto* pass into allegiance and service of another prince."[114] Wesley's statement in 1780 is similar: "Setting then religion aside, it is plain, that upon principles of reason, no Government ought to tolerate men who cannot give any security to that Government for their allegiance and peaceable behaviour."[115]

George Whitefield and Howel Harris

Another influence on the writing of Wesley's *Catholic Spirit* may have been his fellow evangelical leaders. This section will focus on the influence of two of his contemporaries: Howel Harris (1714–1773) and George Whitefield.

Whitefield had a vision of a church united and he often wrote about this in his letters. He hoped to see denominational barriers fall in the transatlantic evangelical revival. The earliest record available of Wesley using the phrase *Catholic Spirit* is the sermon, but Whitefield was using it before this. For instance, Whitefield wrote to Wesley in July 1739: "Is it true, honoured sir, that brother Stock is excluded the society because he holds predestination? If so, is it right? Would Jesus have done so? Is this to act with a catholic spirit?"[116] This letter was written at the beginning of Whitefield and Wesley's disagreement over predestination. Whitefield had written to Wesley just over a week earlier after having heard that he was "about to print a sermon against predestination."[117] That sermon was "Free Grace."[118] Whitefield did not attempt to explain *Catholic Spirit* here, so it seems that Whitefield expected Wesley to understand what he

---

113. Rack, "A Man of Reason and Religion," 10.

114. See Haydon, "Eighteenth-Century English," 49.

115. JW, "Letter to the Printer of the *Public Advertiser*," *Works* (Jackson), 10:161.

116. GW to JW, July 2, 1739, *Works*, 25:667.

117. GW to JW, June 25, 1739, *Works*, 25:662.

118. See *Works*, 3:542–63 for the sermon, *Free Grace*. For the *Free Grace* controversy, see Hammond, "Whitefield, John Wesley, and Revival Leadership," 104–14 and Houston, *Wesley, Whitefield*.

meant. Since Whitefield was using the phrase before Wesley, it is probable that Whitefield had some influence on Wesley's later us of the expression in his sermon. Perhaps Whitefield and Wesley discussed *Catholic Spirit* before the writing of this letter. The divide between Wesley and Whitefield and Wesleyan and Calvinistic Methodism may have been one of the several reasons that Wesley wrote the sermon.

Howel Harris was an evangelical preacher and close friend of Wesley and Whitefield. Whitefield described his first meeting with Harris in the following way: "He is of a most Catholick Spirit, loves all that loves our Lord Jesus Christ, and therefore, he is styled by Bigots, a Dissenter."[119] A letter from Harris to Whitefield's society at the Moorfields Tabernacle in February 1742 provides insight into his concept of catholic spirit: "And I believe want of this tenderness and love was one great cause of so many separations, perhaps; and 'tis in vain to preach up a Catholick Spirit, and Love, and Union among all, 'till the Lord has inclin'd every one to renounce all Names, and to be dead to his own Party."[120] Catholic spirit had to do with love and union, to renounce "names," and to disregard party affiliations. This aligns with Wesley's view of catholic spirit.

In 1742, Whitefield expressed longing that God would provide a catholic spirit in a particular society: "Our society is in great order. If the Lord gives us a true catholic spirit, free from a party sectarian zeal, we shall do well."[121] Just a few months later, Whitefield wrote a letter to John Willison, wherein he described his view of catholic spirit:

> I have often declared in the most public manner that I believe the Church of Scotland to be the best-constituted National Church in the World. At the same time, I would bear with, and converse freely with, all others who do not err in Fundamentals, and who give Evidence that they are true Lovers of the Lord Jesus. This is what I mean by a Catholick Spirit: Not that I believe a Jew or a Pagan, continuing such, can be a true Christian, or have true Christianity in them.[122]

119. March 8, 1739, GW, "An Account of the Rev. Mr. Whitefield's First Acquaintance with Mr. Howel Harris," in Lewis, *The Weekly History*, 2.

120. February 12, 1742, Howel Harris to the Society at the Tabernacle, in Lewis, *The Weekly History*, 4.

121. May 27, 1742, GW to Rev. Mr. O[oulton], GW, *Letters of George Whitefield*, 393.

122. August 17, 1742, GW to [Revd John] Willison, *An Account of the Most Remarkable Relating*, 42–43.

Whitefield declared that he would work with any Christian who held to the "Fundamentals" to which he subscribed. Whitefield's "Fundamentals" could be aligned with Wesley's use of "essentials."[123] Additionally, love was the key to unity for Whitefield as well as for Wesley.[124]

Of Whitefield and Wesley's view of catholic spirit, James L. Schwenk remarked: "'Evangelical ecumenicity' best captures the essence of 'catholic spirit' each was attempting to foster. The challenges lay in promoting evangelical ecumenicity, retaining their theological integrity, and doing so to continue the successes of the Evangelical Revival."[125] Both Whitefield and Wesley desired a uniting of Protestants involved in the revival. Whitefield held a negative perception of the Catholic Church, and it is probable that Whitefield, like Wesley, did not believe that *Catholic Spirit* should extend as far as unity with Catholics in doctrine or practice.

Catholic Spirit

The sermon *Catholic Spirit* was chosen for its ecumenical attributes. Although it initially seemed that Wesley was arguing that all Christians, including Catholics, should work together in unity, in-depth research showed that Wesley did not intend this sermon to apply to Catholics.

In his dictionary published six years after preaching *Catholic Spirit*, Wesley defined "catholic" as "universal," and catholic spirit as "universal love."[126] Additionally in *Letter to a Roman Catholic*, he was insistent that "catholic" meant "universal."[127] On the one hand, Wesley would have agreed with Richard Baxter that "Papists" abused the name of Catholic.[128] He took issue with "the priority and universality of the Roman Church."[129] However, on the other hand, in *Letter to a Roman Catholic* he explained that Christ had gathered a church, "this catholic, that is, universal, Church."[130] Even later in *Popery Calmly Considered*, he

---

123. See JW to William Legge, 2nd Earl of Dartmouth, April 19, 1764, *Works*, 27:360; and Campbell, "The Shape of Wesleyan Thought," 27–48.

124. JW, *Catholic Spirit, Works*, 2:81.

125. Schwenk, *Catholic Spirit*, 55.

126. JW, *Complete English Dictionary*, s.vv. "Catholic," and "Catholic Spirit."

127. *Works* (Jackson), 10:82.

128. Baxter, *The Reformed Pastor*, 193.

129. JW to a Roman Catholic Priest [1735], *Works*, 19:92.

130. JW, *Letter to a Roman Catholic, Works* (Jackson), 10:84–85.

asserted that "[The Church of Rome] it is only one particular branch of the catholic or universal Church of Christ, which is the whole body of believers of Christ, scattered over the whole earth."[131]

In *Catholic Spirit*, Wesley referred to the sermon itself as an attempt to correct misunderstanding of the phrase *Catholic Spirit*: "There is scarce any expression which has been more grossly misunderstood and more dangerously misapplied than this. But it would be easy for any who calmly consider the preceding observations to correct any such misapprehensions of it, and to prevent any such misapplication."[132] He pointed to this summary: "Whatsoever love, whatsoever offices of love, whatsoever spiritual or temporal assistance, I claim from him whose heart is right, as my heart is with his, the same I am ready, by the grace of God to give him." And, "I have not made this claim on behalf of myself only, but all whose heart is right toward God and man, that we may all love one another as Christ loved us."[133] This reinforced his definition of catholic spirit as universal love.

This book asserts that Wesley never intended the concept of catholic spirit to apply to Catholics. He aimed the sermon at Dissenters and Anglicans. The purpose of Methodism was "to reform the nation, more particularly the church, and to spread Christian holiness over the land."[134] Wesley did not perceive it impossible for a Catholic to experience New Birth, but he believed it would be difficult since he said Catholics would not hear "true religion" preached. It was only through New Birth that a person could practice a catholic spirit.

Conclusion

"No Popery!" had become a watchword of British identity in the eighteenth century as the clergy of the Established Church desperately tried to keep their country from the tyranny that they thought Catholicism would bring. Yet many Anglicans struggled to form a theology of toleration. Nonconformists such as Richard Baxter and empiricists such as John Locke all formulated ways to instruct Christians to live together in spite of their differences, yet most of them did not believe that Catholics

---

131. *Popery Calmly Considered, Works* (Jackson), 10:142.
132. JW, *Catholic Spirit, Works*, 2:92
133. JW, *Catholic Spirit, Works*, 2:92
134. *The Large Minutes A and B, Works*, 10:845.

deserved toleration. Wesley's contemporaries such as Howel Harris and George Whitefield used the concept of catholic spirit, and this likely influenced Wesley's writing of *Catholic Spirit*.

It has been determined that Wesley used the "Enlightenment" themes of opinion, doubt, and liberty of conscience as drawn from Locke's writings and others in the sermon *Catholic Spirit*. These sources led him to beseech Protestant Christians to distinguish between opinions and doctrines, and to humbly practice liberty of conscience.[135] However, the evidence strongly suggests that the same sources also influenced Wesley's anti-Catholicism.

135. Rack, "A Man of Reason and Religion?," 10.

3

A *Catholic Spirit* and Jacobitism

CHAPTER TWO CONSIDERED THE English Protestant Reformation's influence on the culture of anti-Catholicism. Leading attempts at articulating
toleration were analyzed as well as influences on Wesley's consideration
of toleration in his sermon, *Catholic Spirit*. This chapter explores events
that took place before Wesley's writing of *Catholic Spirit*, when he and the
early Methodists faced criticism for suspected Jacobitism at Oxford, and
encountered oppression from various antagonists during the "Forty-five,"
indicating that these events may have influenced the writing of *Catholic
Spirit*.[1] Understanding the charges of Jacobitism against Wesley and the
early Methodists is essential to the interpretation of *Catholic Spirit* and
Wesley's anti-Catholicism.

Rooted in the Latin form of James ("Jacobus"), "Jacobite" referred
to any attempt at restoring the exiled Stuarts after the removal of James
II and VII during the Glorious Revolution of 1688–1689.[2] The study of
Wesley's alleged Jacobitism leads to an assessment of Wesley's political
views.[3] Evaluating the influence of his family's political sympathies upon

1. This second Jacobite conflict had many labels, including "the '45," and the Second
Jacobite Rebellion, see Fremont-Barnes, *The Jacobite Rebellion*. For consistency, in this
book, the attempt of James's son, Charles Edward Stuart, the "Young Pretender," to
seize the throne and the events thereof in 1745–1746 will be called the "Forty-five."

2. The "Whig account" of the Revolution called it Glorious because limited blood
was shed in England, but other accounts tell of battles across Ireland and Scotland, see
Ciardha, "A lot done, more to do," in Monod, *Loyalty and Identity*, 57–79.

3. On Wesley's politics, see Maddox, *Political Writings*; Semmel, *The Methodist
Revolution*; Hynson, "John Wesley and Political Reality," 37–42; Hynson, "Human
Liberty as Divine Right," 57–85; Rack, *Reasonable Enthusiast*, 370–80; Weber, *Politics*;
and Vickers, *Guide*, 60–82.

him, and the setting at Oxford in which he lived will shed light on his political views. To further explore his political leanings, Wesley's reading, published essays and pamphlets, and his associations with known Jacobite sympathizers provide valuable insight. Along with these, the letters and journals of Wesley and his family, the diary of Benjamin Ingham (1712–1772), another Oxford Methodist, will be explored. For the "Forty-five," the political writings of Wesley such as *A Word in Season, or Advice to an Englishman* (1774), among others, will be analyzed. John Nelson's (bap. 1707, d. 1774) journal provides a perspective of a forcibly conscripted Methodist preacher during the "Forty-five." Wesley's contemporaries wondered whether he was a Jacobite, and scholars today still debate his exact political affiliation. In this chapter, the religious and political context of Jacobitism in eighteenth-century Great Britain will be provided as context to Wesley's religious and political perspectives.

After this context is explored, and the Jacobite accusations against Wesley and the Methodists are evaluated, it will emerge that these allegations can be included in Wesley's reasons for formulating a method of toleration in his sermon, *Catholic Spirit*, even though there is a lack of written documentation on this. First, Jacobitism and its complex implications in eighteenth-century Britain must be understood in order to place Wesley into his context.

The Religious and Political Context of Jacobitism

The two opposing parties, Whig and Tory, of the English Parliament worked together to bring about the Glorious Revolution, for both agreed that James's Catholicism was not in the best interest of the nation, especially since his wife had given birth to an heir, James Francis Edward Stuart (1688–1766), later called "the Old Pretender," in June 1688. Wesley acknowledged that the Revolution was "brought about by a coalition of Whigs and Tories."[4] The following is a brief description of the seventeenth- and eighteenth-century Whigs and Tories.

Whigs and Tories were two opposing political parties. They were first used as terms of abuse beginning in 1679 during the clash over the bill to exclude James, Duke of York (James II) from succession. "Whig," which probably has its origin in Scottish Gaelic, was a word used to refer to horse thieves and then to Scottish Presbyterians. "Tory" has its origin

---

4. JW, *A Concise History of England*, 4:5.

in Irish Gaelic meaning a papist outlaw. This term was used to refer to those who supported James II.[5]

The two parties had fears that England would become nothing more than a satellite state under the control of the Pope and France. William III and Mary II, James's son-in-law and daughter, who replaced him, ruled together until her death in 1694, with William ruling until he died in 1702. William and Mary left no heir, and Mary's sister Anne ascended the throne in 1702. Although she had multiple pregnancies, no child survived, and again, the sovereign died without issue. From 1688 to 1714, the Tory party remained strong opponents of the Whigs and swapped control through various elections. William and Mary's early government was mostly Tory, and Anne was perceived as a champion of the Tories. Yet, when the Whigs were instrumental in bringing George I (1660–1727) of Hanover to Britain in 1714, the Tories' influence declined. Henry St. John, First Viscount Bolingbroke (1678–1751), Tory leader and Secretary of State, fled to France in 1715, and this has been understood as the end of a period of Tory power.[6]

After the Glorious Revolution, most Tories accepted the Whig view of limited constitutional monarchy rather than promoting only passive obedience to the monarchy. The Whigs focused on constitutional monarchism and opposition to absolute rule, or tyranny, and had control of the British government from 1715 to 1760. In a general sense, Whigs asserted the power of Parliament over the monarchy, and Tories the opposite. Whigs became associated with Protestant Dissent. Tories opposed Whig liberalism and Protestant Dissent. They were usually associated with the High Church party, preservation of the privileges of the Established Church, and conservativism.[7] However, a movement, an ideology, and an

5. *Encyclopaedia Britannica Online*, s.v. "Whig and Tory," https://www.britannica.com/topic/Whig-Party-England.

6. For Bolingbroke's life, see MacKnight, *The Life of Henry St. John*.

7. David Hume defined a Tory "as a lover of monarchy, tho' without abandoning liberty; and a partisan of the family of Stuart." A Whig he defined as "a lover of liberty, tho' without renouncing monarchy; a friend to the settlement in the Protestant line," see "Of the Parties of Great Britain," in *Essays, Moral and Political*, 131. Samuel Johnson showed the complexity of the definitions of Whig and Tory. "Tory" he defined as "one who adheres to the ancient constitution of the state, and the apostolical hierarchy of the Church of England, opposed to a Whig." "Whig" he listed as "the name of a faction" after giving explanation of the origin of the word in Scotland he said, "it is now one of our unhappy terms of disunion." Johnson, *Dictionary*, 2: s.v. "Whig."

ethos remained with a group of people who still believed that James II's heirs belonged on the British throne. These were the Jacobites.[8]

There is variance among scholars in their interpretation of Jacobitism as it relates to Toryism.[9] However, the purpose of this section is not to enter into the debate on the Jacobite-Tory connection. Instead the aim is to provide examples of the varied views of eighteenth-century British politics, even among people who claimed to be of the same political affiliation. The complexion of this diversity is still debated between scholars today as not all agree on the political connections between Tories and Jacobites. One illustration of the Jacobite-Tory relationship comes from a voice of an eighteenth-century Member of Parliament, George Lyttelton (1709–1773). In *A Letter to the Tories* (1747), he declared, "all Jacobites are Tories, tho' all Tories are not Jacobites. A Jacobite is a Tory and something more, as a Dissenter is a Whig and something more."[10] Many Tories were High Churchmen, and Wesley was no exception. Yet there remained many politically diverse opinions within the Church of England.

John Walsh and Stephen Taylor noted: "the major schools of Churchmanship—High, liberal, Evangelical existed as identifiable tendencies in the Georgian Church. For the most part their relationship was one of peaceful coexistence."[11] Wesley identified himself as a High Churchman, as he said: "for I am an High Churchman, the son of an High Churchman, bred up from my childhood in the highest notions of passive obedience and non-resistance."[12] Defining "High Church" proves difficult. Chamberlain described High Churchmanship in terms of ethos rather than specific doctrines or practices, with two predominant

---

8. Clark, *English Society*, 107; and Monod, *Jacobitism and the English People*, 6–12.

9. For example, Cruickshanks asserted that the Tory party had survived forty years of proscription after 1714 by adopting the Old Pretender's cause. Colley disagreed, pointing out that Tories had more options than Jacobitism, that they were never committed to Stuarts as a party, and that the Tory party was predominately Hanoverian after 1714. Andrew Hanham disagreed with Colley's conclusion, as he implied that she founded her case on "British Tory archival material" but did not examine the Jacobite factor systematically. Sedgwick, *The History of Parliament*, 1:62–78; Cruickshanks, *Political Untouchables*, 1–13; Colley, *In Defiance of Oligarchy*, 36–45; and Andrew Hanham, "'So Few Facts,'" 233–35.

10. Lyttelton, *A Letter to the Tories*, 12.

11. Walsh and Taylor, "Introduction," in Walsh et al., *The Church of England*, 45.

12. JW to the Earl of Dartmouth, June 14, 1775, in Telford, 6:156.

principles concerning the High Churchmen: loyalty to the Church of England and to the Crown.[13]

Peter Nockles offered the following characteristics of eighteenth-century High Churchmen. They believed in some form of apostolic succession—that the Church of England was a branch of the universal catholic church. They held to the authority of Scripture but taught that the Bible should be interpreted through the Book of Common Prayer, the creeds, and the catechism. Valuing the writings of the early Church Fathers, they placed vast importance on the sacraments. Therefore, spirituality was based upon sacramental grace rather than a personal conversion experience. They stressed the vitality of the religious establishment alongside the state being divinely ordained. The state existed to uphold the well-being of the Church.[14] During Anne's reign, "High Church" was delineated politically as synonymous with "Tory."[15] This lumping together of High Church and Tory was encouraged by Whigs and Dissenters to align High Churchmen with Jacobitism, but just as it is a wrong assumption that all Tories were Jacobites, it is a false conjecture that all High Churchmen were Tories.[16] Early in the eighteenth century it was usually the case that to be a High Churchman was to be a Tory, and vice versa, but Chamberlain provided evidence that later in the century many High Churchmen tended towards Whiggism, in part, for the purpose of survival.[17] High Churchmen were partial to the liturgy of either the 1549 or the 1662 Book of Common Prayer, and resisted any further modifications to the version of the book to which they were loyal. They "gloried in the moderation of the Church of England," and believed that more moderation would be dilution.[18] They were against changes that would bring Dissenters into the Church unless they "repented" of their nonconformity and communicated wholly with the Established Church, for moderation was *not* a virtue when the Church was threatened. High Churchmen were loyal to a specific vision of the Church: episcopal,

---

13. Chamberlain, *Accommodating High Churchmen*, 14; and Nockles, "Church Parties," 334.

14. Nockles, "Church Parties," 335–36.

15. Nockles, "Church Parties," 336.

16. Nockles, "Church Parties," 336–37.

17. Chamberlain, *High Churchmen*, 79–105.

18. Chamberlain, *High Churchmen*, 17.

sacramental, liturgical, and uniform. They viewed episcopacy, the governing of the Church by bishops in apostolic succession, as ordained of God.[19]

High Church Tories believed in the doctrine of passive obedience to the monarch. They saw themselves as subjects and not citizens. They held tightly to these beliefs because they thought that any alternative would lead to anarchy.[20] Wesley's famous claim about his churchmanship is as follows, "I am a Church-of-England man . . . in the Church I will live and die unless I am thrust out."[21] While he identified himself as a High Church Tory, over time, he relaxed his views that went along with this as indicated in *Catholic Spirit*.[22]

The "Fifteen" was the befuddled attempt of James Stuart, the "Old Pretender," at starting an uprising in 1715.[23] Louis XIV (1638–1715) of France had recognized James as James III, *de jure* king of England after his father's passing in 1701. James Stuart arrived in Scotland intending to gather an army, but he fell ill, and ultimately abandoned his retreating army at Montrose. He boarded a ship for France in February 1716, but when he arrived, he found that Louis XIV had died.[24] No longer welcome in France, James and his supporters settled in Rome by invitation of Pope Clement XI (1649–1721) in 1717.[25] The "Old Pretender" did not give up hope that he would return to what he believed was his right as king of Great Britain. He married Maria Clementina Sobieski (1702–1735) in 1719, and their union produced two sons, Charles Edward (1720–1788) and Henry Benedict (1725–1807).[26] Charles Edward would lead his own rebellion against the Crown in 1745–1746, which will be discussed below.

The atmosphere at Oxford during the "Fifteen" had been heated and turbulent.[27] There had been riots, which resulted in military occupation of the city as the Whigs of Oxford alleged that the "Old Pretender" had been proclaimed king in Oxford in October 1715.[28] John Wesley's 1775

19. Chamberlain, *High Churchmen*, 13–14.
20. Vickers, *Guide*, 62–63.
21. JW to Henry Moore, May 6, 1788, in Telford, 8:58.
22. JW, *Catholic Spirit*, *Works*, 2:86.
23. See Szechi, *1715*.
24. Szechi, "Retrieving Captain Le Cocq's Plunder," 98.
25. Szechi, *1715*, 215.
26. For the life of Charles Edward Stuart, see McLynn, *Bonnie Prince Charlie*.
27. Langford, "Tories and Jacobites 1714–1751," 5:99–103.
28. Ward, *Georgian Oxford*, 61.

account of the "Fifteen" indicated that the British ambassador to Paris had sent the king all the intelligence he could, yet none of this kept the Pretender from attempted invasion.[29] Wesley commented further that the Pretender should have known that the nation would not support him.[30] When Wesley went up to Christ Church, Oxford, it had been only five years since the 1715 Jacobite Rising. Even into the 1730s, Oxford's Tory High Churchmen were labelled Jacobites, and consequently faced criticism. Most of the colleges were predominately controlled by Tories of diverse opinions, and only a few became Whig in complexion.[31] The heads of houses leaned towards moderation, but the junior members leaned towards Jacobitism. The result was a string of squabbles within and between colleges, worsened by religious fears, personal antipathies, and the environment of senior common rooms where university gossip occurred.[32] This is the environment in which Wesley lived and breathed while a student and later as a fellow.

Wesley's Politics

Unfortunately, not much is known about Wesley's undergraduate years other than the books he studied as required by Christ Church.[33] We can only deduce what his political views were during this time from what he was reading, his later writings, or assume that he shared the perspectives of one or both of his parents.[34] Susanna Wesley possibly maintained her Jacobite views throughout her life. Susanna declared in her journal in 1709 that a king "derives his power from God, so to him only must he answer for using it."[35] However, this was a High Church view and not necessarily Jacobite. When Wesley was a student, he wrote to his mother mentioning the "abdication of King James II."[36] Calling the removal of

29. JW, *Concise History*, 4:126.

30. JW, *Concise History*, 4:128.

31. Rack, *Reasonable Enthusiast*, 63. The colleges that were predominantly Whig were: Exeter, Jesus, Wadham, and from the 1730s, Christ Church.

32. Rack, *Reasonable Enthusiast*, 63; and Sutherland, *History of Oxford*, 5:3.

33. English, "John Wesley's Studies," 29.

34. Rack, *Reasonable Enthusiast*, 69–71; and Green, *The Young Mr. Wesley*, 61–83.

35. See Susanna Wesley, Journal entry, 1709, Susanna Wesley, *Complete Writings*, 204.

36. JW to Susanna Wesley, [December 18, 1724], *Works*, 25:154; and Weber, *Politics*, 53.

James II an abdication was a claim of the Whigs to suggest that James II had left on his own accord. Wesley may have been imprecise with his words, or he may have been showing his mother his support of the Revolution. Susanna Wesley most likely would not have agreed with her son's words, but we do not have record of her reaction. Weber was correct when he said that Susanna's Jacobitism was a matter of conscience rather than of active effort for a restoration of the male line of James II.[37]

Some have argued that Samuel Wesley, Sr. held Jacobite leanings because John Wesley reported that his father wrote the speech that the Jacobite Tory Henry Sacheverell (c. 1674–1724) made before Parliament in 1710 when tried for sedition.[38] Historians of the trial do not believe that Wesley was correct that his father wrote the speech.[39] Samuel Wesley, Sr. wrote verses in 1688 to honour the birth of James II's son, but this was before the Glorious Revolution, and it was expected that he would support the reigning king.[40] Nevertheless, even if he did help write the speech and wrote in honour of the infant "Pretender," there is other evidence to show that he did not hold Jacobite views.[41] For example, he seems have supported the Glorious Revolution. Luke Tyerman stated that he was not a Jacobite because he praised God for the 1688–1689 Revolution. There is no evidence that he was attached to the interests of James; but on the contrary, there is evidence that he was disgusted with James's tyranny at Oxford. Samuel was the author of a pamphlet published in defense of the Revolution.[42] Adam Clarke said of the Epworth rector, "he left a remarkable memorial of King William's character in one of his *Dissertations on the Book of Job* wherein remarking on the description of the war horse, he introduces the deceased monarch as he appeared at the Battle of the

37. Weber, *Politics*, 53.

38. JW, *Concise History*, 4:75n. Wesley said of Sacheverell's speech, "it was wrote by the Rector of Epworth, in Lincolnshire." See also Southey, *Life of Wesley*, 1:21n; and Weber, *Politics*, 45.

39. Scudi, *The Sacheverell Affair*, 90, mentioned that Wesley said his father wrote the speech, but said there is no evidence that Samuel Wesley wrote it. The speech is in John Rylands Library, Manchester, with handwriting listing Samuel Wesley as the author. There also is evidence in Tyerman and *Concise Ecclesiastical History* of Samuel's authorship. No author is printed on the tract itself. See MARC DDwf 1/18, *Dr. Sacheverell's Answer to the Articles of Impeachment &c.*

40. Rack, "Wesley, Samuel (bap. 1662 d. 1735)," *ODNB*.

41. Tyerman, *Samuel Wesley*, 177.

42. Tyerman, *Samuel Wesley*, 177.

Boyne in Ireland July 1, 1690." He [Samuel] pointed out that William was *"the fittest hero* to have managed the *warlike animal* just described."[43]

Samuel Wesley, Sr. published a poem in 1695 on the death of Queen Mary II, given that Mary died in 1694, and he supported the Hanoverians' right to the throne when Queen Anne died in 1714. There is record that during family prayers the rector led his household in praying for King George I.[44]

John Wesley's older brother, Samuel Wesley, Jr. (1690/91–1739) was a protégé of the Jacobite Bishop of Rochester Francis Atterbury (1662–1732), who was exiled in 1723 for a Jacobite plot.[45] Maldwyn Edwards stated outright, "Samuel [Jr.] was the Jacobite in the family."[46] Yet Edwards argued that the oldest Wesley brother was a Jacobite only because of his friendship with Atterbury.[47] John Wesley denied that this brother ever was a Jacobite in the *Gentlemen's Magazine* in 1785, pointing out that those who gave Samuel Wesley Jr. this label did not "distinguish between a Jacobite and a Tory; whereby I mean, 'one that believes God, not the people, to be the origin of all civil power.' In this sense he was a Tory; so was my father, and so am I."[48] Nevertheless, Samuel's association with Atterbury tarnished his reputation, and most likely added to the accusations against Wesley and the Methodists.[49] John Wesley was influenced by his family's political sympathies, but he seems to have, like many other Tories, transferred his ideas of divine right to the Hanoverian dynasty.[50]

Wesley's family shaped his politics, and there is no denying that Oxford High Churchmanship in the 1720s and 1730s affected him. V.

43. Clarke, *Memoirs*, 158.

44. See Samuel Wesley, "On the Death," 1–17; Tyerman, *Samuel Wesley*, 353–54, reprinted Samuel Wesley's journal as describing the Wesley family praying for "King George and the prince."

45. See Atterbury, *Memoirs and Correspondence of Francis Atterbury*, 2:465; Bennett, *The Tory Crisis in the Church and State*; Ward, "Wesley and his Evangelical Past;" Ward, *The Protestant Evangelical Awakening*, 309; Hammond, *JW in America*, 67; and Rack, *Reasonable Enthusiast*, 69. Atterbury, *The Axe Laid to the Root of Christianity* is included in JW's book collection at his London House. See Maddox, "John Wesley's Reading," 120. For Atterbury's exile, see Szechi, *The Jacobites*, 92–93.

46. Edwards, *Family Circle*, 115.

47. Edwards, *Family Circle*, 115.

48. JW to the Editor of the *Gentlemen's Magazine*, December 24, 1785, in Telford, 7:305–6.

49. JW to Susanna Wesley, January 24, 1726/7, *Works*, 25:208–9.

50. Rack, "Wesley, John (1703–1791)," *ODNB*.

H. H. Green disclosed: "His High-Churchmanship carried with it a dislike of the Hanoverian regime which suggested an inclination to flirt with Jacobitism, but his inherent sense of loyalty and dislike of Roman Catholicism would never have made him a Jacobite in fact."[51] Henry Rack echoed Green's observations by stating, "Though possibly flirting with Jacobitism and certainly criticizing the Walpole administration during his Oxford period, Wesley soon adopted his father's position."[52]

Wesley at Oxford

During his Oxford years, Wesley was in close touch with known Jacobites.[53] For instance, Thomas Hearne (1678–1735), a family friend, had lost his position as second librarian at the Bodleian for refusing to take the oath to George I when asked in 1716.[54] In his journal, Hearne wrote that he heard Wesley preach twice in 1733.[55] Wesley indicated that he had talked with a friend in December 1725 against King George [I], and the next Saturday he resolved not to speak against the king.[56] As late as 1775, when he wrote about the first Hanoverian king, his words were controlled, but not affirming: "the new-elected monarch did not seem sensible, the men around him soured him with all their own prejudices."[57] Wesley blamed the Whigs for some of George I's problems: "The Whigs governed the senate and the court; whom they would, they opposed; bound the lower orders of people with severe laws, and kept them at a distance by vile distinctions; and then taught them to call this—Liberty."[58] In *A Concise History*, Wesley described George I:

> Before he ascended the throne of Great Britain, he had acquired
> the character of a circumspect general, a just and merciful

51. Green, *Young Mr. Wesley*, 78.

52. JW to Earl of Dartmouth, June 14, 1775, in Telford, 6:156; Rack, "Wesley, John (1703–1791)," *ODNB*; see also Hempton, "Wesley in Context," 70; and Ward, *Protestant Evangelical Awakening*, 114.

53. Weber, *Politics*, 48; Green, *Young Mr. Wesley*, 78–79; and Clark, *English Society*, 286n.

54. Harmsen, "Hearne, Thomas (bap. 1678, d. 1735)," *ODNB*; and Hearne, *Remarks and Collections*, 1:11, 49–50.

55. Hearne, *Remarks and Collections*, 11:180.

56. Green, *Young Mr. Wesley*, 81.

57. JW, *Concise History*, 4:111.

58. JW, *Concise History*, 4:111.

prince, and a wise politician who perfectly understood, and steadily pursued his own interests. With these qualities, it cannot be doubted that he came to England extremely well disposed to govern his new subjects according to the maxims of the British constitution, and the genius of the people; and if he ever seemed to deviate from these principles, we may take it for granted, that he was misled by the venal suggestions of a ministry, whose power and influence were founded on corruption.[59]

Wesley's speaking ill of George I at Oxford and hesitancy later to say anything against this monarch is notable. However, he had no scruples in criticizing the rest of the government, as is shown by several conversations he recorded in his diary while a Lincoln College Fellow. On November 5, 1725, he had talked of passive obedience and had engaged in "evil speaking of [Robert] Walpole."[60] He had breakfasted with Lord Dupplin in February 1727 and talked of Walpole and Bolingbroke.[61] These things he wrote in cipher in his Oxford diary.[62] Another friend, Nonjuror Thomas Deacon, allegedly associated with two men who had been hanged for their actions in the 1715 Rising. In 1733 Wesley had journeyed to Manchester twice where he visited Deacon.[63] During his later Oxford and Georgia days, the Nonjuror influence was a major influence on his theology and practice. This could have led some to suspect him of Jacobitism, as many, but not all, the Nonjurors were Jacobites. Wesley and his brother, Charles, were also in contact with known Jacobite Nonjuror, John Byrom (1692–1763).[64] However, it seems that Wesley's

59. JW, *Concise History*, 4:159. For more on *Concise History*, see Black, "John Wesley and History," 1–17.

60. Green, *Young Mr. Wesley*, 78–79. Robert Walpole (1676–1745), 1st Earl of Orford, is generally regarded as the first Prime Minister of Great Britain, even though the title was not used. He was appointed the first Lord of the Treasury in 1715, and resigned the post in 1717. The start of his period as "Prime Minister" is dated as 1720, 1721, and 1722 in different accounts (1721 is the "traditional" date). See Gregory and Stevenson, *The Routledge Companion to Britain*, 67; and Sedgwick, *House of Commons*, 2:513–17.

61. Most likely George Hay, eighth earl of Kinnoull (1689–1758) who took the title Viscount Dupplin in 1709, and was detained in London for support of Stuarts during the 1715 Jacobite Rising. See Carter, "Hay, George, Eighth Earl of Kinnoull (1689–1758)," *ODNB*; and Green, *Young Mr. Wesley*, 78–79.

62. Green, *Young Mr. Wesley*, 78n.

63. For the life of Deacon, see Broxap, *A Biography of Thomas Deacon*. See also Tyerman, *Oxford Methodists*, 34; and Rack, *Reasonable Enthusiast*, 90.

64. Byrom, *The Private Journal*, 336, 375–76, 383; and Best, *Charles Wesley*, 170–71.

fascination with the Nonjurors was a spiritual rather than a political one. Green stated that Wesley sympathized with the Nonjurors, but that he was not one of them.[65]

Although there is not space to give a full account of Wesley's political readings at Oxford, a few shall be examined. There are some books that he read that give insight into his political sympathies. Interestingly, he read Richard Venn's (1691–1739) *King George's Title Asserted*, which was Venn's attempt to persuade his friend, Thomas Baker (1656–1740), to take the Oath to King George I.[66] Baker was married to the daughter of John Ashton (c. 1653–1691), who had been executed for his part in the Jacobite Preston Plot of 1691. Therefore, it seems this convincing of Baker by Venn would have been a difficult task.[67] However, Wesley read widely and did not necessarily agree with everything he read. Another writer, philosopher George Berkeley, had refused to take the Oath of Allegiance to William and Mary, but recanted and took the oath to Queen Anne, publishing a justification of this decision in *Passive Obedience* (1712), a book that Wesley read in December 1730.[68]

Bernard Semmel and Leon Hynson argued that Wesley was a Jacobite and Nonjuror during Oxford days, but his persuasions shifted from a Jacobite High Church Tory to a more Whiggish view over a period of thirty years from 1734 to 1764.[69] Hynson claimed Wesley's political evolution from Jacobite to Hanoverian commenced after Wesley read William Higden's (1662/3–1715) *A View of the English Constitution* in 1733.[70] Higden was a Nonjuror, but recanted, and wrote to defend his retraction. Theodore Weber criticized Hynson's view that Higden 'converted' Wesley from the belief in divine hereditary right and passive obedience to an advocate of limited monarchy and civil liberties.[71]

---

65. Green, *Young Mr. Wesley*, 28.

66. Venn, *King George's Title Asserted*.

67. Sharp, "Venn, Richard (1691–1739)," *ODNB*.

68. Berkeley, *Passive Obedience*; and Ross, "Was Berkeley a Jacobite?," 17–30. For a record of Wesley's reading at Oxford, see Heitzenrater, "Oxford Methodists," appendix IV.

69. Semmel, *Methodist Revolution*, 59–60; and Hynson, "Human Liberty," 71.

70. Higden, *A View of the English Constitution*. JW owned the book as his initials are on the inside cover, see Maddox, "John Wesley's Reading," 49, 54. See also Heitzenrater, "Oxford Methodists," appendix iv; and Hynson, "Human Liberty," 59.

71. Weber, *Politics*, 58–66.

In 1750 Wesley wrote that "With regard to my political principles I never had any doubt since I read Mr. Higden's *View of the English Constitution*, which I look upon as one of the best wrote books I have ever seen in the English tongue."[72] Weber pointed out that Wesley never stated that Higden changed his mind, but: "what Wesley read in Higden is what he believed already."[73] Clark described Wesley's political views in 1730 in the following way:

> Wesley had always practiced the political virtue of non-resis-
> tance under a *de facto* government. After he had come in the
> 1730s to acknowledge the Hanoverians a divine right, he de-
> vised for them a defense in dynastic terms. His *Concise History
> of England* announced that since the marriage in 1209 between
> King John and Isabella was not "lawful" their children were
> illegitimate, and the Stuarts' title "by birth" unfounded; King
> George I was "lineally descended" from Matilda who had a
> "prior right."[74]

George Ballantyne had asserted the same thing in 1743.[75] Wesley's indication in his *Concise History* that George I was descended from Matilda reflected the teaching of many churchmen, as they would refer to John 19:11 where Jesus declared to Pilate, "you can have no authority over me except it were given from above."[76] These churchmen interpreted this verse to mean that *de facto* monarchs are the rulers that are ordained by God. As Wesley emphasized, "what right then could they or any of their posterity, the Stuarts in particular, have to the crown of England?"[77] Ward remarked that Wesley wrote, in *A Concise History*, "with the radicalism of a party [Tory] defeated in the struggle for a first class establishment."[78] This makes sense, as Wesley had remarked negatively on Walpole's Whig

---

72. JW to Samuel Brewster, February 22, 1750, *Works*, 26:410–11.

73. Weber, *Politics*, 60. David Hempton expressed the same interpretation in *Religion of the People*, 80.

74. JW, *Concise History*, 1:189; and Clark, *English Society*, 287.

75. Ballantyne, *A Vindication of the Hereditary Right*, 10–11. Clark indicated this similarity in *English Society*, 95.

76. JW, *Concise History*, 1:189; and Clark, *English Society*, 287.

77. JW, *Concise History*, 1:189.

78. Ward, *Protestant*, 301.

administration during his Oxford days.[79] Nonetheless, no matter Wesley's true political sympathies, he was accused of Jacobitism while at Oxford.[80]

The Oxford Methodists and Jacobitism

The first rumor that Wesley might be a Jacobite surfaced while he served as Fellow at Lincoln College, Oxford. Wesley called the story of the Oxford Methodists "the first rise of Methodism," describing them as a "few young gentlemen at Oxford" who met together soon after 1729, and by 1731 they were called the Godly Club, the Reforming Club, Methodists, or the Holy Club.[81] The next summer they visited prisoners, the sick, and the poor. Thomas Broughton (1712–1777) from Exeter, Benjamin Ingham from Queen's, James Hervey (1714–1758) from Lincoln, and George Whitefield (1714–1770) from Pembroke are just a few of the men who were eventually branded "Oxford Methodists."[82]

The Methodists were accused of making Oxford into a "monastery" in a letter published in *Fog's Weekly Journal* in late 1732.[83] This charge related to the strictness of the lifestyle that the Methodists promoted. The way of life of the Methodists was strict: times for rising, praying, eating, reading, fasting, group confession, and self-examination could be interpreted as similar to a monastic order of the Catholic Church. Yet their central focus was the goal of Christian perfection, and they did not wish to let the particular spiritual disciplines become primary. They practiced meditation and denied themselves with early rising and fasting.[84] Although the letter did not use the words "Roman Catholic," the implication seems to be there. The eighteenth-century stereotypical English understanding was that anything Catholic could logically lead to Jacobitism. The author of this letter remains unknown, but the newspaper must have

---

79. Green, *Young Mr. Wesley*, 78–79.

80. Heitzenrater, "Oxford Methodists," 276.

81. For JW's account of the Oxford Methodists, see *A Short History of Methodism*, 4–6; and *Works*, 9:367–72; for CW's account, see CW to Dr. [Thomas Bradbury] Chandler, April 28, 1785, MARC DDWes 1/38.

82. For the list of those who were participants in Oxford Methodism, see Heitzenrater, "Oxford Methodists," 334.

83. "To the Author of *Fog's Weekly Journal*"; Heitzenrater, "Oxford Methodists," 190; Heitzenrater, *Elusive Mr. Wesley*, 2:28–35; and Colley, *In Defiance of Oligarchy*, 114.

84. Heitzenrater, "Oxford Methodists," 352–64.

obtained a copy of a letter that Richard Morgan, Sr. (c. 1679–1742), wrote in complaint to Charles Wesley blaming the Methodists' strict lifestyle for the death of his son, William (d. 1732).[85] Morgan insisted that he had not given the letter to the newspaper.[86]

An unexpected answer to this letter in *Fog's Weekly Journal,* a Jacobite publication, came in the form of a pamphlet titled *The Oxford Methodists.*[87] It was not completely positive towards them, but Wesley was generally pleased with it.[88] The authorship of this pamphlet has been a mystery: Rack speculated that it could have been William Law, but John Dussinger has made a convincing case that it was the printer of the first edition, Samuel Richardson (bap. 1689, d. 1761).[89] The controversy that Wesley and the Oxford Methodists experienced was far from over, as two years later, when Wesley preached at the University Church of St. Mary the Virgin, he was accused of Jacobitism.

Wesley preached "The One Thing Needful" on St. Barnabas Day, 1734.[90] His text was Luke 10:42, "but one thing is needful: and Mary hath chosen that good part, which shall not be taken away from her."[91] For years it was thought that the manuscript of the sermon did not exist but Heitzenrater determined it was "The One Thing Needful" transcribed by Charles Wesley and published by his widow, Sarah Gwynne Wesley (1726–1822).[92] Charles Wesley noted in a manuscript collection of sermons that John Wesley preached the sermon nine times after this occasion, but it is unknown whether he altered the sermon based on the

---

85. Richard Morgan, Sr. to CW, September 5, 1732, in Telford, 1:122–23.

86. Richard Morgan, Sr. to JW, March 10, 1733, *Works,* 25:349.

87. [Richardson], *The Oxford Methodists.*

88. Heitzenrater, *Elusive Mr. Wesley,* 2:32.

89. See Dussinger, "The Oxford Methodists."

90. JW, "The One Thing Needful" (1734), *Works,* 4:352–59; Heitzenrater, "Oxford Methodists," 276; and Ingham, *Diary,* 217. Heitzenrater deduced this based upon the record in Wesley's *Diary* that said he preached at St. Mary's twice that year: February 10 and June 11; on February 10, he preached "On the Love of God," according to Ingham, *Diary,* 112–13, and Heitzenrater, "John Wesley's Early Sermons," 124.

91. *Works,* 4:352–59; and CW, *The Sermons of Charles Wesley,* 360–68. Newport indicates that the MS said John Wesley also preached the sermon, but does not comment on who might be the original author in 360n. CW published a poem on "The One Thing Needful" in 1762; see Kimbrough and Beckerlegge, *Unpublished Poetry of Charles Wesley,* 2:125–26. See also MARC DDcw 8/13.

92. *Works,* 4:351–52; and Weber, *Politics,* 52.

accusations as the only manuscript copy that is known to exist is this one in the handwriting of Charles.[93]

Charles Wesley wrote to his brother, Samuel Wesley, Jr., a few weeks after John Wesley preached the sermon that John had been "much mauled, and threatened more for his Jacobite Sermon on June 11: but he was wise enough to get the Vice Chancellor to read it, and approve it before he preached it, and may therefore bid Wadham, Merton, Exeter, and Christ Church to do their work."[94] However, detecting John Wesley's thoughts during this period of time is especially difficult as his diary entries stopped in April 1734, and he did not start them again until August for reasons still unknown.[95]

Heitzenrater indicated that the occasion (but he did not name the occasion) might have "lent itself to the expressing of Jacobite sympathies," but nothing in the text of the sermon gave a hint of what caused the controversy.[96] Like Heitzenrater, Weber asserted that there is nothing political in the sermon text as it has survived in Charles Wesley's manuscript.[97] This makes sense, because if there had been words in the sermon that Charles thought would lead to the accusation of Jacobitism, then Charles probably would have edited them in transcription. It is impossible to know the difference between the oral sermon, and the written sermon: John's written manuscript, and then Charles's manuscript. Yet there had to be something in the sermon that caused the accusation of Jacobitism. A general analysis of the sermon can be made from the text that remains, but first the occasion must be considered.

The Feast of St. Barnabas the Apostle was celebrated June 11 in the Church of England, so the day itself would not have engendered anything particularly Jacobite.[98] Wesley's sermon even reflected the description of the Anglican observation of the festival as it was described as a time to "to despise ease, and even life itself when we have any happy opportunity of

---

93. *Works*, 4:352–59; and MARC DDcw/8/13.

94. CW to Samuel Wesley Jr., July 31, 1734, CW, *Letters of Charles Wesley*, 40.

95. Heitzenrater, "Oxford Methodists," 272. Nehemiah Curnock gives an overall summary of the Oxford Diaries 1–4 in his introduction to volume 1 of JW, *The Journal of the Rev. John Wesley*, 1:3–77.

96. Ingham, *Diary*, 217n.

97. Weber, *Politics*, 52.

98. See Nelson, *A Companion for the Festivals*, 142–52. Wesley read this book in 1731; see Heitzenrater, "Oxford Methodists," 539.

propagating Christian knowledge."[99] For Wesley asked: "Is the entertainment of the senses the one thing needful? Or the gratifying imagination with uncommon, or great, or beautiful objects? Our Lord saith not so."[100]

The Old Pretender's birthday was June 10, and June 11 was the seventh anniversary of the accession of George II (1683–1760).[101] Together these two dates may have caused anxiety at Oxford as sometimes Jacobites would celebrate an anniversary related to James Stuart that was close to the "national one" to show their opposition, and the Pretender's birthday was known as a day that could spark riots.[102] There had been riots on June 10 in 1695, 1715, 1718, and 1721.[103] Since he was known for his High Church Toryism, Whig listeners could have been on edge and waiting for this Lincoln fellow to say anything which they could relate to Jacobitism, especially since *Fog's Weekly Journal* had already accused the Oxford Methodists of Catholicism less than two years previously. Another reason for the accusation could have been the political strife between the Whigs and the Tories in 1734. The general election had been held between April 22 and June 6, 1734, when Robert Walpole's Whigs had lost multiple seats in Parliament to the Tories, even though the Whigs kept the majority. Whigs had identified Oxford's Tory High Churchmen with the Jacobite cause. It is possible that Wesley and the Oxford Methodists could have fallen victim to this Whig propaganda, especially since "Whig governments after 1714 saw the real or imaginary Jacobitism of Oxford as infecting young men with scabrous ideas."[104]

Of the sermon itself, Weber suggested that the words "riches, or honour, or power" in the sermon could have stirred some trouble, as it could have led some to believe that the "one thing needful" could be to gain power. Weber called these typical Tory complaints when the Whigs were in power.[105] It may have been subtle, but there may have been enough political language in the sermon to convince the Whig listeners this High Church Tory sided with the Stuarts. Not much has been recorded about the ramifications of Wesley and the Oxford Methodists'

99. Nelson, *Companion*, 148.

100. JW, "The One Thing Needful," *Works,* 4:358.

101. Haydon, *Anti-Catholicism*, 33n; Szechi, *Jacobites*, 25; and Cannon, "George II (1683–1760)," *ODNB.*

102. Harris, *The Politics of the Excluded*, 14.

103. Monod, *Jacobitism*, 213–14.

104. Sutherland, *History of Oxford*, 4.

105. Weber, *Politics*, 52.

experience of being accused of Jacobitism at Oxford. Heitzenrater said, "in the midst of the minor turmoil that followed [the preaching of "The One Thing Needful"], one of Wesley's strongest supporters left the University [Benjamin Ingham]."[106] Heitzenrater did not elaborate on the turmoil.

It may not have helped matters that he would travel to Georgia at the invitation of the son of a known Jacobite insurrectionist, James Oglethorpe (1696–1785). Raised in a Jacobite family, Oglethorpe invited Wesley to travel to the colony of Georgia in 1735.[107] Wesley accepted the challenge, taking Charles Wesley and Benjamin Ingham with him. John Wesley's Georgia mission lasted from October 1735 to December 1737 when he returned to England after the scandal involving Sophia Hopkey Williamson.[108] Shortly after his return, he felt his heart "strangely warmed" at Aldersgate, and began field preaching in the following year. A few years later, the "Forty-five" commenced, and Wesley and the Methodists were caught up in it.

The "Forty-Five"

Rumors of Charles Edward Stuart's (the Young Pretender) invasion swept the country in the early 1740s.[109] Methodism had become a visible movement by 1745, and in this period of heightened concern there was gossip that Methodist activities were a cover for Jacobite collaboration.[110] Those spreading these rumors were some Church of England priests and bishops concerned about the preaching of unauthorized Methodist lay preachers who they believed were teaching heresy. Others targeting the Methodists were factory owners who complained that Methodist preaching took workers away from labour, and bar owners and pimps who were

106. Heitzenrater, "Oxford Methodists," 276–77.

107. Ward, *Protestant Evangelical Awakening*, 309. For the life of Oglethorpe see Wright, *A Memoir of James Oglethorpe*. Oglethorpe's father had not only refused the oath to William and Mary, but a warrant was issued for his arrest in 1689 for plotting an insurrection, see "Oglethorpe, Sir Theophilus (1650–1702)" in Hayton et al., *The House of Commons*, 5:10–12.

108. Hammond, *JW in America*, 13; for JW's account of his Georgia ministry, see MSS *Journal, Works* 18:312–571.

109. See Walsh, "Methodism and the Mob," 226.

110. Weber, *Politics*, 69; and Rack, *Reasonable Enthusiast*, 280–81; David Hempton, *Methodism and Politics*, 32.

angered over drunks and prostitutes being converted.[111] Soon Charles Edward Stuart landed in Scotland, gathered an army of highlanders, and marched towards Edinburgh, taking the city in September 1745.[112]

Even before the Young Pretender invaded, it was whispered in April 1744 that Wesley had been seen with James Stuart. Shortly thereafter Wesley wrote a "loyalty letter" to George II, saying that the Methodists had been "traduced as inclined to Popery' and 'consequently disaffected to your Majesty.'"[113] He assured the king that the Methodists were Protestant and in full support of him, even going so far as to saying, "that we detest and abhor the fundamental doctrines of the Church of Rome."[114] Charles Wesley talked him out of sending it because he said the Methodists would be labelled sectarians.[115]

In this case, John Wesley listened to his brother, but the letter was printed in his *Journal* in 1746. Charles Wesley, too, was accused of siding with the Jacobites as he received word that a warrant was being written, calling for "information against one Westley, or any other of the Methodist speakers, for speaking any treasonable words or exhortations, as praying for the banished, or for the Pretender."[116] Charles had to face his accusers and explain that his prayer "for the banished," had not meant the Stuart usurper of the throne but all those who were pilgrims on this earth.[117] Yet Charles's trials continued. He was shown a warrant for his arrest in March 1744 by an unnamed constable.[118] While riding away from the one who showed it to him, he cried, but instead of fleeing, he rode to Wakefield and confronted the justices who had issued the warrant.[119] Charles endured a day of questioning, but when the justices listened close enough to realize that he was an ordained clergyman, they administered the oaths to the Crown, and let him go.[120] Charles's response to the Jacobite Rising was to write poetry, including the following verse:

111. Weber, *Politics*, 79.

112. Szechi, *Jacobites*, xxii.

113. JW to George II, March 5, 1744, *Works*, 20:16.

114. *Works*, 20:16.

115. *Works*, 20:17; and March 6, 1744, *MJCW*, 2:397.

116. CW, March 15, 1744, *MJCW*, 2:395.

117. *MJCW*, 2:396; Baker, "Methodism and the '45 Rebellion," 326–27.

118. CW, March 15, 1744, *MJCW*, 2:397.

119. *MJCW*, 2:396.

120. *MJCW*, 2:398–400.

Thou in danger's darkest hour
Didst on our side appear
Snatch us from the wasting power
Of Rome and Satan near.[121]

When Charles published the *Hymns for Times of Trouble and Persecution* (1745) he included an appendix containing fifteen hymns against the Jacobites.[122] Yet, his trials continued.

Unlike John and Charles Wesley, the Methodist itinerant lay preachers who did not have the security of ecclesiastical immunity were seen as prime targets for forced military conscription, or "impressment."[123] The fear of the Young Pretender, along with threats to national welfare from the French provoked the need for a sizable army, and some magistrates decided it was time to enforce a law that had been passed in 1706. The magistrates could conscript anyone into the military who did not have visible means of employment, called "pressing."[124] Several Methodist preachers were "pressed," including but not limited to: John Nelson, John Downes, Thomas Beard (d. 1744), and Thomas Maxfield (d. 1784).[125]

In May 1744, "*John Gibson* (an Alehouse keeper, who had found *his craft was in danger*), the Constable's Deputy, pressed me for a soldier," wrote John Nelson, Yorkshire stonemason and Methodist preacher, in his account of his pressing during the "Forty-five."[126] Nelson asked Gibson, "by whose order?"[127] Gibson informed Nelson that the people of the town did not like "so much preaching."[128] Gibson arrested Nelson, and someone offered £500 bail, but Gibson refused the bail. The local officials took Nelson and others who had been pressed to the army commissioners where a captain read Nelson the "Articles of War," and warned him: "You hear your doom is death, if you disobey us."[129] Nelson informed him that all he feared was God. They threw Nelson into the dungeon where he

121. JW and CW, *Hymns for Times*, 54.

122. JW and CW, *Hymns for Times*, 54–70.

123. Best, *Charles Wesley*, 171–72.

124. 4 & 5 Anne, c. 21.

125. May 14, 1744, *Journal, Works*, 20:29. JW's only reference to Downes's arrest is that the constable who arrested Downes was in the congregation at Epworth while he preached. JW, *Journal*, June 11, 1744, *Works*, 20:32.

126. Nelson, *The Case*, 3; and Jackson, *Lives*, 1:95. This is Nelson's use of italics.

127. Nelson, *The Case*, 3.

128. Nelson, *The Case*, 3.

129. Nelson, *The Case*, 6.

prayed for his enemies. He was eventually taken to join a soldiers' company, but he still refused to fight, and his major reported that one-third of the men in the company had stopped swearing and smoking while Nelson was there. The entire time Nelson was in the army, he refused shoot or hold a weapon, and he earned the respect of his companions.[130] John Wesley wrote to Nelson in May 1744 a word of encouragement: "Who knows how many souls God may by this means deliver into your hands[?]"[131] George Whitefield had speculated only five years previously that he or Wesley might end up in a dungeon. They did not, but one wonders whether Wesley and Whitefield remembered these words as they worked to get Nelson released: "Today I was thinking, supposed my honoured friend was laid in a dungeon, for preaching Christ; Oh how would I visit him! How would I kiss his chain, and continue with him till midnight singing psalms! Perhaps our friends think none of these things shall befall us. But I know they may be nigh, even at the door."[132]

It was requested that the Countess of Huntingdon (1707–1791) use her influence to get Nelson released from military service.[133] She did, and James Erskine, Lord Grange (1679–1754), a former Scottish judge, who was serving as secretary to Frederick, Prince of Wales (1707–1751), arranged to have a soldier bought to redeem Nelson.[134] Ward called Erskine's aid to Nelson, "Jacobitism coming to the aid of the revival," because Ward was convinced that Erskine was a double agent, therefore, a Jacobite spy.[135]

In June 1745, Thomas Maxfield was captured and pressed for service in the navy while preaching in Cornwall.[136] A captain of a man-of-war refused to take him on board, saying he had not the authority, so they tossed him in a dungeon. Then a rumor surfaced that Methodists would rescue him, so they took him to a house where John Wesley found him, and

130. Nelson, *The Case*, 7–30.

131. JW to John Nelson, [May 12? 1744], *Works*, 26:106.

132. GW to JW, February 13, 1739, Thomas, "George Whitefield and Friends," 77–78.

133. See Ward, *Protestant Evangelical Awakening*, 334.

134. Jackson, *Life of the CW*, 1:307; Ward, *Protestant Evangelical Awakening*, 334–35; and Nelson, *The Case*, 36.

135. Ward, *Protestant*, 334.

136. For Maxfield, see Lee, "Thomas Maxfield," 161–63. In the 1760s, he had a falling-out with Wesley for preaching "eschatological sinless perfection" see Rack, *Reasonable Enthusiast*, 339.

remarked that Maxfield was not afraid. After a trial, they heard Maxfield had been sentenced to serve as a soldier, and he was not released until July 1746 according to Charles Wesley.[137] His presence is noted at the May 1746 Methodist Conference in Bristol.[138] Unlike Nelson, Maxfield did not leave a written account of his impressment, so it is not known whether he refused to fight as Nelson had done. John and Charles Wesley did all they could to get him released as they had done with Nelson.[139] Nelson and Maxfield survived their pressing, but at least one Methodist preacher did not. Thomas Beard, lay preacher, was pressed in York in 1744 and imprisoned with Nelson. He died in Newcastle, most likely because of the way he was treated in the army.[140]

Unlike the others, John Haime (bap. 1708, d. 1784) was an enlisted soldier who became a Methodist while in the army. After Haime heard John Cennick (1718–1755) preach, Haime was convicted, but not converted.[141] Later he heard Charles Wesley preach, whose words blessed him. Haime wrote to John Wesley, and Wesley's answer was what Haime needed for his soul to be at peace. Later Wesley wrote to him again, words of encouragement: "Speak and spare not: declare what God has done for your soul; regard not worldly prudence; be not ashamed of Christ, or of His word, or of His servants."[142] Haime formed a Society in his regiment and it soon grew to three hundred. Many of the officers and chaplains tried to stop it. Writing his memoir, the enlisted soldier reported that during the "Forty-five:" "The duke, hearing many complaints of me, inquired who I was; if I did my duty, if I would fight, and if I prayed for a blessing on the king and his arms: they told his royal highness, I did all this as well as any man in the regiment."[143] The duke then asked the grumblers why they had criticized Haime. They confessed they were concerned that Haime preached and prayed so much that he never got rest. Haime inserted that he preached sometimes as much as thirty-five times a week. The duke interviewed Haime until he was happy with the

---

137. *JWJ*, June 20–22, 1745, *Works*, 20:70–71; and CW, July 6, 1745, *MJCW*, 2:444.

138. *Works*, 10:169.

139. *Works*, 20:71.

140. Jackson, *Life of CW*, 1:386–87; and Lenton, *John Wesley's Preachers*, 303.

141. Jackson, *Lives*, 1:276.

142. Jackson, *Lives*, 1:279.

143. Most likely Prince William Augustus (1721–1765), Duke of Cumberland, the third son of George II, and general of the Crown's army. His antagonists later called him "Butcher Cumberland." See Jackson, *Lives*, 1:290–91.

answers and told Haime that he should preach anywhere and that no one would trouble him.[144]

Michael Snape asserted that there were so many Methodist soldiers and society members in the military that the Duke of Cumberland was asked to put an end to Methodist meetings in the army camps.[145] The Duke had heard a Methodist preacher-soldier pray on behalf of king and country and declared: "I would to God all the soldiers in the British army were like these men."[146] Perhaps the Duke was referring to John Haime. Wesley indicated later that Cumberland had a religious conversion at this time, but this may have been exaggerated.[147] The Duke may not have converted, but this does show that the Methodists were influencing the army. However, Wesley's comments on the Duke were not so kind when he described the "Forty-five" thirty years later in his *Concise History of the English People*. His criticism of the punishment of the Jacobites instigated by the Duke revealed Wesley's abhorrence of injustice and physical violence. Wesley described the gory punishment of the rebels:

> But no mercy was shewn; the conquerors were seen to refuse quarter to the wounded, the unarmed, and the defenseless; and soldiers to anticipate the base employment of the executioner. The duke afterwards ordered six and thirty deserters to be executed, the conquerors spread terror wherever they came; and after a short space, the whole country round was one dreadful scene of plunder, slaughter and desolation; justice was forgotten, and vengeance assumed the name.[148]

He expressed his views further: "civil war is in itself terrible, but more when heightened by unnecessary cruelty."[149]

Wesley showed his concern for the souls of the soldiers who would die in the Rising by writing an appeal directly to them, *A Word in Season: or, Advice to a Soldier* (1745). The entire pamphlet was a reminder to the men they were on the verge of eternity. He described the life of the children of God in contrast to the wicked. He acknowledged the soldiers might already be experiencing inner turmoil,

144. Jackson, *Lives*, 1:291.

145. Snape, *Redcoat and Religion*, 25. Snape did not list a source for his claim.

146. Snape, *Redcoat and Religion*, 25.

147. Snape, *Redcoat and Religion*, 25.

148. JW, *Concise History*, 4:228.

149. JW, *Concise History*, 4:227.

"but if there were no other Hell, thou hast hell within thee."[150] He ended with a reminder that the soldiers had limited time in which to repent.

Wesley wrote in 1775 of the fears they had all experienced before the royal army overcame the Jacobites: "if the young pretender had made it to the capital, he might have been joined by a considerable number of his well-wishers, who waited impatiently for his approach."[151] He did not make it to the capital, for the "Forty-five" was crushed on April 16, 1746 at the Battle of Culloden, and Charles Edward Stuart fled.[152]

Yet the ramifications continued for the Methodists. In July 1746, The Crown issued a reward for capture of the fugitive: £30,000, the rough equivalent of £4 million today.[153] Caught up in the chaos, Charles Wesley was accused of hiding the Young Pretender under the assumed name James Waller, and while he was preaching, the "rebels of Helstone" [Helston, Cornwall] threatened, saying, "a law is to come from London tonight to put us all down, and set £100 upon my head."[154] The next day a crowd gathered, waiting, but no one came from London to arrest him.

Later Allegations and Why Wesley Was Not a Jacobite

As Weber, Rack, and Green have insisted, labelling Wesley as a Jacobite on account of his mother and brother's views, his sermon "The One Thing Needful," and his friendships is not correct. It is understandable that Wesley may have struggled with his conscience over the Jacobite issue in his early Oxford years. Weber said of Wesley's politics: "The fundamental question is whether as a Tory Wesley was a theocratic divine right thinker, which would link him with the Stuart past, or a constitutionalist, which would link him with the Hanoverian future."[155]

In *A Word in Season, or Advice to an Englishman*, Wesley interpreted the "Forty-five" to be a result of God's judgment, and that the end result of the Jacobite Rebellion, if the people did not repent of their sins, could only be "Popery and slavery."[156] It is clear in this treatise that

150. JW, *Advice to a Soldier*, 6.

151. JW, *Concise History*, 4:220.

152. Fremont-Barnes, *Jacobite Rebellion*, 67–74.

153. Fremont-Barnes, *Jacobite Rebellion*, 87.

154. CW, July 19, 1746, *MJCW*, 2:467.

155. Weber, *Politics*, 67.

156. JW, *Word in Season*, 3.

Wesley opposed the restoration of the Stuarts, and his dedication to the Hanoverian monarchy was not just about his concern for his own movement, but for the good of the nation.[157] According to Bernard Semmel, when Wesley preached absolute loyalty to George II: "in this he followed the path of other Jacobites, who as the usurper became better established, extended the principles of non-resistance and passive obedience to him, and as a final gesture, gave him divine right as well."[158] Semmel asserted that Wesley could not remain a Jacobite because he realized that the only way that the Stuarts could regain the throne was by bloodshed. This is incorrect, as Wesley was never a Jacobite.

Wesley arrived in Bristol in early March 1756, finding the city "all in a flame" because an election for a Member of Parliament was proceeding.[159] The Tory candidate was Jarrit Smith, an eminent local attorney; the Whig candidate was John Spencer.[160] John Latimer, writing in the late nineteenth century, suggested that Wesley gave energetic support to the Tory candidate Jarrit Smith (1692–1783), but he gave no source to support this.[161] A letter Wesley wrote to Ebenezer Blackwell (d. 1782), banker, on March 4, 1756 proved Latimer wrong. Wesley supported the Whig, John Spencer (1734–1783), later Earl Spencer.[162] Weber used Latimer's accusing Wesley of supporting Smith as evidence of the persistence of the myth that Wesley was a Jacobite, because Smith was suspected of Jacobitism.[163] Wesley described the election to Blackwell with concern that the Jacobites would win: "And if the Jacobites gain one member now, they will have two the next time."[164] Wesley had talked to the freemen of his society encouraging them to support His Majesty, and his comment that some had promised to vote for Mr. Smith instead showed that Wesley supported Spencer.[165] Yet Smith was elected, and Latimer described one reason why Smith was suspected of Jacobitism: "one of his ornaments was a carved representation of the royal arms of the Stewarts, borrowed from

157. Weber, *Politics*, 76.

158. Semmel, *Methodist Revolution*, 58.

159. JW, *Journal*, March 3, 1756, *Works*, 21:43.

160. Latimer, *Annals of Bristol*, 318.

161. Latimer, *Annals of Bristol*, 318.

162. JW to Ebenezer Blackwell, March 4, 1756, *Works*, 27:16–17; and Weber, *Politics*, 82–83.

163. Weber, *Politics*, 82–83.

164. *Works*, 27:16–17.

165. Latimer, *Annals of Bristol*, 319.

All Saints' Church."[166] The decoration without the heraldic blazon of the Hanoverian family was seen to be a token of sympathy to the Pretender. Wesley may have shown trepidation over this election because it took place at the beginning of what would later be called the Seven Years' War. Wesley was so concerned over this that he wrote to the Honorable James West (1703–1772) in the month the election took place offering to raise a company of two hundred men and to support them from Methodist contributions.[167] Still, this was not the end of people accusing Wesley of Jacobitism.

After writing *A Calm Address to Our American Colonies* (1775), Wesley was accused of "ideological Jacobitism" by Baptist pastor Caleb Evans (1737–1791). Writing directly against *A Calm Address*, he accused Wesley of reviving "the good old Jacobite doctrine of *hereditary, indefeasible, divine right,* and of *passive obedience and non-resistance*" in *Thoughts Concerning the Origins of Power* (1772).[168] It is understandable that Evans interpreted this essay as reviving a Jacobite doctrine, because Wesley asserted in it that the people are never the origin of power, but the origin of power is from God.[169] There is no known record that Wesley called himself a Jacobite, in fact, later in his life Wesley denied that he was a Jacobite, stating clearly, "I am no more a Jacobite than I am a Turk."[170]

Jacobitism and Catholic Spirit

Although Weber called Wesley's actions during the "Forty-five" "damage control," Wesley did more than that. The "Forty-five" brought suffering to his preachers, and he desired a method to stop this.[171] The 1744 and 1745 Conferences confronted the issues that arose during the conflict. The first Methodist conference convened in June 1744 in London.[172] Found

166. Latimer, *Annals of Bristol,* 319.

167. See JW to James West [MP for St. Albans and Joint Secretary of the Treasury], March 1, 1756, *Works,* 27:15; and Stone, *John Wesley's Life and Ethics,* 101. Stone incorrectly stated Wesley offered to raise an army during the "Forty-five."

168. JW, *A Calm Address to Our American Colonies;* Americanus [Caleb Evans], *A Letter to the Rev. Mr. John Wesley,* 11; JW, *Thoughts;* and Weber, *Politics,* 84.

169. JW, *Thoughts,* 1.

170. JW to the Editor of the *Gentlemen's Magazine,* December 24, 1785, in Telford, 7:305–6.

171. Weber, *Politics,* 73.

172. *Works,* 10:120.

in the Conference *Minutes* is the question: "is it lawful to bear arms?" They declared, "we incline to think it is."[173] They decided that it was lawful because there was no command against it in the New Testament, and Cornelius was commended and not asked to lay down his arms.[174] Recorded in the *Minutes* was another question: "Is it lawful to use the law?"[175] The reply was: "As defendant, doubtless. And perhaps as plaintiff in some cases, seeing magistrates are an ordinance of God."[176]

The Methodists were still struggling with the issue of the use of weapons a year later when the second Conference convened at Bristol in August 1745.[177] This time they did not seem as certain as they were in 1744, possibly because of the pressing of the preachers. After all, John Nelson had shown his commitment to non-resistance by refusing to take up arms even when forced, defying the law, and others had been pressed. Some of the preachers' names, especially deceased Thomas Beard's, were painfully absent from the roster of preachers in the *Minutes*. To the question of: "is it lawful to bear arms?" They answered, "We cannot tell. We will endeavour to hear Mr E. and K. together."[178] Since they were uncertain, Wesley called in what was most likely a person on each side of the issue. Henry Rack said that Mr. E. was most likely James Erskine, whom he labelled a "secret Jacobite sympathiser, though much concerned with religion in an ecumenical spirit," but it could have been any number of men with the last initial "E."[179] Mr. K. may have been Abraham Kershaw (1716–1789), a Quaker, who would have argued for non-violence. The Methodists may have heard arguments from both sides on whether to take up arms before deciding, yet there is no decision noted in the *Minutes*.[180] This suggests that they were struggling to find an answer. The question of bearing arms does not appear in the 1746 *Minutes*, most likely because by this time, the "Forty-five" had been crushed by the King's troops, and there was no reason for Methodists to use weapons.[181]

173. June 1, 1744 (printed on the agenda), *Works*, 10:122; and June 29, 1744 (*Minutes* of the Conference), *Works*, 10:145.

174. *Works*, 10:145; Acts 10:34–38.

175. *Works*, 10:122, 145–46.

176. *Works*, 10:146.

177. August 1–3, 1745, *Works*, 10:147–68.

178. *Works*, 10:160–61.

179. *Works*, 10:161n.

180. *Works*, 10:161n.

181. May 12–15, 1746, see *Works*, 10:168–85.

Outside the Conferences, some of Wesley's other publications dealt with issues that could possibility have related to the "Forty-five." Gerald R. Cragg summarized Wesley's writing of *A Farther Appeal to Men of Reason and Religion*, commissioned by the 1744 Conference and published during the Jacobite rebellion, asserting that this was Wesley encouraging what he believed would heal the nation and aid in ending the attacks on his movement: the remedy lay in a recovery of the heritage of a Christian nation. "Every segment of the religious spectrum had its place in his appeal. Presbyterians, Independents, Baptists, Quakers, Roman Catholics–each denomination had its distinctive traditions and each had in some measure forsaken its heritage."[182] *A Farther Appeal* was a theological argument, an attempt to explain to "men of reason and religion," mostly Church of England clergy, especially bishops, what the Methodists believed and practiced. This illustrates the intricate ties between religion and politics in the world in which Wesley and the early Methodists moved.

Wesley warned that a king who practiced Catholicism would force British people to bow down to images. All of this has happened to Britain "because of our sins; because we have well-nigh *fill'd up the measure of our iniquities*."[183] He listed multiple sins of the English such as theft, cheating, and violence. Especially harsh were his words against the aristocracy: "who in *Europe* can compare with the *sloth, laziness, luxury*, and *effeminacy* of the English Gentry?"[184] Then Wesley spoke as the voice of a prophet saying that God had been patient long enough, and now judgment was coming. Next, Wesley urged the people of England to confess their sins, and avoid damnation.[185] Living by faith and practicing virtues such as courage, knowledge, and kindness was the answer.[186] Wesley believed that Methodism could and would spread these virtues, and he asserted this in another pamphlet published that same month. Whereas the above tract spoke to the nation, this next treatise had the purpose of encouraging and uplifting the Methodists. He called it *Advice to the People called Methodists* (1745).[187]

182. JW, *Farther Appeal, Works*, 11:102–325. Cragg, "Introduction to a Further Appeal," *Works*, 11:100.

183. JW, *Advice to an Englishman*, 3.

184. JW, *Advice to an Englishman*, 4.

185. JW, *Advice to an Englishman*, 4–5.

186. JW, *Advice to an Englishman*, 6.

187. JW, *Advice to the People Called Methodist, Works*, 9:123–31.

The thrust of the message of the *Advice to the People Called Methodists* was almost the opposite of the message of *Advice to an Englishman*. There was no condemnation, but only words of motivation and inspiration. The difference in the Methodists and other religious groups, according to Wesley, was that they had not separated themselves from their congregations. They were united, rather than divided. Wesley explained this unity:

> What makes even your *principles* more offensive is this *uniting* of yourselves *together*: because this union renders you more *conspicuous*, placing you more in the eye of men; more *suspicious*–I mean, liable to be suspected of carrying on some sinister design (especially by those who do not, or *will* not, know your inviolable attachment to His present Majesty King George).[188]

He declared: "condemn no man for not thinking as you think. Let everyone enjoy the full and free liberty of thinking for himself. Let every man use his own judgment, since every man must give an account of himself to God."[189] The Methodists had been called "Papists" or heretics because of their abstinence from reading plays, romances, their plain dress, and their avoidance of liquor.[190] Yet Wesley urged the Methodists to be true to their principles. As for worship, their leader encouraged the Methodists to "conform" to those modes of worship they used, yet to love as brothers and sisters in Christ those whose conscience did not allow them to conform. They were not to hold any malice towards anyone with different opinions than theirs.[191] These same ideas about "opinions," "modes of worship," "liberty of thinking," and "leaving the judgment to God" would be further developed in *Catholic Spirit*.

No analysis of Wesley's writings in the years 1744 to 1746 can be complete without the sermon "Scriptural Christianity" preached August 24, 1744.[192] A few months before he wrote *Advice to the People Called Methodists* and *A Word in Season or Advice to an Englishman*, Wesley preached before the University Church of St. Mary the Virgin. Ten years had passed since he had preached "The One Thing Needful" in the same church. He had spent time in the New World, experimenting with extreme High Church practices influenced by the Nonjurors, where he had

188. *Works*, 9:128.
189. *Works*, 9:130.
190. *Works*, 9:126–27.
191. *Works*, 9:130.
192. *Works*, 1:159–80.

been heavily criticized for the same.[193] He returned home to examine his own spiritual life, and both he and his brother Charles experienced their "Days of Pentecost" in May 1738. Nearly five years had passed since he took the advice of George Whitefield and preached in the fields. There were Methodist societies growing in England and Wales, despite multiple Methodist lay preachers serving "pressed" time in the army. As when he preached "The One Thing Needful" on St. Barnabas Day and the anniversary of George II's accession, this day too held meaning. It was St. Bartholomew's Day, and of special meaning to Wesley, the eighty-second anniversary of the Great Ejection after the Act of Uniformity when Wesley's grandfathers were driven from their parishes for refusal to conform.[194]

After mounting the steps to the tall wooden pulpit, he stood above the congregation at the university church gazing at the doctors, masters, graduates, and scholars in their regal robes. His words painted a picture of what the world would look like if the Kingdom came, as he proclaimed: "Where does this Christianity now exist? Where, I pray, do the Christians live? Which is the country, the inhabitants whereof are "all (thus) filled with the Holy Ghost?" Are all "of one heart and one soul?" Cannot suffer one among them to "lack anything?""[195] The fear of the Young Pretender's invasion was still just that in August 1744: trepidation. Surely the community who had seen riots and hangings during the "Fifteen" needed to hear a message of comfort. Wesley did not have gentle words: "many of you are a generation of *triflers*, triflers with God and one another, and with your own souls?"[196] How dare he say that to a university that upheld righteousness, truth, and the Church of England? Yet he knew that some of the wickedness of England sat in the pews in front of him, for his belief was that all had sinned. Most likely his listeners believed a wicked force was coming, a power that could enslave them all to the Stuarts, France, and Pope Benedict XIV's (1675-1758) tyranny. Wesley acknowledged this, but he said that perhaps God might send "armies of Romish aliens" to reform them.[197] That he said God would send "Romish armies," refer-

193. Hammond, *JW in America*, 37–41.
194. Outler, "Introduction to Sermons 1–4," *Works*, 1:113.
195. JW, "Scriptural Christianity," *Works*, 1:172–73.
196. *Works*, 1:179.
197. *Works*, 1:180.

ring to the possible Jacobite invasion, could have caused his listeners to believe that he was on the side of the Stuarts.

Only two years later when he published "Scriptural Christianity" along with many other sermons, he would articulate his theology of preaching in the preface to *Sermons on Several Occasions*: "I design plain truth for plain people."[198] He acknowledged that his preaching had provoked anger from some saying, "nay perhaps if you are angry so I shall be too, and then there will be small hopes of finding the truth."[199] Even in this preface, he had begun to use the words, phrases, and concepts he would later employ in *Catholic Spirit*: "for how far is love, even with many wrong opinions, to be preferred before truth itself without love?"[200] For a decade he had seen conflict within and without the Church, perhaps his words could lessen the hostility and aid in bringing peace. "Scriptural Christianity" would be the last sermon he preached inside St. Mary before the community that had raised him in academia. When he received the message that he was no longer welcome in this particular church, he might have thought of the Ejection. Almost forty years later he remembered:

> I preached for the last time before the University of Oxford. I am now clear of the blood of these men. I have fully delivered my own soul. And I am well pleased that it should be the very day on which, in the last century, nearly two thousand burning and shining lights were put out at one stroke.[201]

He spoke of the two thousand ejected men, yet in his spirit of optimism, he rejoiced that unlike them he had not been cast out of his home but only from taking his turn as a fellow in preaching at the university.

After the "Forty-five" was over, Wesley penned *A Word to a Protestant* in January 1746, this time using the patriotic pride of the people against them. National pride that "we are Protestant and not Catholic" had swept the nation during the young Pretender's rebellion. Wesley's argument was that they had not acted as true Protestants and loved their brothers and sisters. The nature of Protestantism involved allowing people to have the right to their opinions.[202] He would articulate this at greater length in

198. *Works*, 1:104.
199. *Works*, 1:107.
200. *Works*, 1:107.
201. *Works*, 1:115.
202. JW, *Word to a Protestant*, 5; *Works* (Jackson), 11:187–91.

Catholic Spirit two years later. Haydon asserted that the peak of British anti-Catholicism took place in 1745.[203] This makes sense as Jacobitism was associated with Catholicism, and the "Forty-five" had wreaked havoc over the land. This havoc, too, may have influenced the writing of *Catholic Spirit*.

Conclusion

This chapter has examined the allegations of Jacobitism thrust upon John Wesley and the early Methodists at Oxford and during the "Forty-five," and the ramifications of these accusations to nearly the end of Wesley's life. The disciplined practices of the Oxford Methodists were perceived as "monastic," which led some onlookers to believe they were under Catholic influence. Some perceived that if the Methodists were under Catholic influence, then they were Jacobites. Due to the intricate ties of theology and politics, Wesley could not remain outside of the line of fire from Whig opposition when he preached alleged "Jacobite" doctrines at Oxford. Like his father, Wesley claimed he was a High Church Tory, and some assumed this inevitably meant he identified as Jacobite as well. This was a false assumption.

The "Forty-five" found the Methodist local preachers pressed for service in the army. The first two Methodist conferences addressed the issues concerning the Rising. Wesley sought to bring peace to his wounded homeland by inviting opposing voices to speak in the conference. He was a Methodist, trying to work out his own salvation and lead others to do the same. If they would all practice a catholic spirit maybe they could bring peace.

The troubles the Methodist movement faced during the "Forty-five" tragically provided Wesley with a living example of religious and political intolerance that turned to violence. *Catholic Spirit* would emerge from his brokenness, pain, and weariness over religious strife escalating to physical hostility. Amid the Jacobite conflicts, perhaps Wesley remembered the words of his mother, "no pretence of zeal should make us lay aside our humanity, or exercise any act of injustice or cruelty towards our neighbour. Nor must we suffer a bad man to perish for want of our relief."[204]

---

203. Haydon, *Anti-Catholicism*, 118.

204. Susanna Wesley to JW, November 10, 1725, *Works*, 25:185.

4

A *Catholic Spirit*
and Conversion in Ireland

CHAPTER TWO INTRODUCED ANTI-CATHOLICISM as the result of the English Protestant Reformation, evaluated leading Anglican attempts at religious toleration, and analyzed these influences on the writing of John Wesley's sermon, *Catholic Spirit*. Although his opponents accused Wesley of Jacobitism, chapter three determined that Wesley was not a Jacobite, and that the opposition the Methodists suffered during the "Forty-five" may have influenced the writing of a *Catholic Spirit*. The present chapter takes into account that Wesley composed and preached *Catholic Spirit* after his tumultuous second journey to Ireland, and wrote *Letter to a Roman Catholic* three months later.[1] Wesley urged Protestants in *Catholic Spirit* to practice Christian love and religious tolerance, and pleaded in *Letter to a Roman Catholic* for Catholics to do the same. This chapter argues that *Letter to a Roman Catholic* was a message to Catholics to convince them to stop rioting, and allow Wesley to preach his message of evangelical conversion: "to reform the nation, more particularly the church, and to spread scriptural holiness over the land."[2] Only after Catholics experienced the New Birth could they could practice a catholic spirit.

This chapter falls into six sections: first an overview of Wesley in Ireland and the political issues he faced is given. The second section provides reasons why *Letter to a Roman Catholic* lacks a catholic spirit. Third, a brief overview of Wesley's view of evangelical conversion is provided, and the fourth section examines the renunciation of Popery that the Catholic

1. JW, *Works* (Jackson), 10:80–86.
2. *The Large Minutes A and B, Works*, 10:845.

converts to Methodism made. Fifth, the Cork Riots of 1748–1750 and their relation to conversion in Ireland are considered, and finally, the outcome of Wesley's attempt to convert Catholics in Ireland is appraised. Although four studies of Wesley's twenty-one visits to Ireland and the early Methodist movement in Ireland were published in the last century, none have been as extensive as Charles Henry Crookshank's three volume *History of Methodism in Ireland* (1885–1888).[3] Nevertheless, Crookshank must be carefully compared to the primary sources as his works contain not only anti-Catholic bias, but elements of Victorian triumphalist historiography as he sets up the Methodist preachers as heroes led by a venerated Wesley.[4] The primary sources used in this chapter include Wesley's published essays, and his and other early Methodists' sermons, journals, and letters.[5]

Biographers have indicated that the tolerant message of *Letter to a Roman Catholic* contradicts some of Wesley's other writings that are much more critical of Catholicism. Henry Rack, for instance, pointed out: "The remarkable thing about the *Letter* is not so much its content as the fact that it was addressed to Catholics. It is essentially an appeal for brotherly love on the basis of a few fundamental Christian beliefs, each side retaining its 'opinions.'"[6] Further, Rack commented that the *Letter* has been reprinted in recent years as an example of ecumenism, but that "it is anachronistic to see Wesley as an ecumenical pioneer in the perspective of the modern ecumenical movement."[7] Rack referred to the fact that after Michael Hurley published comments on *Letter to a Roman Catholic* in the 1960s, it gained ecumenical attention.[8] Although it is to be acknowledged that church leaders can still choose to interpret *Letter to a Roman Catholic* for today, this present chapter takes up the statement that "it is anachronistic to see Wesley as an ecumenical

3. Haire, *Wesley's One-and-Twenty Visits to Ireland*; Jeffrey, *Irish Methodism*; Rogal, *John Wesley in Ireland*; Cooney, *The Methodists in Ireland*; and Crookshank, *History*. Smith, *A Consecutive History*, is the oldest history of Methodism in Ireland.

4. For instance, Crookshank refers to Catholics as "poor ignorant papists" or "the poor deluded" Catholics, the Methodist mission is a "hallowed enterprise," and the preachers are "noble itinerants." Crookshank, *History*, 1:2, 3, 11, 18.

5. For Wesley's published essays, see *A Short Address to the Inhabitants of Ireland*; *A Short Method of Converting all the Roman Catholicks*; *The Advantage of the Members of the Church of England*; and *A Compassionate Address to the Inhabitants of Ireland*.

6. Rack, *Reasonable Enthusiast*, 310.

7. Rack, *Reasonable Enthusiast*, 310–11.

8. Hurley, *John Wesley's Letter to a Roman Catholic*.

pioneer" from Rack and attempts to address the problem of classify-ing *Letter to a Roman Catholic* as an ecumenical declaration. Wesley's attempt to convert Irish Catholics further revealed that Wesley did not intend the message of *Catholic Spirit* to apply to Catholics. In order to ad-dress the context needed to explain the subversionary nature of the *Letter to a Roman Catholic*, this chapter will take a thematic approach to the first fifty years of Methodism in Ireland rather than a chronological one.

John Wesley and Ireland

It is important to understand that Wesley's preaching was a part of a transatlantic evangelical revival. The Methodists sought to convert the masses to "heart religion," whether from a Protestant, Catholic, or "heathen" background. George Whitefield had preached in Ireland in 1738, but the first permanent "Methodist" inroad to Ireland was with John Cennick's preaching in 1745, although by then he had joined the Moravians.[9] During the Bristol Conference of 1746, it was asked: "What is a sufficient call of providence to a new place, suppose to Edinburgh or Dublin?" They answered that they would consider it a call to a new place if an invitation came from "someone that is worthy; from a serious man, fearing God, who has a house to receive us," and "A probability of doing more good by going thither than staying longer where we are."[10] Unknown to Wesley and the Conference, Benjamin LaTrobe (1728–1786), a Baptist, formed a society in response to preaching from an un-known soldier in Dublin.[11] Cennick preached to this group in 1746 about the "babe wrapped in swaddling clothes," and earned the Methodists the nickname "swaddlers."[12] In 1747, Thomas Williams (c. 1720–1787), a Welsh Methodist lay preacher, preached in Dublin, formed a society, and invited John Wesley to Ireland.[13]

When Wesley arrived in Dublin in 1747, a banker named William Lunell (1699–1774), the son of a Huguenot refugee who had been

9. See GW to Samuel Mason, November 16, 1738, Thomas, "George Whitefield and Friends," 394–95. For Whitefield in Ireland, see Beebe and Jones, "Whitefield and the 'Celtic Revivals'"; Lineham, "Cennick, John (1718–1755)," *ODNB*.

10. Conference *Minutes*, May 15, 1746, *Works*, 10:181.

11. Newport, "Charles Wesley in Ireland," 16. See also Mason, "LaTrobe, Benjamin (1728–1786)," *ODNB*.

12. Crookshank, *History*, 1:13.

13. JW, *A Short History of People Called Methodists*, *Works*, 9:448–49.

converted by Williams, showed him hospitality. This warm welcome most likely influenced Wesley to write of the Irish: "For natural sweetness of temper, for courtesy and hospitality, I have never seen any people like the Irish. Indeed, all I converse with are only English transplanted to another soil; and they are much mended by the removal, having left all their roughness and surliness behind them."[14] However, it should be noted that his first encounters were with "transplanted" English people and their descendants, and not with the native Irish.

Wesley had been in Dublin less than a week when he preached in St. Mary's Church [of Ireland], and promptly received orders never to preach in St. Mary's again by the Archbishop of Dublin Charles Cobbe (1687–1765). The curate of St. Mary's, relaying the Archbishop's orders, spoke to Wesley, and Wesley recorded in his *Journal*: "the most rooted prejudice against lay preachers or preaching out of a church, and said the Archbishop of Dublin was resolved to suffer no such irregularities in his diocese."[15] In a "Letter to a Clergyman" (1748), Wesley answered these critiques. The problem this clergyman had with Wesley was not with Wesley himself, but with the unordained preachers who could preach to save souls.[16] Wesley argued that ordination did not give anyone the right to "murder souls, either by his neglect, by his smooth if not false doctrine, or by hindering another from plucking them out of the fire, and bringing them to life everlasting."[17] When Wesley wrote the sermon "A Caution against Bigotry," he discussed whether the lay preachers should be forbidden to preach based upon Scripture, insisting that they had every right to preach.[18] To William Legge in 1761, Wesley gave an extensive argument for the allowance of lay preaching.[19]

After a fortnight's stay in Dublin, John Wesley wrote and asked Charles Wesley to visit.[20] Charles arrived with two preachers to discover the Methodist society under constant attack by rioting Catholic mobs. More riots ensued, mostly in Dublin and Cork. John Wesley wrote a few letters and essays to address this problem. Writing alone did not change

14. JW to Ebenezer Blackwell, August 13, 1747, *Works*, 26:256.

15. *JWJ*, August 10, 1747, *Works*, 20:187–88. For Wesley's rational for the use of lay preachers, see Wood, "Tensions," 113–38.

16. Davies, "An Introductory Comment," *Works*, 9:247.

17. JW, "Letter to a Clergyman," *Works*, 9:251.

18. JW, "A Caution against Bigotry," *Works*, 2:61–78.

19. JW to William Legge, April 10, 1761, *Works*, 27:251–56.

20. Newport, "Charles Wesley in Ireland," 17.

the situation, but engaging the law did. The Riot Act of 1715 did not apply to Ireland, but connections through the Countess of Huntingdon with the persistence of George Whitefield finally brought a declaration from the Lent Assizes of 1750 that no more riots would be tolerated, at least in Cork.[21] This reduced but did not end all the opposition to the Methodists in Ireland during Wesley's lifetime.

During his first days in Ireland, Wesley supposed that ninety-nine out of one hundred Irish "remain in the religion of their forefathers" when he observed the Catholicism of Ireland during his visit to Dublin.[22] The hearthmoney survey of Ireland in 1732–1733 reported that the proportion of Catholics to Protestants was nine to four outside of Ulster.[23] Since not long before the Methodists arrived in Ireland the country had faced enforcement of the penal laws because of the "Forty-five," some Irish men and women would have been on edge. Three years before the Methodists arrived, priests were arrested, and the Catholic chapels closed in County Cork. An elderly Catholic bishop, Theodore McCarthy (bishop from 1727–1747), who had built a chapel on the site now occupied by the present Cathedral of St. Mary and St. Anne, in defiance of the penal code, remained in hiding for two years.[24] There had been a fatal shooting of an aged Catholic priest in Killygarven (County Donegal), and the Catholic bishop of Ossory had been accused of being chaplain to the Old Pretender in 1744.[25]

Further, due to the penal laws, Catholics in Ireland were fined for sending their sons overseas to Catholic schools. They could not sit in Parliament, nor have legal or military careers, and they could lose their property to a Protestant relative.[26] In consequence, identifying as Protestant or Catholic in Georgian Ireland denoted much more than religion, it demonstrated clashing politics, for English and Protestant were viewed as one and the same by many native Irish.[27] Hence, it is not diffi-

---

21. Riot Act, 1 Geo. 1, st. 2, c. 5. GW to William Lunell, December 9, 1749, Tyerman, *Life of Whitefield,* 2:240.

22. *JWJ,* August 15, 1747, *Works,* 20:189.

23. Bindon, *An Abstract,* 12. The hearthmoney survey was the closest thing to a census in Ireland at this time, and it counted families, not individuals.

24. See Herbermann, *Catholic Encyclopedia,* s.v. "Cork," 4:371; and Dickson, "Jacobitism in Eighteenth-century Ireland," 58.

25. Ó Ciardha, *Ireland and the Jacobite Cause,* 304.

26. Haydon, *Anti-Catholicism,* 14.

27. Vaudry, *Anglicans and the Atlantic World,* 47–48.

cult to comprehend that "eighteenth-century [Irish] resistance to English rule came as much from anger at what England had done and continued to do as from fear of what she might do."[28] Eamon Ó Ciardha described the Irish Catholic attitude towards the British after the "Forty-five:"

> If people believed they were subject to discrimination, they were being persecuted and it is immaterial whether the legislation was being imposed or not. Irrespective of the views of Irish historians, the penal laws were inexorably linked to the Jacobite cause in the minds of Irish Catholics. They rejoiced at the Jacobite succession, lauded the imminent eclipse of the Protestant religion, the restoration of the ancient rights, and the Catholicisation of the army and judiciary.[29]

Given John Wesley's loyalty to the British crown, some might suspect that his aim of converting Catholics in Ireland was politically motivated. Did he go to Ireland as an agent of the British empire, or did the Irish view him as such? It seems that the belief that Catholics had massacred defenseless Protestants during the Rebellion of 1641 had been entrenched in him. Further, Wesley's perception of Ireland in 1748 had been: "I fear God still hath a controversy with this land, because it is defiled with blood."[30] Wesley gave no insight into his meaning in this 1748 *Journal* entry for why he thought Ireland was "defiled with blood." However, in his 1779 *Journal*, he wrote that he believed the Irish had been "plundering and murdering each other from the earliest ages" before "they were restrained by the English."[31] On the one hand, this quotation reveals that Wesley thought that the Irish were not civilized until the English arrived, and uncovers a prejudice that Wesley communicated. This aligns with a perception of "natives" as people who need to acquire the English language and religion in order to be civilised.[32] On the other hand, Theodore Jennings has accurately asserted that Wesley criticized the British Empire, especially those who had wealth and power.[33] He wrote against slavery, and he reprimanded the British for "wantoning

28. McLoughlin, *Contesting Ireland*, 9.

29. Ó Ciardha, *Ireland and the Jacobite Cause*, 28.

30. *JWJ*, August 15, 1747, *Works*, 20:189; and *JWJ*, April 9, 1748, *Works*, 20:218.

31. *JWJ*, November 26, 1779, *Works*, 23:156.

32. Strong, *Anglicanism and the British Empire*, 54.

33. Jennings, "John Wesley," 268.

in blood" and "exterminating whole nations."[34] Jennings argued that "Wesley was not taken in by pretensions to social virtue that too often serve as a cloak for naked self-interest on the part of the stronger nations at the expense of weaker ones," but Wesley's statement about the native Irish benefiting from being restrained by the English makes one wonder if he thought differently of the Irish than of other groups.[35] Wesley spent a considerable amount of his preaching time in Ireland speaking to the military as 12,000–15,000 British troops were garrisoned in Ireland. He also preached in courthouses and other places of ascendancy control, and this may have affected the limited number of conversions of Catholics to Methodism.[36] Even associating with the Church of Ireland clergy may have colored the Methodists in the eyes of the native Irish, as they represented not only the Empire, but the social elite.[37]

However, Wesley criticized the penal laws the British enforced against Catholics because he saw that the laws had done nothing to convert them.[38] Yet, Wesley probably did not help matters when he preached in court houses which the Irish Catholics could have perceived as him associating with the British government, nor would it had helped matters that he preached to British troops garrisoned in Ireland.[39] W. R. Ward criticized Wesley's preaching at Birr (County Offaly) in 1748 in front of the memorial to the Duke of Cumberland, the "butcher of Culloden," who would have been seen as an enemy to those who had supported the "Forty-five."[40] Nothing in his *Journal* suggests that this crossed Wesley's mind as he preached where there was space to hold a crowd, and where people gathered. Furthermore, Wesley may have loved the Irish people, but he had no taste for their nationalism, and he remained firmly English even in his attempt to convert the Irish.[41] The Irish may have viewed Wesley and the English Methodist preachers as just another attempt to force the British Empire upon them.

---

34. See JW, *Thoughts upon Slavery*, and JW, "A Caution against Bigotry," *Works*, 2:67.

35. Jennings, "John Wesley," 268.

36. Hempton, *Religion and Political*, 153.

37. Vaudry, *Anglicans and the Atlantic World*, 48–50.

38. *JWJ*, August 15, 1747, *Works*, 20:189.

39. Ward, "Methodist Evangelistic Strategy," 295.

40. Ward, "Methodist Evangelistic Strategy," 296.

41. *Works*, 3:309n.

Catholic Spirit and Letter to a Roman Catholic

Although Wesley wrote *Catholic Spirit* after his second journey across Ireland, he preached the message in Newcastle and Bristol, and there is no record that he ever preached it in Ireland.[42] Additionally, there are two main reasons why it is clear that Wesley did not intend the message of *Catholic Spirit* to apply to Catholics. First, explaining that he had once been zealous concerning that "the place of our birth fixes the church to which we ought to belong," he stated the main problem of this persuasion: "not the least of which that if this rule had took place, there could have been no Reformation from Popery, seeing it entirely destroys the right of private judgement on which the Reformation stands."[43] If Wesley had meant this message for Catholics, he would not likely have placed value on the Protestant Reformation, or have used the word, "Popery." Furthermore, Wesley took issue with Catholicism's denial of the right of private judgement. In *Catholic Spirit* Wesley argued that "every wise man will allow others the same liberty of thinking of which he desires they should allow him."[44] For after reading Catholic Bishop Richard Challoner's statement that private judgement had no place in religion, Wesley asserted his disagreement.[45]

If Wesley did not intend *Catholic Spirit* for a Catholic audience, he certainly aimed *Letter to a Roman Catholic* at Catholic listeners. He wrote it after experiencing violent opposition from Catholics in Dublin and Cork, while on his third journey across Ireland. However, it is in the context of evangelical conversion that *Letter to a Roman Catholic* must be understood. There is nothing in the letter that would lead one to believe that it was written to a specific person, but it was rather an address to all Catholics in Ireland. In the *Letter*, Wesley implored Catholics to agree with him that they should not hurt one another, speak nothing harsh of each other, nor harbour unkind thoughts. Both Catholics and Protestants were to endeavour to help each other in whatever way might promote to the Kingdom of God, and to strengthen each other's hands in God.[46] He stated: "I believe that Christ gathered unto himself a church . . . That this catholic that is, universal, Church, extending to all nations and ages,

---

42. Baker, *John Wesley*, 124.

43. JW, *Catholic Spirit*, *Works*, 2:86.

44. JW, *Catholic Spirit*, *Works*, 2:84.

45. *JWJ*, March 25, 1743, *Works*, 19:320; see Challoner, *Grounds of the Old Religion*.

46. JW, *Letter to a Roman Catholic*, *Works* (Jackson), 10:82–83.

is holy in all its members."[47] Wesley asked his Catholic listeners to join hearts and hands in the work, just as he had written to Protestants in *Catholic Spirit*.[48]

In *Letter to a Roman Catholic*, Wesley listed the beliefs that Catholics and Protestants held in common, perhaps shocking Catholics that he agreed with them that Jesus was "born of the Virgin Mary, who, as well after as before she brought Him forth, continued a pure and unspotted virgin."[49] Although some may think it odd that Wesley professed something so Catholic as the perpetual virginity of Mary, he shared this perspective with the Protestant Reformers, Martin Luther (1483–1586) and Huldrych Zwingli (1484–1531).[50] Zwingli (1522) wrote that Jesus assumed flesh of the "immaculate and perpetual virgin Mary," and Luther (1537) that "He was the only Son of Mary, and the Virgin Mary bore no children besides him."[51] John Calvin (1509–1564) wrote in his commentary in 1555 on Matthew 1:25, "He is called first-born; but it is for the sole purpose of informing us he was born of a virgin."[52] Yet, Calvin continued, "What took place afterwards, the historian does not inform us."[53] Commenting on Matthew 1:25 in *Explanatory Notes on the New Testament* (1754), Wesley came to a similar conclusion: "He knew her not, till after she had brought forth–It cannot be inferred from hence, that he knew her afterward: no more than it can be inferred from that expression."[54] That Wesley expressed a stronger statement regarding the perpetual virginity of Mary in *Letter to a Roman Catholic* than he did in *Explanatory Notes*, suggests he may have emphasized this belief in the *Letter* to establish common ground with Catholics.

47. JW, *Letter to a Roman Catholic*, *Works* (Jackson), 10:84–85.

48. JW, *Catholic Spirit*, *Works*, 2:94–95.

49. JW, *Letter to a Roman Catholic*, *Works* (Jackson), 10:81–82.

50. The perpetual virginity of Mary was first articulated as a Christian doctrine at the Second Ecumenical Council of Constantinople in 553, see Tanner, *Decrees of the Ecumenical Councils*, 1:116.

51. Zwingli, *The Latin Works*, 2:36; and Luther, *Luther's Works*, 22:214–15.

52. Calvin, *Commentary*, 1:107.

53. Calvin, *Commentary*, 1:107.

54. JW, *Explanatory Notes on the New Testament*, 1:16. See also his notes on Mark 3:34 for more on Mary: "but [he] seems to guard against those excessive and idolatrous honours, which he foresaw would in after ages be paid to her," 1:155; and his comment on John 2:4, "how absurd it is to address her as if she had a right to command him [Christ]," 1:328.

He mentioned his belief in the perpetual virginity of Mary in *Letter*, and did not address his disagreements of other aspects of Mariology as he did in *Advantage of the Members of the Church of England over Those of the Church of Rome*. In *Advantage*, Wesley wrote of Catholicism: "that this forgiveness [penance] is obtained not thro' the merits of *Christ* alone, but also thro' the merits and intercession of the Virgin *Mary* and other saints."[55]

Yet a Catholic priest, Robert Manning (1655–1731), wrote in the early eighteenth century that for Catholics it was wrong to worship the Virgin, and that it is only through her intercession to Jesus Christ that those who pray find mercy. Manning emphasized that Christ alone forgives sins; the Virgin only intercedes; and finally, that Mary's authority is subject to Christ's.[56] Likewise, Richard Challoner addressed the issue of Catholic devotion to Mary in his *Catholick Christian* (1737), stating that the Church condemns those who do not honor Mary as the Mother of God, but condemns more those that "would give her divine worship."[57]

Additionally, a portion of *Letter to a Roman Catholic* summarized the main points of the Apostles' and Nicene Creeds, which the readers would have recognized.[58] Wesley may have used Bishop of Chester John Pearson's (1613–1686) *Exposition of the Creed* as a source for this section, for his mother, Susanna Wesley, had written a commentary on the Nicene Creed based on Pearson's work.[59] Ted Campbell correctly summarized: "the creedal passage from the 'Letter to a Roman Catholic' then, weaves together themes of Christian doctrine inherited from the ancient church, from the Reformation, and from the Methodist movement."[60]

Although he focused on similarities between Catholics and Protestants in the *Letter*, in addition to his dispute with Catholics on his understanding of aspects of Mariology, Wesley took strong issue with other aspects of Catholic doctrine according to a letter he wrote in 1735. He repudiated the worship of images, the seven sacraments, transubstantiation, "communion in one kind only," "purgatory and praying for the

55. JW, *Advantage of the Members*, 6.

56. Manning, "The Catholic Devotion to the Blessed Virgin," 3:154–56.

57. Challoner, *Catholick Christian*, 236.

58. JW, *Letter to a Roman Catholic*, *Works* (Jackson), 10:81–82; Pearson, *An Exposition of the Creed*; and Campbell, "Shape of Wesleyan Thought," 32.

59. Campbell, "Shape of Wesleyan Thought," 32; Susanna Wesley, *Complete Writings*, 377–408.

60. Campbell, "Shape of Wesleyan Thought," 33.

dead therein," "praying to saints," veneration of relics, indulgences, "the priority and universality of the Roman Church," and the "supremacy of the bishop of Rome."[61] Additionally, in *Advantage*, Wesley elaborated on his disagreements with Catholicism. In writing this, Wesley used John Williams's *Catechism* (1686) which he reprinted in 1756, three years after writing *Advantage*.[62] His contentions with Catholicism were in line with Anglican disagreements with Catholicism from the seventeenth century.[63] His misinterpretations could possibly be attributed to his drawing on other Anglican clergymen's work. Although Wesley engaged in literary battle with Catholic scholars, he seemed to dismiss their interpretation of Catholic doctrine.

The similarities that Wesley demonstrated between Catholics and Protestants cannot be denied, but the heart of the problem with aligning *Letter to a Roman Catholic* with Wesley's intentions for the Catholics of Ireland emerges in this line: "I am not persuading you to leave or change your religion, but to follow after the fear and love of God without which all religion is vain."[64] How could Wesley claim this if he had every intention of preaching New Birth to them? For it cannot be denied that conversion is the foundation of evangelical Protestantism.[65] The answer to the question of "why convert Catholics?" does not particularly lie in the Irish mission, but in the overall Methodist message of evangelical conversion. As did the Reformers before him, Wesley as an evangelical accentuated that God's grace outpouring on people's lives could transform them.[66] In addition, Wesley perceived Methodism as an attempt to practice primitive Christianity. This was why he could say he was not asking them to "change their religion." He was asking them to live out their religion, the primitive and "old religion," and the only way to practice this religion according to Wesley, was to repent of one's sins and be transformed by God's love, or to convert.

---

61. JW to a Roman Catholic Priest [1735], *Works*, 19:92.

62. See Williams, *A Catechism Truly Representing the Doctrines*; and [JW] *A Roman Catechism: With a Reply Hereto*. JW rewrote *A Roman Catechism* in 1779 and published it as *Popery Calmly Considered*.

63. See Tillotson, *The Hazard of Being Saved*. JW read Tillotson's sermons in 1732; see Heitzenrater, "Oxford Methodists," 522.

64. JW, *Letter to a Roman Catholic*, *Works* (Jackson), 10:83.

65. Bebbington, *Evangelicalism in Modern Britain*, 2–3.

66. Locke, *The Church in Anglican Theology*, 30.

Wesley's *Letter to a Roman Catholic* was a product of the moment. Ireland had given the government little trouble during the "Forty-five." There were problems ahead in the second half of the century that had not yet taken place in 1749. Wesley chose a convenient time to deliver his plea for Protestants and Catholics to work together, even if his purpose was to convince Catholics to allow the Methodists to preach evangelical conversion. Wesley seemed optimistic about Ireland in the *Letter*, but by 1758 he was not. In his 1758 *Journal* he wrote: "Most of them [the Irish] retain the same bitterness, yea, and thirst for blood, as ever and would as freely now cut the throats of all Protestants as they did in the last century."[67]

"True Religion" and Conversion

Although Wesley left the word "religion" out of his own dictionary, he may have agreed with Samuel Johnson's 1755 definition of religion: "virtue, as founded upon reverence of God, and expectation of future rewards and punishments."[68] According to *Catholic Spirit*, "true religion" had nothing to do with outward ceremonies or forms of worship, or right opinions.[69] Wesley would attempt to explain this to the Rector of Hollymount (County Mayo), James Clark, who attacked *Catholic Spirit* in 1756.[70] Clark accused the Methodists of being enthusiasts, Montanists, schismatical, and illegal lay preachers. When Wesley heard that Clark had preached this, he sent a copy of *Catholic Spirit* to him.[71] Clark's issues with *Catholic Spirit* centered on his perception that Wesley blatantly disregarded ecclesial law, especially through his use of lay preachers. However, in reply, Wesley tied this all back to the argument that he used when confronted about such things: ordination or church membership or denomination mattered less than "true religion."[72]

---

67. *Works*, 21:150.

68. Johnson, *Dictionary*, 2: s.v. "Religion."

69. JW, *Catholic Spirit*, *Works*, 2:83–85.

70. JW to James Clark, September 18, 1756, *Works*, 27:62. See also Field, *Bid Our Jarring Conflicts Cease*, 52.

71. JW to James Clark, July 3, 1756, *Works*, 27:36–37; and Crookshank, *History*, 1:111.

72. JW to James Clark, September 18, 1756, *Works*, 27:62.

Additionally, Wesley believed that "true religion," or "heart religion," was neither Catholic nor Protestant, but harkened back to primitive Christianity, the practice of Christians in the first three centuries after Christ. This was the purest form of Christianity in Wesley's view.[73] Wesley believed that Constantine's calling himself a Christian brought wealth upon Christianity and thereby "struck at the root of that humble, gentle, patient love, which is the fulfilling of the Christian law," and corrupted primitive Christianity.[74] Thus, the way to "true religion" was not through *any* church, not the Catholic Church, nor the Church of England, but through the New Birth, also called evangelical conversion, defined by Wesley as "a thorough change of heart and life from sin to holiness, a turning," which provided the only way to true religion.[75] Later, in his sermon, "The Way to the Kingdom," Wesley expounded that a person could "espouse all three creeds" and "have no religion at all."[76] Thus he explained the reason for preaching conversion to Protestants in England. His observations of the lives of many of the Catholics in Ireland did not provide proof of "true religion." George Whitefield's observations on his first visit to Ireland in 1738 were that both Catholics and Protestants were ignorant of the "nature of purity and the holiness of God," and Wesley's observations nine years later were similar.[77] If "true religion," to Wesley, only came through evangelical conversion, then it is understandable that he thought Catholics needed to experience conversion.

Wesley's placed considerable emphasis on the importance of Christians, including Catholics, having a personal experience of New Birth. Alongside this, Wesley held concerns regarding the dangers of Popery, and one of these worries was that the Catholic priest held such a high status in the eyes of his flock. This could have influenced the Catholics to think that they must go through a priest to pray to experience New Birth. Further, in his treatise, *A Short Method of Converting All the Roman Catholicks in the Kingdom of Ireland: Humbly Proposed to the Bishops and Clergy of this Kingdom*, Wesley stated:

> It was observed that the grand difficulty of the work lies, in the strong attachment of the Papists to their Clergy. Here therefore

73. Hammond, *JW in America*, 30–37; and Danker, *Wesley and the Anglicans*, 233.

74. JW, "The Mystery of Iniquity," *Works*, 2:463.

75. JW, *Complete English Dictionary*, s.v. "New Birth."

76. JW, "The Way to the Kingdom," *Works*, 1:220.

77. GW, *A Continuation of the Reverend Mr. Whitefield's Journal*, 31–32.

we are to begin; we are to strike at the root; and if this bigotry be
but removed, whatever error or superstition is built upon it will
of course fall to the ground.[78]

This was the solution he proposed to the problem: if the Church of
England clergy embodied the holiness of the Apostles, it would aid in the
evangelical conversion of many. This was because the Catholics revered
the Apostles as higher than priests.[79]

Wesley's own evangelical conversion motivated his preaching about
it to others, although what Wesley experienced at Aldersgate when his
"heart strangely warmed" on May 24, 1738 has been the subject of extensive debate.[80] There is no need to rehearse what Henry Rack, Kenneth
Collins, Randy Maddox, and most recently, Mark Olson have already said
on the subject.[81] Since Wesley's view of the way of salvation has been the
focus of much discussion, this chapter will only touch briefly on the subject.[82] However, it is important to indicate that although his soteriological
themes remained constant, Wesley's view of conversion progressed over
time.[83] For simplicity, Wesley's perception of conversion at the onset of
the mission to Ireland will be explained. Wesley taught that each person
is born in sin, and totally depraved. However, he believed that everyone
was totally depraved apart from the prevenient grace of God.[84] The preventing grace of God allowed for the awakening of the heart, convicting
one of sin. Without this grace, no conviction could take place. When an
individual heard the message of the Gospel preached, his or her heart
either responded with repentance through faith, or rejection. If a person repented of his or her sins, God forgave. The heart, then, became

78. *Works* (Jackson), 10:130.

79. *Works* (Jackson), 10:131–33.

80. *JWJ*, May 24, 1738, *Works*, 18:249–50.

81. See Rack, *Reasonable Enthusiast*, 147; Collins, "Twentieth-Century
Interpretations," 18–31; Maddox, *Aldersgate Reconsidered*; and Olson, "Exegeting
Aldersgate."

82. Maddox, *Responsible Grace*, 157–90; Collins and Tyson, *Conversion in the
Wesleyan Tradition*; Collins, *Theological Journey*, 183–93; and Hindmarsh, *Evangelical
Conversion Narrative*, 89–161.

83. Olson, "Exegeting Aldersgate," 147–51.

84. JW, "Free Grace," *Works*, 3:544–63.

transformed.[85] True repentance, Wesley believed, was "a thorough conviction of sin, an entire change of heart and life."[86]

Wesley believed that the only way anyone could practice a catholic
spirit was to experience God's transformation in the form of New Birth. In
his manuscript journal in May 1737, he wrote of his concern about "over-
grown zeal for Protestantism, quite swallowing up zeal for our common
Christianity."[87] In the same entry, he expressed his view of Catholicism
at the time: "as bad as a religion Popery is, no religion is still worse" and
"that as dangerous a state as a Papist is in, with regard to eternity, a Deist
is in a far more dangerous state if he be not an assured heir of damnation,
and Because as difficult as it is to recover a Papist, 'tis far more difficult to
recover an infidel."[88] Neither zeal for Protestantism nor Catholicism mattered if there was no repentance. Thus, both Protestants and Catholics
must experience evangelical conversion, or New Birth, before either will
ever have the power of God to practice a catholic spirit.

Wesley, in response to Richard Challoner's *Caveat against the
Methodists*, wrote "it must be said that the Catholics in general are not
the 'people of God.'"[89] He did not say that all Catholics are not the people
of God, nor would he ever say that *all* Protestants were the people of God.
This Wesley demonstrated in a letter to John Newton in April 1765:

> "Oh, but Mr. Hervey says you are *half* a papist." What if he
> had proved it too? What if he had proved I was a *whole* papist
> (though he might as easily have proved me a Mahometan)? Is
> not a papist a child of God? Is Thomas à Kempis, Mr [Gaston
> Jean Baptiste] de Renty, Gregory Lopez gone to hell? Believe
> it who can. Yet still of such (though papists), the same is my
> brother and sister and mother.[90]

Wesley valued other Catholic devotional writers such as: John of
Avila (1500–1569), Francis Xavier (1506–1552), and Madame Guyon
(1648–1717).[91] Although he valued these writers, Wesley believed that

85. See JW, "Salvation by Faith," *Works*, 1:117–30; JW, "Justification by Faith,"
Works, 1:188; JW, "The Spirit of Bondage and Adoption," *Works*, 1:249; and JW, "The
Witness of the Spirit I," *Works*, 1:269–84.

86. JW, *Complete English Dictionary*, s.v. "Repentance."

87. JW, MSS *Journal*, May 25, 1737, *Works*, 18:511.

88. *Works*, 18:511.

89. *JWJ*, February 13, 1761, *Works*, 21:306.

90. JW to John Newton, April 9, 1765, *Works*, 27:421.

91. See JW to Samuel Wesley [his nephew], September 16, 1789, in Telford, 8:171;
and Khoo, *Wesleyan Eucharistic Spirituality*, 142–43.

Catholicism held responsibility for the religious and political problems of Ireland, and he perceived that the continued dominance of Catholicism in Ireland was to be blamed on the lack of true Christianity in the Church of Ireland clergy.[92] He thought that the Catholic priests deceived the people, and that the Anglican clergy did not preach "true religion," thus: "The Methodists could understand that an illiterate and ignorant peasantry would be strangers to the truth, but they could not understand or forgive their educated representatives continuing in error."[93] This sentiment Charles Wesley echoed in his hymn "For the Roman Catholics in Ireland," stating that Catholics did not have knowledge of God's "pardoning love."[94]

When John Wesley compiled *A Short History of the People Called Methodists* (1781), he declared that by 1759:

> the plain, old Bible religion had made its way into every county in Ireland, save Kerry. And many in each county, and in most large towns, were happy witnesses of it. But I doubt not there would have been double the number had not true pains been taken by Protestants (so called) as well as Papists, either to prevent their hearing, or at least prevent their laying to heart, the word that is able to save their souls.[95]

The above quotation explains two aspects of the Methodist Irish mission: that within ten years of the first permanent Methodist inroad into Ireland, they had preached and planted societies in every county except Kerry. The other aspect illustrates Wesley's insistence throughout the remainder of his life as he clashed with both Catholic and Protestant opposition in Ireland: if the communicants and the clergy of the Established Church would have lived "the plain, old Bible religion," there would have been a much larger "harvest of souls" in the country.[96]

Conversion and Renouncing "Popery"

The overall Methodist method of promoting conversion, preaching by both ordained and laymen and forming societies, did not change in

92. JW, *Short Method.*
93. Hempton, *Methodism and Politics*, 36–37.
94. CW and JW, *Poetical Works of John and Charles Wesley*, 8:398.
95. JW, *A Short History of the People Called Methodists*, *Works*, 9:469.
96. JW, *Short Method*, 9.

Ireland, nor did their expectation of persecution.[97] Nonetheless, since Wesley preached to dominant Catholic rather than Protestant audiences, his practice necessitated slight adjustments. Any overt anti-Catholicism would only alienate Methodist preachers from their listeners. Through trials they learned that preaching in buildings rather than fields usually brought fewer injuries, and sometimes the societies met secretly in barns to avoid discovery by mobs bent on mischief. Though they altered their methods, Wesley and his preachers still irritated the Anglican clergy. Yet this was nothing new, as some clergy of the Established Church in England had been attacking the Methodists for over a decade.[98] However, the most obvious difference in method between England and Ireland was the renunciation of Popery by the converts.

In 1726 John Wesley read Thomas à Kempis's, *De Imitatione Christi*, and discovered "the nature of true religion" as centered in the heart.[99] He discussed it with his mother, who had also read it.[100] One of his earliest publications was a translation of à Kempis, for which he had been criticized by the Society for Promoting Christian Knowledge for not purging it enough of its "Popery." He often recommended à Kempis to others, and proposed that every house should have a copy.[101] Further, he quoted à Kempis after preaching in Mountmellick (County Laois), noting that "Papists stood in the skirts of the congregation, though liable to heavy penance for it. Well might Kempis might say, 'He rides easily whom the grace of God carries.'"[102]

Wesley did not say whether he intentionally used à Kempis to connect to the Catholics of Ireland, but Charles Wesley preached from *The Imitation of Christ*, on his first visit to Dublin, realizing the benefits of preaching something familiar. After he preached from à Kempis, he remarked: "the Papists stood like lambs. I quoted Kempis, which makes some of them confident I am a good Catholic."[103] Similarly, once, after

97. Heitzenrater, "John Wesley's Principles," 89–106.

98. Lyles, *Methodism Mocked*, 17.

99. JW, *Plain Account*, *Works*, 13:137. For more on Wesley and à Kempis, see Hammond, "John Wesley and 'Imitating Christ,'" 197–212.

100. Susanna Wesley to JW, June 8, 1725, *Works*, 25:164.

101. à Kempis, *The Christian Pattern*, translated by John Wesley; and "Register of Books, April 1735," *Gentlemen's Magazine* 6 (1735), 222. JW to Samuel Wesley [his nephew], September 16, 1789, in Telford, 8:171; and Hammond, *JW in America*, 163.

102. *JWJ*, April 20, 1758, *Works*, 21:144.

103. September 27, 1747, *MJCW*, 2:510.

preaching in Dublin, John Wesley heard a voice exclaim: "aye! He is a Jesuit; that's plain!" A Catholic priest who heard the exclamation replied, "No, he is not, I would to God that he was."[104] However, a quiet crowd was not the norm in the first days of Methodist preaching in Ireland. Less than a week later, Charles encountered a "popish mob" in Dublin:

> Some time since a Popish mob with some Protestants, so called, at their head & the Romish priests behind the curtains, broke open our preaching room, tore away the benches, pulpit, wainscot etc. & burnt them in the face of the sun, after they had cruelly abused & only not murdered several of the society. The riot in all its circumstances was laid before the Grand Jury; who were so widely dealt with by the persecutors, that they threw it out & thereby gave them full license to murder us all, if they were so minded. They concluded we should at least be broke into pieces hereby, & scattered & come to nought.[105]

Nonetheless, after preaching from à Kempis to the calm crowd, surprisingly, he "advised them to go to their respective places of worship."[106] This was well received by all, "especially the papists."[107] Was this the case, however, for his brother John? John did not comment on the declaration that he was Jesuit, only that the next day he had preached: "What does it profit a man if he should gain the whole world and lose his own soul?"[108] Further, John Wesley wrote to Charles Wesley from Cork in 1749 that "The number of communicants daily increased. And among these were many who had been Papists, but had now relinquished the Church of Rome. These are facts which no man can deny."[109] "Communicants" meant these former Catholics who had become Anglican, for they had received the Holy Sacrament. Bishop George Lavington (1749) said of John Wesley, "People of *every communion* are among his *disciples*, and he rejects with indignation any design to convert others *from any communion*, and consequently *not from Popery*."[110] Wesley answered that this was false: "I have, by the blessing of God, converted several from popery,

---

104. *JWJ*, May 16, 1748, *Works*, 20:226.

105. CW to Hannah Dewel, October 6, 1747, CW, *Letters of Charles Wesley*, 135.

106. *MJCW*, September 20, 1747, 2:509.

107. *MJCW*, September 20, 1747, 2:509.

108. *JWJ*, May 16, 1748, *Works*, 20:226.

109. JW to CW, [June 17, 1749], *Works*, 26:366.

110. [Lavington], *Enthusiasm*, 166.

who are now alive and ready to testify it."[111] By 1756 he wrote to Nicholas Norton: "We have many members in Ireland that *were* Papists, but not one that continues so." Norton, who oversaw Wesley's Book Room in Bristol, had heard that a person could remain a Catholic and continue a member in a Methodist society.[112]

That John Wesley insisted to Nicholas Norton that he had converted some from Popery and that none of his members remained "papist" seems to contradict the message of *Catholic Spirit* and *Letter to a Roman Catholic*. It is likely that multiple converts of Catholicism in Ireland did not communicate with the Church of Ireland as this is one reason why Thomas Walsh (c. 1730–1759), a Methodist lay preacher who had been "trained a strict Roman Catholic," begged Wesley to register the Methodists as a dissenting church so that the preachers could be licensed to administer the sacraments.[113] Walsh experienced conversion under the preaching of Robert Swindells (d. 1783), one of Wesley's first itinerant preachers, in Limerick in 1749.[114] Walsh, who spoke fluent Gaelic, was received into the itinerancy shortly thereafter.[115] Crookshank wrote of Walsh: "Even the poor Romanists listened willingly when they were addressed in their mother tongue, and frequently shed silent tears or cried aloud for mercy."[116] James Morgan, Walsh's biographer, was convinced that Wesley's inflexibility on the matter of refusal to register as a dissenting church hastened the death of Walsh at the age of twenty-eight in 1759.[117]

Although Methodism "attracted thousands of curious Irishmen to outdoor meetings," only a small proportion joined societies.[118] Yet not all who began the journey in a society remained, for Wesley desired all to experience conversion and "grow in grace," and he regularly questioned them. Perhaps preachers who had converted from Catholicism, like Walsh, required less of the society members. Walsh specifically stated that the Catholic converts refused to attend the Established Churches

111. JW, *Second Letter, Works*, 11:423.

112. JW to Nicholas Norton, September 3, 1756, *Works*, 27:49.

113. Baker, *John Wesley*, 132.

114. Crookshank, *History*, 1:47.

115. Crookshank, *History*, 1:76.

116. Crookshank, *History*, 1:78.

117. Morgan, *Life of Thomas Walsh*, 205.

118. Hempton and Hull, *Evangelical Protestantism*, 34.

who had clergy of less than desirable character, and after all Wesley him-self stated that the lack of integrity of the Anglican clergy kept Catholics from converting in the first place.[119]

Societies in Ireland were not new, for the Church of Ireland formed societies in Dublin as early as 1695. The meetings, scheduled on Sunday before and after services, attempted to keep people out of the drinking establishments. These societies did not last long, dying from apathy, so why, then did Wesley's societies in Ireland thrive?[120] First, they may have flourished because Wesley did not require membership in the Established Church to join. Second, societies provided a social life for the members, as Wesley proclaimed: "we *introduce* Christian fellowship where it was *utterly destroyed*."[121] Davies pointed out that by allowing anyone in the societies Wesley "broke down the theological barrier of Calvinistic ex-clusiveness," but perhaps Wesley shattered some Catholic walls as well. His father, Samuel Wesley, had remarked of societies within Catholicism, most likely referring to religious orders: "The church of Rome owes, per-haps, her very *substinence* [sic] at the least, most of the *progress* she has made of late years, to those several societies she nourishes in her bosom: why may not we learn from *enemies*; and what better to way to fight with their own *weapons*?"[122] Perhaps Wesley took this cue from his father.

Methodist society leaders encouraged all members to seek personal piety. Every participant had "equal liberty of speaking, there being none greater or lesser than another."[123] John Murray (1741–1815), a young convert from Cork in the early 1750s, described the Methodist system this way:

> The congregation, who, as outer-court worshippers, were only *hearers*, and *seekers*; members of the society, who were classed; and members of the band society, who were *genuine believers*. The two latter met every Sunday evening after meeting, and no individual who was not furnished with a ticket could gain admittance. The ticket was a badge of distinction; it gave the possessor entrance; all others were shut out and the door was locked. No words can describe my sensations when I obtained a

119. For Walsh's statement see, Baker, *John Wesley*, 132. JW, *Short Method*, 3–4.

120. Barnard, *Irish Protestant Ascents and Descents*, 150–53.

121. JW, *Plain Account of Methodists*, *Works*, 9:259.

122. "Introduction," *Works*, 9:25; and Wesley, "Letter Concerning the Religious Societies," appendix.

123. JW, *Plain Account of Methodists*, *Works*, 9:270.

seat *inside* the closed door, when I listened while the preacher in a low voice addressed the children of God.[124]

Wesley claimed that his societies were denominationally inclusive, but Murray, who Wesley had appointed to lead a society, said Wesley put him under censorship for his Calvinism: "Wesley received information against me. He set a watch over me; thus fixing upon me the evil eye of suspicion."[125]

During the first years in Ireland (1747–1750), the Methodists saw many Catholic converts. Sufficient numbers converted, it seems, that both Catholic and Anglican priests were alarmed, some trying to convince converted Methodists to abandon their new beliefs. Wesley had not known what to expect, for he remarked after his first visit to Rathcormack: "I found we were mistaken in thinking the papists would not come to the church. They were the larger half of the congregation. Though I should scarce have imagined it by their behavior. For they were all serious and deeply attentive."[126] Within the first year of the commencement of Methodist preaching in Ireland, Charles Wesley penned a hymn: "Thanksgiving for the success of the gospel in Ireland."[127] Although they had experienced harsh resistance, Charles thanked God for the conversions they had witnessed, as this is how he measured the success of the mission to Ireland. Likewise, after Charles preached in Dublin he wrote, "A Papist behind the wall at first lifted up his voice in curses, but in the end cried out, the 'Lord bless you!'"[128] Moreover, writing to William Holland, Charles Wesley, in optimism, shared: "surely he [God] has much people in Ireland . . . yet in spite of all opposition, we pick up every day more lost sheep of the Romish Communion. Remember them, & me."[129] They saw results, for in April 1748, less than a year after his first journey to Dublin, John Wesley wrote to Charles that the Society in Tyrrellspass (County Westmeath) had about one hundred members, "nine or ten of whom were papists."[130]

124. Murray, *Life*, 21.

125. Murray, *Life*, 47.

126. JW to CW, [May 30, 1749], *Works*, 26:364–65.

127. CW, *Poetical Works*, 8:400–1; and Crookshank, *History*, 1:44.

128. *MJCW*, October 4, 1747, 2:511.

129. CW to William Holland, August 13–October 8, 1748, CW, *Letters*, 1:159.

130. JW to CW, April 16, 1748, *Works*, 26:306.

There are multiple accounts of Catholics in Methodist society meetings "renouncing Popery." For instance, in 1748, the rector of Rathcormack (County Cork), Richard Lloyd (1699–1778), wrote to Wesley: "Michael Poor, lately a Roman, who is now of your society, read his recantation Sunday last."[131] Moreover, Edward Drumgoole (c. 1751–1835) publicly renounced Popery, and became a member of the society in County Sligo, and Matthias Joyce (1754–1814), who became a preacher, had once been a Catholic who "renounced Popery."[132] On the other hand, Crookshank wrote of Catholics who did not "openly renounce Popery" but stopped believing the "dogmas of the system and gave up going to confession" at the influence of the Methodists.[133]

What "renouncing Popery" specifically meant for Wesley and the Methodists in Ireland remains unclear. It is understandable that the Methodists' encouragement of renunciations of Popery angered Irish Catholics; however, no records survive to show whether the renunciations were a simple statement or a formal oath. George Whitefield, while preaching on repentance referred to

> a particular office in the large prayer book, to be used when any one publicly renounces Popery in the great congregation. When this is done, that prayer read, and the person said Amen to the collects upon the occasion, everybody wishes him joy, and thanks God he is converted; whereas if this be all, he is as much unconverted to God as ever; he has in words renounced Popery, but never took leave of the sins of his heart.[134]

Since there is no particular office in the Book of Common Prayer for "renouncing Popery," it is difficult to determine what Whitefield meant. One possibility is that he referred to a 1714 document: "A form for admitting converts from the Church of Rome and such as shall renounce other errors, to be used for such persons only as shall desire to be solemnly admitted into the Church thereby."[135] This brief ceremony was to be used

131. Richard Lloyd to JW, August 29, 1749, *Works*, 26:377.

132. Crookshank, *History*, 1:240, 286.

133. Crookshank, *History*, 3:320.

134. GW, "Repentance and Conversion," in *Eighteen Sermons*, 111. This is a transcription of GW's sermon, which gives a reason to be cautious about its accuracy.

135. Tenison, "20, Anno Christi 1714," 4:660–62. It is acknowledged that Wilkins may have made some errors in transcription of the original document, Bodleian Library Rawlinson D 843, fol. 150r-156v., according to Jacob, "Wilkins's *Concilia* and the Fifteenth Century," 91–131. See also Questier, *Conversion, Politics, and Religion*, 108–12.

with a penitent in "separation" from the Church of England, a dissenter; or a penitent from "the Church of Rome."[136] It is possible that Whitefield could have viewed this form bound with a Book of Common Prayer, as a person who requested a bound prayer book could request that other documents be bound with it.[137] Furthermore, this form of the prayer book could have been used in Whitefield's chapels. If this is the form to which Whitefield referred, the ceremony was diocesan, with the bishop offering absolution. Wesley's societies in Ireland certainly would not have had a bishop present, but Wesley and his preachers assigned to Ireland could have adapted the form for their own use. However, his societies in Ireland may not have had a standard or universal ritual for renouncing Popery.

It is likely that multiple converts from Catholicism in Ireland did not communicate with the Church of Ireland as this is one reason why Thomas Walsh begged Wesley to register the Methodist chapels as dissenting churches to grant permission to the preachers to administer the sacraments, for the converted Catholics would not attend the Established Church because they believed most of the Anglican clergy did not practice "true religion."[138] Of course, Wesley refused. The Irish Conference would not allow Methodist preachers to serve the sacrament until 1816, twenty-five years after Wesley's death.[139] Whether Wesley, Walsh, or other Methodist preachers ever forbade converted Catholics from attending mass is unknown.

Since Wesley allowed anyone who "desired to flee the wrath to come" into the societies, it is not known whether he required every Catholic to "renounce Popery" to continue in the society. Although Wesley stated clearly in *Catholic Spirit* that it was up to a person's own conscience to choose his or her particular congregation in which to worship, the evidence suggests that he would not have approved of a Methodist society member choosing to kneel at mass.[140] This among many reasons reveals why the irritation of the Irish towards Methodists, especially Irish Catholics, continued at various levels of intensity throughout Wesley's lifetime.

136. "A Form for Admitting Converts," 661.

137. Maltby, *Prayer Book and People*, 26–27.

138. Baker, *John Wesley*, 132.

139. Crookshank, 2:408–9.

140. JW, *Catholic Spirit, Works*, 2:85–86.

The Cork Riots and Conversion

After John Wesley had experienced riots against the Methodists in Cork he wrote *A Short Address to the Inhabitants of Ireland* (1749), and in this he assured the people of Ireland that if allowed to do their work, the Methodist preachers would advance solid virtue and community peace, thereby bringing happiness as part of the overall plan "to reform the nation."[141] This treatise did not specifically address Catholics, but all of the people of Ireland. Wesley insisted that the Methodist preachers were agents of truth, change, goodwill, virtue, and happiness. If they were allowed to do as God called them to do, then "holiness and happiness would certainly cover the land."[142] In Wesley's view, the people of Ireland should praise God that God had spoken through the Methodist preachers, because the preachers advanced "solid rational virtue."[143] Such virtue, to Wesley, resulted only in "true religion."

Advancing virtue took time, but even amidst the riots, most Methodists continued preaching and meeting in societies. Even among those who chose not to convert, some respected and aided the Methodists. Although happy to make friends and have assistance in their work, indubitably Wesley and the Methodists believed that the most vital fruit of their work was evangelical conversion.[144] The tiny glimpses of the change, goodwill, virtue, and happiness that Wesley had assured to Ireland in *A Short Address* began to surface, for Charles Wesley said: "Much good has been done already in this place [Cork]. Outward wickedness has disappeared, outward religion succeeded. Swearing is seldom heard in the streets. The churches and altars are crowded to the astonishment of our adversaries. Yet some of our clergy and all the Catholic priests take wretched pains to hinder their people from hearing us."[145] Although there had been riots against the Methodists in Dublin 1747, they did not amount to the level of violence which they experienced in Cork. Shortly before Wesley published *A Short Address*, Jonathan Reeves (d. 1787), Methodist lay preacher, wrote an appeal to the opposition in Cork, asking them to allow the Methodists to work in peace.[146] Reeves echoed

141. JW, *Short Address*, 8.

142. JW, *Short Address*, 8; and Crookshank, *History*, 1:53.

143. JW, *Short Address*, 8.

144. JW, *Short History, Works*, 9:477–79.

145. August 21, 1748, *MJCW*, 2:536–37.

146. Reeves, *Affectionate Address*.

Wesley's preaching when he wrote that Methodists work for the "revival of vital religion," and added a plea that if the readers would not work with them, they should just "let them alone."[147] "Vital religion," a synonym to "true religion," according to the Methodists, only came through evangelical conversion. When speaking of "assurance," Reeves made his only mention of Catholicism in the pamphlet: "And I know no church that denies this doctrine of assurance, but that of Rome."[148] With this phrase, he likely sought to gather the support of the Protestants of Cork, as some had joined with the Catholics in rioting against the Methodists.

Despite Wesley and Reeves's efforts, hostility towards the Methodists exploded in Cork in August 1748.[149] Writing to William Lunell from Cork that same month, Charles Wesley reported, "[God] has brought us safe through various trials & difficulties in this place; when a door is opened great & effectual. I preached repentance & remission of sins to above 7000 listening souls at 5 this morning. They seem all to have ears to hear."[150] Nevertheless, by May 1749, John Wesley wrote to Charles of Reeves' warning of Cork's chaos: "The town is set on fire of hell, and all the powers of hell are stirred up against your coming."[151] At one point, John Wesley expressed apprehension at riding through town, for when he visited Cork, a mob attempted to tear the house down in which he had preached.[152] This took place in front of the Lord Mayor, William Holmes, who stood by and did nothing. Wesley sent for his friend, a retired alderman who walked with him until he was out of danger. He made it out of Cork unscathed, but word reached him that the mob had burned his effigy.[153]

The Cork riots led Wesley to exclaim: "Upon the whole one question readily occurs, whether, setting aside both Christianity and common humanity, it be *prudent* thus to encourage a popish mob to tear Protestants in pieces. And such Protestants as are essentially and remarkably

147. Reeves, *Affectionate Address*, 43.

148. Reeves, *Affectionate Address*, 41.

149. Jeffery, *Irish Methodism*, 11.

150. CW to William Lunell, August 21, 1748, MARC DDcw 1/17a. See Bradshaw, "William Lunell, of Dublin," 73–76.

151. JW to CW, May 14, 1749, *Works*, 26:358.

152. JW to CW, May 30, 1749, *Works*, 26:365.

153. JW to Mr. Baily of Cork, June 8, 1750, *Works*, 9:298; and JW to CW, June 17, 1749, *Works*, 26:367–72.

attached to the present government!"[154] Wesley's perception was that Lord Mayor Holmes had done nothing to stop the rioting. Further, John Bailey, the Rector of Kilcully, just north of Cork, challenged the right of the Methodists to preach in Cork.[155] By the next year, the new mayor, Daniel Crone, had allowed Nicholas Butler, a hired ballad singer who instigated the riots, to do as he wished.[156] It is understandable that Wesley took to his pen to advocate Christian unity and tolerance after facing these obstacles.

Yet, "truth, goodwill, and virtue" materialized in the worst conflict. At the height of the mob rioting in Cork in 1749, the Philosophical Society of Cork composed a letter to John Wesley. They wrote: "You will be beforehand with us, in applying this, to Mr Whitefield and yourself, and in the allusion to the many real or pretended reformers that preceded."[157] They were not unanimous in their agreement on what they all thought about the Methodists, but they knew that Whitefield and Wesley must be "exceptional men." The society issued an invitation to Wesley to join them in their meetings when he next visited, but it is not known whether Wesley acted on this invitation.[158] They waited impatiently for Wesley to come, but meanwhile the "Preachers appeared," and hearing a preacher out of church was a novelty to them. The Philosophical Society was amazed at the preacher (whom they did not name) because he described his own conversion in an "emphatic way and had a great effect on the audience." The society had agreed that someone from their group should always attend the meetings and report back to the rest as they were trying to consider the preachers' words in a philosophical capacity.[159] The first set of Wesley's missionaries had had the "Rules" printed and went off to another town.[160] More preachers came and formed societies. In spite of the rioting mobs, the Philosophical Society observed that the Methodists' overall influence on the city was positive, as several drunkards reformed and the people in the societies acted in an orderly way. In all of the accounts of the rioting in Cork, it seems that the only Methodist who acted

154. JW to CW, June 17, 1749, *Works*, 26:372.

155. Davies, "Introductory Comment," *Works*, 9:288.

156. JW to Mr. Baily of Cork, June 8, 1750, *Works*, 9:290; and JW to CW, June 17, 1749, *Works*, 26:367–72.

157. Ozello, *An Account*, 4.

158. Ozello, *An Account*, 5.

159. Ozello, *An Account*, 6–7.

160. Most likely JW, *The Nature, Design, and General Rules of the United Societies*, see *Works*, 9:69–75.

contrary to a catholic spirit was Daniel Sullivan, a convert, who in fear and anger "fired a pistol without any ball" over the heads of the mob.[161] Not only did the Philosophical Society of Cork accept the Methodists as Wesley had hoped when he wrote *A Short Address to the Inhabitants of Ireland*, it seems as if they were so enthralled with the Methodists that they were willing to pay Nicholas Butler, the instigator of the riots, to stop. The Philosophical Society enquired of Wesley: "Is it lawful to countermine? What if his employers were outbid?"[162] They closed the letter promising Wesley that they would attend the meetings and keep him informed of anything he needed to know.[163]

However, this was not necessary as, from the beginning, William Lunell had been in correspondence with George Whitefield concerning opposition to the Methodists at Cork. As soon as Whitefield heard of the riots he dispatched a letter to Lady Huntingdon so that she could wield her influence with the government to get the riots to stop.[164] Whitefield requested that his friend Mr. Gifford, a "dissenting minister," advocate to the Speaker of the House of Commons, Arthur Onslow (1691–1761), about the Cork Riots, who suggested that Gifford go to the Secretary of State (Chesterfield) and the Lord Lieutenant of Ireland (Harrington) (c. 1683–1756).[165] Wesley wrote a narrative of the persecution with many first-hand accounts of it, which was presented to Harrington. This seems to have led to the case being brought to court. Thereby through the effort of many supporters, the judges of the Lent Assizes of 1750 declared that no riots would be tolerated in Cork.[166]

Whitefield's visit to Cork in May 1751 showed that peace finally reigned as the people received him with gladness. As he left, many prayed for his blessing, and numerous Catholics maintained that if he

161. JW, *A Letter to the Rev Mr. Bailey of Cork, Works*, 9:296–97.

162. Ozello, *An Account*, 11.

163. Ozello, *An Account*, 16.

164. GW to William Lunell, December 9, 1749, in Tyerman, *Life of Whitefield*, 2:240–41. Whitefield mentioned to Lunell he had written to the Countess.

165. See Laundy, "Onslow, Arthur (1691–1786)," *ODNB*. Most likely the Baptist minister Andrew Gifford; see Cannon and Hayden, "Gifford, Andrew (1700–1784)," *ODNB*. GW to Lady Huntingdon, January 12, 1750, in Tyerman, *Life of Whitefield*, 2:244.

166. JW to Mr. Baily of Cork, June 8, 1750, *Works*, 9:297; and Tyerman, *Life of Whitefield*, 2:245–46.

would remain in the city, they would "leave their priests."[167] No doubt this promise to leave their priests would have angered the Catholic clergy, but it is not known whether the priests knew of the promises made by their flocks to Whitefield. Although they experienced opposition from many, the Methodists encountered friendliness in some towns.

The (Mostly) Positive Outcome of the Attempt to Convert Ireland

Some Church of Ireland clergy agreed with John Wesley, and even allowed him to preach from their pulpits. One of these clergymen, Richard Lloyd, reported to Wesley in August 1749: "Your society here keeps well, and is, I believe considerably increased since you left it. I frequently attend preaching."[168] He experienced opposition for attending the preaching, and for allowing Wesley to preach from his pulpit. Archdeacon Michael Davies wrote to Lloyd in July 1750 with concerns from Bishop of Cloyne, George Berkeley, that Lloyd had allowed Methodists [lay preachers] to preach in his church.[169] Lloyd assured Berkeley that he had only allowed John Wesley to preach.[170] The bishop told Lloyd that he trusted him with his pulpit, and that he would avoid anything that would provide a reason for riots.[171]

Berkeley had just published *A Word to the Wise: Or an Exhortation to the Roman Catholic Clergy of Ireland by a Member of the Established Church* (1749). This message has similarities to *Letter to a Roman Catholic*, but it was published ten months later.[172] Berkeley appealed to the similar beliefs of Protestants and Catholics, and like Wesley, he asked Catholics to "suspend our animosities, forgetting our religious feuds, consider ourselves in the amiable light of countrymen and neighbours," closing with "we believe in the same Christ."[173] Eight years later, Wesley discovered that Archbishop Cobbe had instructed his clergy to begin a society for the purpose of distributing books to the poor. This excited

167. Crookshank, *History*, 1:83.

168. Richard Lloyd to JW, August 29, 1749, *Works*, 26:377.

169. Michael Davies to Richard Lloyd, July 4, 1750, *Works*, 26:436–37.

170. Richard Lloyd to George Berkeley, July 4, 1750, *Works*, 26:437.

171. George Berkeley to Richard Lloyd, July 4, 1750, *Works*, 26:437.

172. Hurley, *Letter to a Roman Catholic*, 44n.

173. Berkeley, *Word to the Wise*, 3; see also Hurley, *Letter to a Roman Catholic*, 42.

Wesley as he recognized a catholic spirit at work: "whether we or they, it is all one, so God be known, loved, and obeyed."[174]

Augustus Toplady (1740–78), an evangelical Anglican priest who had attended Trinity College, Dublin, criticized Wesley's *Letter to a Roman Catholic*: "Far be it from me, to charge Mr. Wesley with a fondness for *all* the grosser parts of Popery. Yet, I fear, the partition between that Church and him, is somewhat *thinner* than might be wished."[175] An anonymous author had a similar complaint about *Letter to a Roman Catholic*, because Wesley did not criticize Catholic liturgy or theology but emphasized their commonalities instead. The writer quoted Wesley's phrase: "I am not persuading you to leave or change your religion, but to follow after that fear and love of God without which all religion is in vain," and stated: "Hence, some have concluded that Mr. Wesley's sentiments are nearly allied to those of the Church of Rome."[176]

Throughout Ireland, the Methodists encountered friendly people. Wesley wrote of an unnamed man who rode next to him in Kilmallock: "I soon perceived he was a priest, and found he was a sensible man. I gave him a book or two at parting, and he dismissed me with 'God bless you' earnestly repeated twice or thrice," but it is unknown whether he meant a Catholic or an Anglican priest.[177] Even on his first journey through Ireland, Charles Wesley recorded: "It is worth observing that in Kinsale I am of every religion. The Presbyterians say I am a Presbyterian; the Church-goers, that I am a minister of theirs; and the Catholics are sure I am a good Catholic in my heart."[178] Additionally, the Wesleys formed friendships with Catholics who did not seem to convert. On Charles Wesley's first visit to Dublin in September 1747, he referred to Catholic friends that would walk him and other Methodists place to place for their safety, and in Athlone, a "well-disposed Roman Catholic" lent a house for a society meeting, "to the great distress of his co-religionists," and a Catholic provided a barn in which to preach.[179] A further small change was displayed as John Rutty (1698–1775) discovered "a glimmer of

174. *JWJ*, April 18, 1758, *Works*, 21:141.

175. Toplady, *A Letter*, 16.

176. *A Faithful Warning to the Followers*, iv.

177. *JWJ*, May 29, 1749, *Works*, 20:277.

178. *MJCW*, September 8, 1748, 2:546.

179. *MJCW*, September 13, 1747, 2:507, 551–52.

hope on the improvement of the nation from the Methodists."[180] Rutty, a Dublin Quaker physician and friend of John Wesley's, gave no indication that he joined a Methodist society in his spiritual diary, but he did hope "to catch the fire of the Methodists."[181]

Yet, in spite of John Wesley's reassurances to the people of Ireland that Methodist preachers only had pure intentions, not all of the Methodist preachers displayed "solid rational virtue." Of the 110 preachers: English, Welsh, and Irish that Wesley assigned to Ireland, he eventually expelled twenty. When Wesley discovered that a preacher had departed from the rules of the Conference, he took action, but this did not prevent the damage done to Methodism's reputation. For instance, David Barrowclough "got a woman with child," and Hugh Saunderson (b. 1746) "seduced Mrs Willis." Furthermore, Wesley expelled Jonathan Hern (b. 1734), Thomas Halliday, James Hall (b. 1751), Barnabas Thomas (1734–?1793), and Isaac Waldron (?1731–1782) for their "drunkenness."[182]

Despite the fact that some magistrates had been apathetic or outright vicious towards the Methodists, some proved helpful. For instance, in Kinsale, "a lady who belonged to the church of Rome insisted on the servant of God going to her house and assured him that Mr. Walter Bowler, the Sovereign or Governor of the town had issued orders that none should dare disturb him [John Wesley]."[183] Likewise, a Catholic priest forbade his parishioners from listening to Charles Wesley preach in Passage (County Cork). Charles took this to "an honest attorney," who went with him to speak with the local justice. The justice informed the priest that he would shut down the Catholic chapel and send the priest to jail for a year if he continued forbidding his people to listen to the Methodists. Still, it took the justice informing the Catholics that he "would himself take off the curse" the priest had sworn upon them before they would listen to the preaching.[184]

Although glad for the assistance of friendly Anglicans priests, magistrates, and philosophers, Wesley continued to seek evangelical converts. Wesley perceived that preaching holiness and forming societies so that people experienced the transforming love of Christ led to a truly

180. Rutty, *Spiritual Diary*, September 24, 1756, 69.

181. *JWJ*, April 25, 1748, *Works*, 20:220; and Rutty, *Spiritual Diary*, August 3, 1760, 155.

182. Roddie, "Register of Irish Methodist Preachers."

183. Crookshank, *History*, 1:40.

184. August 28, 1748, *MJCW*, 2:539.

"reformed nation." The Catholics kept converting, for an intense revival broke out in July 1762 in Dublin.[185] Moreover, Thomas Rourke, Catholic convert, began preaching in 1762, and John Bredin (1737–1819), a Catholic schoolmaster was converted in 1766.[186] Indeed, people came to Methodist preachers, "desirous of salvation," including "papists," according to Thomas Walsh.[187]

John Lenton indicated that several historians including Rack and Hempton agreed "that in general, Wesley had little success with the Catholic majority in Ireland."[188] This is not an easy matter to determine as the lists of society members that survive do not indicate whether a convert was a former Catholic. Lenton indicated as well that many Catholics who converted emigrated to America or other places to escape persecution from family or former associates.[189] However, when it came to preachers, few came from Catholic backgrounds. Lenton specified that only six of the 110 preachers active in Ireland during Wesley's lifetime can be verified as having been raised Catholic, but at least fifteen others had surnames of Irish origin and may have been Catholics, although there is no evidence of their religious affiliation.[190]

Although not a Catholic convert, the most detailed account of an early Irish Methodist conversion comes from Elizabeth Bennis (1725–1802) of Limerick, who described her conversion to Wesley in August 1763.[191] She had heard Robert Swindells preach in May 1749, and was "much affected."[192] Struggling with conviction of her sin for a month, when "the preacher offered Christ to all, I found my burden in a moment taken off, and my soul set at liberty."[193] In the year of Wesley's death, a concerned Catholic priest wrote to Elizabeth Bennis in an attempt to correct her. By now Bennis had been a Methodist for almost forty years. The

185. JW, *Short History, Works*, 9:478.

186. Crookshank, *History*, 1:196–97.

187. Morgan, *Life of Walsh*, 92.

188. Hempton, "The Methodist Crusade in Ireland," 33–48; Rack, *Reasonable Enthusiast*, 235–36; Lenton, "British Preachers," 205.

189. Lenton, "British Preachers," 205.

190. Lenton, "British Preachers," 205.

191. Elizabeth Bennis to JW, August 2, 1763, in Bennis, *Correspondence*, 2–10.

192. Elizabeth Bennis to Unknown, October 18, 1765, in Bennis, *Correspondence*, 308.

193. Elizabeth Bennis to Unknown, October 18, 1765, in Bennis, *Correspondence*, 309–11.

priest assured her that there was only one church, and that the church is united under one head, the Pope. Not to be deterred, she replied: "My faith is not founded on St. Peter or St. Paul; on pope or bishop of any sect, but on the Lord Jesus Christ alone who died for my sin, and rose again for my justification."[194] Bennis's testimony reveals that she had internalized Wesley's teachings as she explained to the priest:

> I would not dare to confine the mercy of God to any particular body of people; nor would I strain any text in the book of God to exclude any from his mercy. . . . I belive [sic] the whole Christian Church of every denomination is the visible church of Christ; but that only those who worship him in spirit and in truth; who love him, and keep his commandments, are members of his invisible church, and are accepted of him. . . . This is, and has been for many years my faith; In which I find myself happy in life, and willing to die; and by the grace of God resolved not to change.[195]

This insightful first-hand testimony demonstrates that by the time of his death, not only had Wesley's message reached Ireland, but it had been preached by Swindells, and other Methodists, to the point where Bennis could articulate it clearly. In *A Plain Account of the People Called Methodists* (1749), Wesley argued that: "*orthodoxy* or *right opinions*, is at best but a very a slender part of religion" and "the only way under heaven to this religion is to 'repent and believe the gospel.'"[196] This accords with the view he had taken in a *Catholic Spirit*. Thus, Thomas Walsh, an Irish former Catholic, and Methodist convert communicated the message of conversion and a catholic spirit to an Irish Catholic priest.

Wesley's influence on Thomas Walsh concerning a catholic spirit was evident when Walsh encountered priests who attempted to convert him. He had been on his way to Roscrea, when a mile from town in January 1752, he was attacked by nearly sixty men, "armed with sticks and bound by oath in confederacy against him."[197] Apparently, their goal was to try to get him to leave Methodism behind, as they brought both Catholic and Church of Ireland priests to convince him. Walsh argued that "he contended with no man concerning opinions, nor preached

194. Joseph C. to Elizabeth Bennis, November 23, 1791, in Bennis, *Correspondence*, 298.

195. Elizabeth Bennis to Joseph C., November 26, 1791, in Bennis, *Correspondence*, 298–99.

196. JW, *A Plain Account of the People Called Methodists*, *Works*, 9:254–55.

197. Crookshank, *History*, 1:87.

against particular churches, but against sin and wickedness in all."[198] This statement expressed the message of *Catholic Spirit*, and probably demonstrates Wesley's influence on Walsh. They agreed to let him go if he swore to never return to their town, and if he did not, they would throw him into a well. Thankfully a friendly Church of Ireland priest walked by and saved him.[199]

In 1757 Thomas Walsh explained the Methodist understanding of the process of conversion to Bennis:

> First . . . the soul by the *spirit of God*, applying the commandment, is deeply convinced of its darkness, guilt, misery and helplessness, then a man is poor in spirit, he has nothing to pay, but being weary and heavy laden, seeks and groans to be delivered. Secondly . . . the same *spirit* works faith in the broken heart; giving divine light, whereby the soul sees God, gracious in Christ; and divine power whereby the soul can trust God; then is given the spirit of Adoption, and the heaven born soul rejoices in God through Christ; loves and delights in the Lord Jesus, has free access to the throne of grace.[200]

Walsh articulated Wesley's conversion model: conviction of sin, repentance, and faith.[201] John or Charles Wesley examined the preachers every year at Conference.[202] Walsh, present at the first Irish Conference in 1752 and subsequent conferences, learned, and thereby communicated, the Methodist message of New Birth.[203]

In 1778, at a time when many Irish people feared French invasion after the French Alliance, an agreement between the Americans and the French government, Wesley comforted the Irish people with *A Compassionate Address to the People of Ireland*. He reminded them of God's promise to Abraham interceding for Sodom: that God would not allow destruction of a kingdom so full of righteous people, and "Religion, true scriptural religion, the love of God and our neighbour," is "continually increasing in every part of the kingdom."[204] Overall, the Methodists

198. Crookshank, *History*, 1:87; and Morgan, *Life of Walsh*, 79.

199. Crookshank, *History*, 1:87.

200. Thomas Walsh to Elizabeth Bennis, February 5, 1757, in Bennis, *Correspondence*, 114–15.

201. JW, "Salvation by Faith," *Works*, 1:117–30.

202. Heitzenrater, "John Wesley's Principles," 100.

203. *The Limerick Conference of August 14–15, 1752*, *Works*, 10:251.

204. JW, *A Compassionate Address to the Inhabitants of Ireland*, *Works* (Jackson), 11:154.

may have experienced a lower level of success in maintaining member-ship in societies in Ireland than in England (Methodism had a member-ship of 22,410 in England in 1767 and grew to 56,605 by 1791), but they still saw an increase in membership. In 1767, there was a membership of 2,801 in Ireland, and by 1791: 14,158, an increase of over 11,000 in twenty-five years.[205]

Conclusion

This chapter has attempted to show that the message of *Catholic Spirit* was not principally intended for Catholics, and that *Letter to a Roman Catholic*, rather than being an ecumenical declaration, was written as a message to gain the trust of Catholics so that they might experience evangelical conversion. Wesley did ask for Catholics to work with him in love, but his intention was to convince Catholics to repent and experi-ence New Birth, thereby "true religion." To Wesley, only a "real Christian" practicing "true religion" could practice a catholic spirit. The message was the same to any person; no matter which was the church of their bap-tism, or if they had no knowledge of God. In order to practice a catholic spirit, people had to have the love of God "shed abroad in their hearts," and the only way to experience this love of God, according to Wesley, was to experience evangelical conversion. By preaching the message of conversion to Catholics, Wesley believed he was spreading the possibility of catholic spirit.

That Wesley did not intend the sermon *Catholic Spirit* as a mes-sage to Catholics is suggested by the emphasis given to the Protestant Reformation in the sermon. Further, Wesley rejected what he perceived as the Catholic Church's denial of the right of private judgement. Since Wesley asserted that "true religion" could only be practiced by those who had experienced the New Birth, it naturally follows that he would say to Catholics that he was not trying to get them to leave their religion, but to "follow the fear and love of God."[206] As for the lack of "true religion" of Catholics of Ireland, Wesley placed the highest blame on the Anglican clergy for not practicing primitive Christianity.

---

205. For statistics on Methodism in England, see Bocock and Thompson, *Religion and Ideology*, 133. For statistics on Methodism in Ireland, see Hempton, *Religion of the People*, 36; and Rogal, *JW in Ireland*, 2:788.

206. JW, *Letter to a Roman Catholic*, *Works* (Jackson), 10:83.

John and Charles Wesley only slightly changed the method used to communicate evangelical conversion in Ireland. They preached and formed people into societies. They adjusted their sermons to reach a predominately Catholic crowd, and sometimes moved societies to secret meeting places to avoid mischief-seeking mobs. The main difference between the ministry in England and the ministry in Ireland had to do with converts renouncing Popery, but it is unknown whether this was a formal or informal renunciation. That Catholics rioted and resisted the Methodists is not surprising. The Cork Riots heavily influenced Wesley in the writing of *Letter to a Roman Catholic*, for "popish" mobs violently opposed the Methodists there.

Despite the twenty preachers Wesley expelled for their behavior, some positive results took place. Some Anglican clergy respected them and allowed them to preach in their pulpits, and even some Catholics proved friendly. However, seeing the Irish experience the New Birth, for Wesley, remained the aim of his efforts. Thomas Walsh had experienced conversion, and he practiced a catholic spirit when confronted by opposition. Elizabeth Bennis, though not a Catholic convert, answered a concerned Catholic priest by stating that she would not limit the mercy of God to one body of people. Eight months before Wesley died, membership in Methodist societies in Ireland was 14,106, although it is not known how many of these had once been Catholic.[207] Although Wesley slightly modified his methods to reach the Catholics of Ireland, he remained forever English. He believed that the Methodist message to Ireland had brought not only New Birth to individuals, but the dawning of a catholic spirit to the land he once called defiled.

207. *Irish Minutes*, 1790, *Works*, 10:1006.

5

Jesuitism, Popery, and a *Catholic Spirit*

THE TWO PREVIOUS CHAPTERS explored events in which John Wesley and the Methodists were involved before the writing of *Catholic Spirit*: the introduction of Methodism to Ireland, and the accusations against Wesley and the preachers during the "Forty-five." The aims of this chapter are as follows: first, Wesley's critique of the Moravians for their "Jesuit" ways is examined. Secondly, the chapter explores critiques by opponents of Wesley and the Methodists of alleged Jesuitism and Popery. The chapter evaluates whether they responded with a catholic spirit to these accusations. The allegations against Wesley and the Methodists concerning Popery and Jesuitism are classified first by the two main groups who provided the critiques: Anglican bishops and Calvinists, followed by specific reasons for the accusations: the alleged use of trickery, magic, and tyranny, especially over women. Finally, the complaints that Wesley displayed Popery and Jesuitism in *A Calm Address to Our American Colonies* (1774) are examined.

According to Luke Tyerman, Wesley "was called a papist times without number."[1] Along with "papist," there were many pejorative terms that British Protestants used regarding Catholics, and those they accused of being Catholic. A person could be called a "papist" if they were thought to practice "papism" or "Popery," consequently, "papism" and "Popery" will be used synonymously in this chapter. In addition, "Popery" will be defined as "a hostile designation for the doctrines and practices of the Roman Catholic Church."[2] Defining Jesuitism as it was used in eighteenth-

---

1. Tyerman, *Life and Times of Wesley*, 3:316.
2. Livingstone, *Concise Oxford Dictionary of the Christian Church*, s.v. "Popery."

century Britain is not quite so simple. A Jesuit is a member of the Society of Jesus, a Catholic order of priests and brothers founded by Ignatius of Loyola (1491–1556) in 1534, and approved by Pope Paul III (1468–1549) in 1540.[3] "Jesuitical," as it was used in eighteenth-century Britain was a slur, a term of abuse often indicating mental reservation, casuistry, and sophistry especially in religious matters.[4] Hence, "Jesuitism" implied the practice of these "Jesuitical" ways. In Georgian Britain, if one wished to slander their opponent, nothing generated as much negative notoriety as casting a Jesuit aspersion. Religious leaders who claimed Protestantism yet seemed to be propagating Catholicism earned the smear "Jesuitical;" or they earned the label simply by being "secretive," or practicing what their opponents perceived as any characteristic of Jesuits. According to Bishop George Lavington of Exeter, John Wesley was a Protestant who promoted "Popery" and demonstrated "a strain of Jesuitical sophistry."[5]

It is an understatement to say that the topic of Wesley and Jesuitism has been neglected by his biographers. Aside from one-sentence acknowledgements in a few biographies and mentions of the same in works concerning the conflicts early Methodism encountered, there are few articles on specific aspects of Wesley, the Methodists, and Jesuitism.[6] Robert Southey said that Wesley could have become the "founder of an order or even the General of the Jesuits had he been in the Roman Catholic Church."[7] This is understandable, even though during Wesley's lifetime in the midst of accusing him of "papism" and "Popery," his many opponents took the opportunity to brand not only him as "Jesuitical," but other Methodists as well. This chapter attempts to fill the gap in Wesley studies concerning Wesley, Popery, and Jesuitism.

Examination of the sources begins with Wesley's *Journal* and letters, where he recorded not only some of the instances when he or his movement was accused of Popery and alignment with the Society of Jesus, but when he himself accused the Moravians of Jesuitism. Additionally,

3. See Padberg, "Ignatius," 1–38.

4. Cannon, *A Dictionary of British History*, s.v. "Jesuits."

5. [Lavington], *Enthusiasm*, 122.

6. Hampson, *Memoirs*, 2:22–23. Moore and Coke, *The Life of the Rev. John Wesley*, 1:193. (Wesley's biographers in the nineteenth century avoided the topic.) Walsh, "Methodism and the Mob," 227. Turner, *Conflict and Reconciliation*, 32; Rack, *Reasonable Enthusiast*, 279; and Byrne, "Ignatius Loyola," 54–66. Lewis, "Papal Emissary," 16–34, mentions allegations of Jesuitism against GW.

7. Southey, *Life of Wesley*, 2:397.

the *Journals* and letters of other key evangelicals, such as Charles Wesley, George Whitefield, Vincent Perronet (1693–1785), and William Seward (1711–1740), illustrate situations in which accusations of Jesuitism surfaced. Furthermore, specific allegation of Jesuitism in anti-Methodist literature is usually buried in works containing accusations of enthusiasm, antinomianism, and/or "Popery." According to W. Stephen Gunter, anti-Methodist writings fall in three categories: "enthusiasm, anti-clericalism, and doctrinal divergence."[8] In all of these categories, allegations pertaining to Popery and Jesuitism may be found.

Even before the Jesuits came to England, they were persecuted; for like "Methodist," "Jesuit," is an appropriated term, its original meaning being "someone who speaks of Jesus too much."[9] Although never official, over time members of the Society accepted the label. The Society of Jesus sent two missionaries to England in 1580: Robert Parsons (1546–1610) and Edmund Campion (1540–1581).[10] Late in 1580 Parsons and Campion separated in order to cover more ground. An informer revealed Campion's identity, and he was imprisoned, interrogated, tortured, and executed in 1581. Parsons managed to escape.[11]

Hatred towards Jesuits raged, especially since four Jesuits were identified as having been involved in the Gunpowder Treason Plot of 1605. This plot ended in the capture of Henry Garnett (1555–1606), the Jesuit superior in England.[12] He was executed though he claimed he only knew of the plot from the confessional. Wesley shared in the prevalent English fear of and opposition to Jesuitism.

John Wesley's Critique of the Moravians

Although tension between Wesley and the Moravians began in Georgia, it did not come to a head until a few years later when Wesley decided he could no longer ignore certain theological differences between himself and the Moravians.[13] In 1750, Wesley, looking back ten years, wrote of

8. Gunter, *Limits*, 267.

9. See O'Malley, *The First Jesuits*, 69.

10. Taunton, *Jesuits in England*; Holt, *English Jesuits*, 1; and South, *The Jesuits*.

11. Taunton, *Jesuits in England*, 63.

12. See A. B., *Ward's Downfall*. See also Cannon, *Oxford Companion to British History*, s.v. "Jesuits."

13. Hammond, *JW in America*, 91–96. See Outler, *John Wesley*, 353–76, for a collection of the documents pertaining to conflict between Wesley and the Moravians.

his issues with the Moravians in a letter to "an old friend whose spirit and life once adorned the gospel;" in it Wesley commented on an unnamed preacher he had heard at Fetter Lane:

> This preaching destroys true, genuine *simplicity*. Let a plain open-hearted man, who hates controversy and loves the religion of the heart, go but a few times to Fetter Lane, and he begins to dispute with every man he meets; he draws the sword and throws away the scabbard. And he if happens to be hard pressed by Scripture or reason, he has many turns and fetches as a Jesuit, so that it is out of the power of a common man even to understand, much more to confute him.[14]

It is certain that in this context, Wesley used the word "Jesuit" as a slur, illustrating a person using deceit and confusion as a means to an end. Philip Molther was most likely the preacher to whom Wesley referred.[15] Wesley had tried to convince the society of what he perceived as Molther's theological errors. His contention with Molther was that Molther's concepts of faith alone and quietism were incompatible.[16] Although his contentions were written in a private letter, his issues with the Moravians culminated in an argument with their leader, Count Nikolaus von Zinzendorf (1700–1760), in which among other things, Wesley accused the Count of acting as a Pope.[17] The Moravian Church replied with an assertion that Zinzendorf was neither their king, nor bishop, nor Pope, nor even a Count to them (although he was a count by birth).[18] After the quarrel went public, both Benjamin Ingham and Charles Wesley perceived that John Wesley had been too harsh. Charles wrote:

> I fear all is not right in your own breast, otherwise you would not think so hardly of them [Moravians]. Is there envy, self-love, emulation, jealousy? Are you not afraid lest they should eclipse your own glory, or lessen your own praise? Do you not give too

---

14. *JWJ*, November 28, 1750, *Works*, 20:371. Ward and Heitzenrater speculated that JW was writing to Rev. George Stonehouse (1714–1793) vicar of Islington, who had been a Moravian from 1741 to 1745. See *Works*, 18:237–38.

15. Gunter, *Limits*, 85–96. A summary of Wesley's break with the Moravians can be found in Podmore, "The Fetter Lane Society 1739–1740," 156–85.

16. Gunter, *Limits*, 270.

17. JW to Count Zinzendorf and the Church at Herrnhut, [August 5–8, 1740], *Works*, 26:24–31.

18. Moravian Church at Marienborn to JW, [October 5, 1740], *Works*, 26:37.

much credit to all that you only hear of them? I am sure they are a true people of God. There is life and power amongst them.[19]

It seems from this letter that Charles Wesley displayed a catholic spirit, on the other hand, a publication of differences between the Moravians and Methodists appeared in 1745, with the names of both brothers, showing that Charles had disagreements with them as well.[20] In spite of Charles's discord with them, it seems that he "always remained sympathetic to the 'Germans,' and especially to their English leader James Hutton."[21] Zinzendorf extended a hand of peace by travelling to London from Germany, attempting to smooth things over with John Wesley. Yet Wesley refused to compromise, and through his leadership the Methodists broke their connexion with the Moravians. Furthermore, the Moravians showed their catholic spirit by agreeing that no one should complain about Wesley when they met for their English Conference in 1741.[22] Less than two weeks later, Whitefield arrived in London, preaching predestination, and Wesley confronted him.[23] John Wesley wrote to Charles stating that the bands had been purged, as he had dismissed those who unnecessarily argued over predestination.[24] Those who disagreed with the Moravians eventually moved from Fetter Lane to the Foundery.

Later, when Wesley outlined his disagreement with the Moravians in a letter, he described their "whole scheme" as mystical, with darkness in their behavior, and guile in their words.[25] Yet in all probability he called them Jesuit because: "the spirit of secrecy is the spirit of their community, often leading into guile and dissimulation. One may observe in them much cunning, much art, much evasion, and disguise. They often *appear* to be what they are not, and not to be what they are."[26] Wesley did not approve of "the way they treated their opponents," for he perceived they treated them without love or humility. Yet Wesley's judgment of

19. Benjamin Ingham to JW, October 3, 1740, *Works*, 26:33–34; and CW to JW, [March 10, 1741], *Works*, 26:53–54.

20. CW and JW, *A Short View of the Differences*, 16. The last page is signed, "John and Charles Wesley." See also Tucker, "Polemic against Stillness," 101–19.

21. Baker, *John Wesley*, 130.

22. Podmore, *Moravian Church*, 77.

23. CW to JW, [March 16–17, 1741], *Works*, 26:54.

24. JW to CW, April 21, 1741, *Works*, 26:55–57; Roberts, "John Acourt," 72; and Gunter, *Limits*, 228–29.

25. *JWJ*, November 28, 1750, *Works*, 20:369.

26. *Works*, 20:369.

them did not seem to be given in a spirit of love, humility, or toleration. Not only was he using "Jesuit" as an insult, he wrote the letter describing his problems with Molther nine years after he separated from the Moravians, implying that he still held animosity.[27] Ultimately, Wesley outlined these differences between himself and the Moravians by printing *Queries Humbly Proposed to the Right Reverend and Right Honourable Count Zinzendorf* (1755).

It seems that Wesley thought the Moravians were adopting what he believed to be Jesuit tactics by using equivocation, mental reservation, and casuistry. "Casuistry" denotes "the art or science of bringing general moral principles to bear upon particular cases, a synonym for sophistry."[28] Casuistry may additionally be defined as: "The art of resolving problems of conscience."[29] Moreover, "equivocation," also known as "doublespeak," is an informal logical fallacy using a pragmatically or lexically ambiguous particular term or phrase twice in the argument, intentionally misleading the listener.[30] Specifically, equivocation is using one word to mean two things. Accordingly, those who taught mental reservation articulated: "It is not lying to make a spoken assertion which you believe to be false, and which you will believe will deceive your hearer, provided that you add in thought some words which make the whole truthful."[31] When John Ward, Catholic priest was captured in 1606, his captors asked him whether he was a priest and whether he had ever been across the seas. He replied "no" to both questions, though the correct answer was "yes." When the Crown produced evidence of his false answer, he claimed he had not lied, for, in denying that he was a priest, he had mentally added, "of Apollo," and in saying he had not been across the seas he had reserved "Indian" before seas.[32] The reason for this practice is not difficult to understand. The Jesuits and other Catholics were persecuted in seventeenth-century England, so they employed the use of mental reservation as a survival tactic.

---

27. *JWJ*, July 20, 1740, *Works*, 19:162.

28. "Casuistry" in *Concise Oxford Dictionary*.

29. Broadie, "Casuistry," in Honderich, *The Oxford Companion to Philosophy*.

30. Watson, *Fallacies Arising from Ambiguity*, 63.

31. Sommerville, "New Art of Lying," in Leites, *Conscience and Casuistry*, 160.

32. Sommerville, "New Art of Lying," 160.

Casuistry

It is important to understand casuistry because it became associated with Jesuitism. It is also vital to comprehend how it was employed in the eighteenth century. Not the first to use mental reservation, the Jesuits may have drawn from Christians as far back as Athanasius of Alexandria (296–373) in its use.[33] Casuistry in the primitive form may also be found in Pope Gregory I (540–604) "who provides the three dilemmas of moral double bind" and gave advice as to the lesser evil.[34] After the first Lateran Council (1215) commanded that Catholics make confession at least once a year, concern about conscience increased. The Council of Trent (1545–1563) brought casuistry into much more common practice. The Society of Jesus trained their priests specifically in casuistry, and by the year 1600, Jesuit colleges had been established in Europe, India, and South America.[35] The doctrine of casuistry eventually became a source of embarrassment for Catholics, with Pope Innocent XI (1611–1689) condemning it in 1679.[36]

Casuistry became well known in England because when the King's Bench tried Jesuit Robert Southwell (1561–1595) for treason in 1595, Archbishop of Canterbury George Abbot (1562–1633) exposed Southwell's equivocation.[37] Sommerville called the assumption that all Jesuits used casuistry unfair, because some were against it. Implying that all Jesuits used casuistry was a way to discredit everything they said, especially their oaths, as it was assumed that the oaths always included equivocation.[38] Robert Parsons wrote that some Jesuits used equivocation, and that he recommended it at certain times.[39] He described equivocation this way:

> Then he may answer, as though he were alone, and no man by, for that he hath no necessary reference to him at all, nor to his demands, questions, or speech, but that he may frame to him self any proposition that is true in it self, and in his own sense

---

33. Newman, *Apologia Pro Vita Sua*, appendix.

34. Jonsen and Toulmin, *The Abuse of Casuistry*, 95.

35. Sorabji, *Moral Conscience*, 122–23.

36. Sommerville, "New Art of Lying," 178.

37. Sommerville, "New Art of Lying," 177.

38. Sommerville, "New Art of Lying," 178–79.

39. P[arsons], *Treatise Tending to Mitigation*, 274–77.

& meaning, though the other that heareth understand it in a
different sense and meaning, & be thereby deceived.[40]

Allegedly Robert Catesby (1573–1605) conferred with a Jesuit ca-
suist in advance of the foiled Gunpowder Plot in 1605. The next year,
James I required every Catholic in the kingdom to swear an oath of allegiance. This was to be done specifically without "any equivocation or
secret reservation," saying that they would not kill the king if the Pope
deposed him.[41] The oaths required by English monarchs from this point
forward triggered dilemmas of conscience not only for Catholics, but for
nonconforming Protestants as well.

Both devout Catholics and Protestants sought moral guidance during the trying times surrounding the Reformation, and casuistry became
an acceptable option. For example, several Puritan divines "engaged
in the direction of conscience," but moderate Puritan William Perkins
(1558–1602), systematized the practice of casuistry.[42] Perkins wrote on
casuistry for many reasons, one being to "temper the rigour of the moral
demands of God as expressed in the Scriptures, just as some Catholic
writers on casuistry can be accused of doing."[43] Keeping the command-
ments, Perkins argued, is the only way of true faith, but the "moral demands on one person are not exactly the same as those on another."[44] The
following is a demonstration of Perkins's view of conscience:

> Whosoever resisteth the power resisteth the ordinance of God;
> and they that resist all receive to themselves judgement: and,
> yet must be subject not only for wrath, but also for conscience
> sake. . . . Magistrate[s] indeed is an ordinance of God to which
> we owe subject but how far subjection is due there is the ques-
> tion. For body & goods & outward conversation I grant all: but
> a subjection of conscience to man's laws, I deny. And between
> these two there is a great difference to be subject to authority in
> conscience, & to be subject to it for conscience, as will be mani-
> fest . . . for the avoiding of sin, & so by consequent for avoiding
> a breach in conscience.[45]

---

40. P[arsons], *Treatise Tending to Mitigation*, 342–43.

41. Sorabji, *Moral Conscience*, 118.

42. Breward, "William Perkins," 8. Perkins, *A Discourse of Conscience*.

43. Patterson, *William Perkins*, 97.

44. Patterson, *William Perkins*, 110.

45. Perkins, *Discourse of Conscience*, 46–47.

Perkins interpreted the Scriptures to allow for individual conscience. He established that a person could choose to "breach" a law made by the government not because the person neglected the law, but because the magistrates who made the law had transgressed against the law of God.[46]

Wesley wrote about casuistry in his sermon, "An Israelite Indeed" (1785), in which he denoted that casuists, "particularly of the Church of Rome," classified lies in three ways. The first way was "malicious," the second was "harmless," and the third, "officious." He stated that all Christians condemn malicious lies. Many, however, are divided on "harmless lies," but Wesley stated that they did not have any place in the mouth of a Christian.[47] Concerning "officious" lies, those that are spoken with a design to do good, there have been numerous controversies in the Christian church. Wesley noted that an abundance of writers had published books on the subject, and regardless of all opposition, commended them as laudable, but Wesley disagreed. He referred to Rom 3:7–8, proclaiming: "If the truth of God hath more abounded through my lie unto his glory, why am I yet judged as a sinner?" Wesley's conclusion is that no matter what the effect of a lie, there is no excuse for it.[48]

After examining Wesley's relationship with the Moravians, his comparison of Ignatius of Loyola to Count Zinzendorf makes sense. While riding his horse in August 1742, he read the *Life of Ignatius of Loyola*. Commenting in his *Journal*, he surmised that Ignatius was a great man who "engaged in support of so bad a cause." According to Wesley, Ignatius had functioned as Count Zinzendorf did in his day: "with a full persuasion that he might use *guile* to promote the glory of God (which he thought the same thing)."[49]

Late in 1763, Wesley visited his "old friend" John Gambold (1711–1771). Gambold had been an Oxford Methodist, and was ordained in the Church of England. Wesley introduced him to the Moravians. Gambold broke with the Church of England and became a Moravian bishop in 1745.[50] In November 1763, Wesley met with Gambold, and afterward wrote: "Who but Count Zinzendorf could have separated such friends as

---

46. Perkins, *Discourse of Conscience*, 47.
47. JW, "An Israelite Indeed," *Works*, 3:285. Wesley had preached this text in 1755.
48. *Works*, 3:285.
49. *JWJ*, August 16, 1742, *Works*, 19:292.
50. *Works*, 18:225n.

we were? Shall we never unite again?"[51] Wesley and Gambold met again a month later. The conversation was "agreeable," according to Wesley, yet disappointing: "O how gladly could I join heart and hand again! But alas! 'thy heart is not as my heart!'"[52] This cry from Wesley was a quotation from 2 Kings 10:15, the text he used for *Catholic Spirit*. Wesley perceived that Gambold's heart was not as his heart, so he could not join heart and hand with him again.

Near the end of his life in 1780, Wesley visited the city of Zeist, Netherlands, calling on "his old friend," a Moravian, Anton Seiffert (1712–1785). This seems to have been a pleasant visit, and this time the leader of the Methodists inscribed no negative appraisal of Moravians in his *Journal*.[53] Perhaps the visit caused him to recall where he had been the last time he saw Seiffert: Savannah, Georgia. He had witnessed Seiffert's ordination, mistaking that he was ordained as a bishop rather than a minister, probably due to his limited German.[54] Soon after the Moravian/Methodist disagreement, the Bishop of Exeter accused Wesley himself of using "Jesuitical arts."

The Episcopal Critique

J. C. D. Clark called Bishop George Lavington's *Enthusiasm of Methodists and Papist Compar'd* (1749–1752) a "lengthy comparison with Popery," and rightly indicated that in its time it spoke effectively to still-powerful anti-Catholicism.[55] Perhaps unknown to Wesley, *Enthusiasm*, according to William Warburton (1698–1779), Bishop of Gloucester, was a "bad copy of Stillingfleet's famous book of *the Fanaticism of the Church of Rome*."[56] Examination of Bishop Edward Stillingfleet's *Discourse Concerning the Idolatry Practiced in the Church of Rome* reveals that Lavington may have used this as a source, but it is not a "copy." Stillingfleet covers the issues of "evangelical poverty," "doctrine of perfection," seeking persecution, and

---

51. *JWJ*, November 3, 1763, *Works*, 21:438.

52. *JWJ*, December 16, 1763, *Works*, 21:440.

53. *JWJ*, February 28, 1736, *Works*, 18:151. *JWJ*, July 28–29, 1783, *Works*, 23:282.

54. Hammond, *JW in America*, 89–90.

55. Clark, "The Eighteenth-Century Context," 18.

56. See William Warburton to Richard Hurd, July 5, 1752, Warburton, *Letters from a Late Eminent Prelate*, 86. He most likely referred to Edward Stillingfleeet (1635–1699), *Discourse*, 5:111–25.

criticizing Jesuits.[57] Stillingfleet summarized what he thought of multiple Catholic orders: "But this is the fruit of leaving the *Scriptures*, and that most plain and certain way of *Religion* delivered therein; there can be no end of phantastical modes of devotion, and every superstitious fanatick will be still inventing more, or reviving old ones."[58] Lavington compared the Methodists with Catholic orders, but did not include an extensive critique of all Catholic orders as Stillingfleet did.

No matter what sources he used, revenge seemed to be the motive for Lavington's publication of *The Enthusiasm of Methodists and Papists Compar'd* in 1749.[59] While John Wesley, his brother, Charles, and other Methodist preachers had been facing riots in Ireland, an unknown antagonist accused Lavington of alignment with the Methodists.[60] Someone who must have known about Lavington's opposition to the Methodists printed a charge to Lavington's clergy with his plagiarized signature, in which the subversive support of the Methodists read, "yet it must be said, that their preaching is right and good in the main, though the persons are immethodical in their practice."[61] Lavington wrote a disclaimer to this charge, saying that he was not a "favourer of the sect," and there were "several well-meaning people among them," but the "sect" was enthusiast and delusional.[62] The stewards of the Foundery immediately published a response, and the Countess of Huntingdon used her influence to force Lavington to print a renunciation.[63] Subsequently, Lavington published *Enthusiasm*. Since this was only three years after the "Forty-five," the accusation was serious.

Labelling the Methodists "enthusiasts" was spiteful, but calling them both enthusiast and papist was vicious. George Whitefield and Methodist preacher Vincent Perronet replied to the first *Enthusiasm* almost immediately, but Wesley waited longer, showing his usual reluctance at entering

57. Stillingfleet, *Discourse*, 5:111–24.

58. Stillingfleet, *Discourse*, 5:125.

59. See Beckerlegge, *The Lavington Correspondence*; Rack, *Reasonable Enthusiast*, 277; and Simon, *John Wesley*, 122–23.

60. See Baker, *John Wesley*, 104–5.

61. Beckerlegge, "A Letter of George Whitefield," 109.

62. See the *General Advertiser* 4329, September 9, 1748; and the *London Evening Post* 3256, September 13–15, 1748.

63. The disclaimer is reprinted in Baker, "Bishop Lavington and the Methodists," 40; for the rebuttal see Seymour, *Life and Times of Selina Lady of Huntingdon*, 1:95–96.

disputes.[64] Upon examining Lavington's subsequent strike, Whitefield wrote to the Countess, expressing: "Mr. Wesley, I think had best attack him now, as he is largely concerned in this second part."[65] Apparently, Wesley agreed, for after the publication of the second letter he replied.[66]

Lavington offered no genuine evidence of a connection between the Methodists and the Jesuits, but the oft-used polemic, "Jesuitical sophistry," was not about evidence of alliance with the Society of Jesus.[67] For instance, Francis Bugg (1640–1727), a former Quaker turned anti-Quaker polemicist, published in 1711 that George Fox (1624–1691) founder of the Society of Friends, was "Jesuit like," as he was good at "Innuendoes"[*sic*].[68] Later, John Philpot Curran (1750–1817), a London lawyer who eloquently advocated Catholic relief earned the title, "the Little Jesuit from St. Omers" in the 1770s, though he had no connection to the Society of Jesus.[69]

Lavington denounced the Methodists for doing "the 'Papists' work for them," and for abiding by the same principles.[70] "The Spirit of Enthusiasm," according to Lavington, was always the same, and having set up himself as a detective of such, he proceeded with a lengthy inventory of what he considered proof. This criterion he gathered from his interpretation of Wesley, George Whitefield, and other Methodists' publications of letters and journals.[71]

Like Ignatius, Wesley and Whitefield preached in the fields, and practiced itinerancy. Lavington claimed that Whitefield invented field preaching, although unknown to Lavington the tradition of field preaching in England dated at least to John Bunyan (1628–1688).[72] Whitefield retorted that it was Jesus who invented it, and claimed that he was not

64. GW, *Some Remarks on a Pamphlet*; and Perronet, *Some Remarks on a Late Anonymous Piece.*

65. GW to Lady Huntingdon, August 24, 1749, in Tyson and Schlenther, *In the Midst of Early Methodism*, 75.

66. Cragg, "Introduction," *Works*, 11:355.

67. [Lavington], *Enthusiasm*, 164.

68. Bugg, *The Quakers Infallibility Shaken All to Pieces*, 607; and Leachman, "Bugg, Francis (1640–1727)," *ODNB.*

69. Kelly, "Curran, John Philpot (1750–1817)," *ODNB.*

70. [Lavington], *Enthusiasm*, 1:8.

71. [Lavington], *Enthusiasm*, preface.

72. Jay, "Field Preaching," in McCalman et al., *The Oxford Companion to the Romantic Age.*

ashamed that others preaching in fields before him included St. Ignatius.[73] The bishop showed exasperation after Whitefield's letter, exclaiming, "you glory in it! [field preaching]!"[74] Although Lavington lumped field preaching and itinerancy together in the same category, they were not the same practice. A preacher did not have to travel far away from his home to preach in a field. The reason he did, nevertheless, often had to do with the unwelcoming attitude of the local clergy towards him. Whitefield and Wesley preached wherever they could. If they could obtain use of a building, such as a town hall, they would preach there. John Bossy asserted that there was "not much warrant in the Protestant tradition" for the itinerancy of preachers, and Jesuits saw it as an application of their idea that the church was apostolic and mission-focused.[75] This seems to be the same reason that Wesley and Whitefield practiced it, although Wesley claimed that he would rather preach in churches, but when forced out, he thought that he had no choice but to proclaim the gospel in fields.[76]

Lavington attacked works that Wesley had written, specifically *A Collection of Forms of Prayers* because it contained prayers for the dead.[77] In this Wesley believed he was justified "by the earliest antiquity, by the Church of England, and by the Lord's Prayer, although the Papists have corrupted this scriptural practice into praying for those who die in their sins."[78] Yet Wesley advocated praying for people who had repented before death. The colonists of Georgia accused Wesley of alignment with Catholicism for the same reason.[79]

The bishop declared that Methodists and Catholics valued "New Birth," and that like Ignatius, Wesley received assurance of salvation.[80] Edmund Gibson (1669–1748), Bishop of London, disapproved of the Methodists for their more than "ordinary assurances of God's grace."[81] Wesley had written of the assurance he received after his "Aldersgate

73. GW, *Some Remarks*, 12. For more on GW's reply see, Haydon, "Bishop George Lavington," 68–69.

74. [Lavington], *Enthusiasm*, ix.

75. Bossy, *English Catholic Community*, 398.

76. JW, *A Second Letter*, *Works*, 11:363.

77. See JW, *A Collection of Forms of Prayers*.

78. JW, *A Second Letter*, *Works*, 11:423.

79. *Works*, 11:423. Tailfer et al., *True Narrative*, 41–42; and Hammond, *JW in America*, 161–64.

80. [Lavington], *Enthusiasm*, 1:31–33.

81. Gibson, *Observations*, 10.

experience." Byrne aligned Wesley's description of his Aldersgate experience, the warming of the heart, as similar to the "deep interior conviction" of the first week of the Ignatian *Exercises*, even though there is no evidence that Wesley read these prior to his evangelical conversion. Furthermore, when Wesley articulated the steps of justification or conversion, he accentuated the role of prevenient grace, and highlighted the vitality of human response.[82] This concerned Bishop Lavington, for it seemed to him as if Wesley was preaching a "papist" view that "works" were required for salvation. However, both Wesley and Ignatius were concerned with "the conviction of sin and a sense of inability to achieve any good apart from the grace and favour of God, as predispositions to the grace of deeper conversion worked by the Spirit."[83] For in Wesley's sermon, "The Witness of the Spirit I" (1767), he described the work of the Holy Spirit as inward impression on the soul.[84] Wesley was not advocating that "works" were required for salvation, but simply that a human responded to God's offer of salvation.

Lavington accused the Methodists of praying for and rejoicing at the thought of imprisonment or persecution. In this Lavington was correct, the Methodists did rejoice in persecution, and even prayed for it.[85] In his study of primitive Christianity, Wesley determined that following Christ led to suffering. While in Georgia, he believed that martyrdom was a real possibility if he ministered to the Indians.[86] Whitefield's response to Lavington was that suffering would come without seeking or praying for it.[87] Yet in a letter in March 1739, Whitefield had confessed: "I look for suffering every day," and in another letter that same month Whitefield reminded a woman that if she was not suffering, he would question her commitment to Jesus.[88] Wesley and Whitefield taught their followers to

82. Byrne, "Ignatius and Wesley," 61.

83. Byrne, "Ignatius and Wesley," 61.

84. JW, "The Witness of the Spirit I," *Works*, 1:282–83.

85. See GW to John Edmonds, May 6, 1738, in Thomas, "George Whitefield and Friends," 391.

86. JW to Boltzius and Gronau, [March 13, 1736], *Works*, 25:448; JW to Timothy Cutler, [July 23, 1737], *Works*, 25:515; JW to [Richard Morgan Jr.], [February 16, 1737], *Works*, 25:491; and Hammond, *JW in America*, 164.

87. GW, *Remarks*, 27.

88. GW to Daniel Abbot, March 10, 1739 in Thomas, "George Whitefield and Friends," 176; and GW to Elizabeth Hankinson, March 20, 1739 in Thomas, "George Whitefield and Friends," 181.

rejoice in suffering, as it was an honour, and synonymous with discipleship.[89] William Warburton (1698–1779), Bishop of Gloucester, accused Wesley of the same over ten years later, insisting that Wesley sought persecution and kept it alive by antagonizing his persecutors.[90]

Lavington may have interpreted the Wesley brothers aligning Methodist suffering with the suffering of Christ as "rejoicing in persecution."[91] Julie Ann Lunn argued that "Charles went beyond simply identifying the believer's suffering with that of Christ, offering comfort and sustaining strength; he seems to suggest that only those who suffer with Christ (the cross) obtain the crown."[92] She quoted this hymn as an example:

> In sorrow, as in grace, we grow,
> With closer fellowship in pain,
> Our Lord more intimately know,
> Till coming to a perfect man
> His sharpest agonies we share,
> And all his marks of passion bear.[93]

Charles seemed to be saying that when times were difficult, God's grace was strongest, and the persecution was, in fact, a blessing. Even in the twentieth century, some, like E. P. Thompson, have considered this a masochistic need for suffering.[94] Joanna Cruickshank in disagreement with Thompson, argued that the theology of suffering that the Wesley brothers upheld was firmly rooted in classical Christology: Christ's agony on the cross.[95] She likewise indicated that theologically, to Charles Wesley, suffering was a progression; it was the path to sanctification. However, Charles, as a Protestant, took care to emphasize that it was Christ's suffering and death that brought salvation, not our own suffering.[96] Long-

---

89. Reed, "From Riots to Revivalism," 180–81.

90. Warburton, *The Doctrine of Grace*, 2:190.

91. [Lavington], *Enthusiasm*, 1:4.

92. Lunn, "'Simply Resign'd and Lost in God,'" 1:30.

93. Lunn, "'Simply Resign'd and Lost in God,'" 1:30; and CW, *Short Hymns*, 2:374.

94. For instance, Thompson, *The Making of the English Working Class*, 40–41.

95. Cruickshank, "Were Early Methodists Masochists?" 81–100.

96. Cruickshank, "Were Early Methodists Masochists?" 91; for example, CW, *The Unpublished Poetry of Charles Wesley*, 2:52.

suffering is likewise the cynosure of *The Introduction to a Devout Life* by de Sales, which Wesley read.[97]

Wesley said that Lavington accused him of mingling with Jesuits, but he could only recount one day when a priest was yelling at Moorfields that the Methodists were all papists, and someone recognized the man as a "Romish priest."[98] Two decades later, Wesley would respond to the accusation that his brother, Charles, was a Jesuit; this time from George Fleury (1741–1825), Archdeacon of Waterford. Fleury attacked Charles Wesley from the pulpit, with Wesley present. John Wesley responded to the public criticism in a letter, saying: "And what do you infer from hence? that my brother who was thought a student of Christ Church in Oxford, was really a Jesuit? and that while I passed for a Fellow of Lincoln College, I was in fact a Dominican friar? Even to hint at such absurdities is an insult on common sense."[99]

Next, Lavington declared that Wesley once a "strict churchman but gradually put on a more catholic spirit, tending at length to Roman Catholic . . . rejects any design to convert others from any communion; and consequently, not from Popery."[100] Likewise, some of the Georgia colonists had accused Wesley of damning "everyone who had a contrary opinion with himself."[101] Wesley admitted that he had changed:

> It is true that for thirty years last past I have 'gradually put on a more catholic spirit,' finding more and more tenderness for those who differed from me either in *opinions* or *modes of worship*. But it is not true that I 'reject any design of converting others from any communion.' I have by the blessing of God converted several from Popery, who are now alive and ready to testify it.[102]

Lavington attacked Wesley's description of opinions as being a slender part of religion in *A Plain Account of the People Called Methodists*.[103] By this time Wesley had published *Catholic Spirit*, but it is unknown whether

97. de Sales, *Introduction*; and JW, *A Second Letter*, *Works*, 11:425–26.

98. *Works*, 11:427.

99. JW to George L. Fleury, May 18, 1771, in Telford, 5:250.

100. *Works*, 11:422–23.

101. Tailfer, *True Narrative*, 48.

102. *Works*, 11:423.

103. *Works*, 11:425. For *A Plain Account of the People Called Methodists*, see *Works*, 9:253–80.

the bishop read it, as he did not comment on it directly. Wesley clarified that in a real Christian, "right opinions are a *very slender part of religion*," and "that in an irreligious, a profane man, they are not *any part of religion at all*, such a man not being one jot more religious because he is *orthodox*." He continued to assert: "Sir, it does not follow from either of these propositions that *wrong opinions* are not a hindrance to religion; and much less, that 'teaching and believing the fundamental errors of Popery, *with the whole train of their abominations and idolatries*' (practiced, I presume you mean, as well as taught and believed) 'are of very little moment, if any.'"[104]

Henry Rack rightly labelled this clash between Lavington and Wesley evidence of "two uncomprehending world-views in collision," for the Methodists "seemed to be reproducing the horrid and far from forgotten behavior of the Interregnum."[105] Some of the Church of England clergy were appalled to see this again, perceiving it would lead to anarchy. Wesley did preach about witchcraft and ghosts, and a return to what may be identified as "popular" or "primary" religion.[106] Many thought that this was superstition, and it stood in juxtaposition to the rationalism of British Empiricism. John Kent's view was that Methodism was wildly popular because the poor and uneducated of Britain were fearful of new ideas and welcomed a return to the familiar old beliefs.[107] If this is true, Lavington represented the modern religion, and Wesley, the primary religion. The two worldviews were substantiated in this dispute, with neither seeing the other person's overall perspective. Connecting "enthusiasm" or "primary religion" to Catholicism was not new, for to the educated Anglican clergyman, Catholicism represented superstition and idolatry. They found it easy to push the allegations further, for a Jesuit mission priest was not only a Catholic, but also stereotypically one who aimed to proselytize through sophistry.

In *The Nature of Enthusiasm* (1750), Wesley addressed empiricist critics by defining enthusiasm as first imputing to God something that ought not to be; secondly, imagining that one has the grace that one does not in fact have; thirdly, believing one has the gifts that one does not have and; finally, expecting to attain the end of religion, holy love, without

---

104. *Works*, 11:425.

105. Rack, *Reasonable Enthusiast*, 277.

106. Kent, *Wesleyans*, 6. For more on Wesley and ghosts, see Yates, "Jeffrey the Jacobite Poltergeist."

107. Kent, *Wesleyans*, 6–24.

employing the means of grace.[108] To Wesley: "religion is the spirit of a sound mind, and consequently stands in direct opposition to madness of every kind."[109] Outler called *The Nature of Enthusiasm*, "an interesting digression" in Wesley's vision of the *ordo salutis*, claiming that the sermon set the stage for *A Caution against Bigotry* and *Catholic Spirit*.[110] However, now that it has been revealed that the context of *The Nature of Enthusiasm* was that he and the Methodists had been accused of enthusiasm likened to Popery and Jesuitism, the stage setting becomes clearer. He spoke against enthusiasm because he had been accused of it himself.

In his *Journal*, Wesley noted that he worshipped in Exeter Cathedral in August 1762, ten years after he wrote to Lavington, and it pleased him to partake of the Lord's Supper with his old opponent.[111] The Bishop died fifteen days later. Opposition from the bishops caused stress for Wesley, but when the conflict came from a friend, it may have been worse. The Lavington uproar had barely settled when a new battle emerged, this time because a former pupil of Wesley's disagreed with him.

The Calvinist Critique

James Hervey, one of Wesley's former students, probably did not intend to start a dispute with Wesley, yet it took place anyway. Hervey had asked Wesley to read his manuscript of *Theron and Aspasio* (1755), and apparently, Wesley's criticism of Hervey's Calvinism offended Hervey.[112] Over a year after Hervey published it, Wesley not only reproached him in a private letter for the way he had taught the "imputed righteousness of Christ," but published the letter as *A Preservative against Unsettled Notions in Religion*.[113] Hervey began a response, but left instructions that it was not to be published even upon his death.[114] However after he died, in 1764 and 1765 versions of Hervey's letters appeared.[115] In reply

108. JW, *The Nature of Enthusiasm, Works*, 2:46–60; and Collins, "Assurance," 608.

109. *Works*, 2:50

110. Albert Outler, "Introductory Comment on Sermon 37," *Works*, 2:45–46.

111. Cragg, "Introduction," *Works*, 11:358.

112. Rack, *Reasonable Enthusiast*, 452. See Hervey, *Theron and Aspasio*.

113. JW, *A Preservative against Unsettled Notions*; and JW to James Hervey, October 15, 1756, *Works*, 13:323–44.

114. Outler, "'The Lord Our Righteousness,' Introductory Comment," *Works*, 1:445.

115. Hervey, *Eleven Letters*.

to these printed versions of Hervey's letters, Wesley printed *A Treatise on Justification Extracted from John Goodwin* (c. 1594–1665), Independent minister, and wrote in the preface the story of his controversy with Hervey.[116] Later, he wrote further on the issue in *An Answer to All That is Material in Letters Just Published under the Name of James Hervey* (1765). He claimed that he had spoken to his friend as a "dear brother," reprinted the letter he had written to Hervey on October 15, 1756, and attempted to further clarify the theological differences between himself and Hervey.[117]

Hervey declared that Wesley vacillated between Protestantism and Catholicism, and warned Wesley that he was in danger of harmony between himself and Rome if he persisted in denying belief in the imputed righteousness of Christ.[118] A supporter of Hervey's letters published *The Jesuit Detected; or the Church of Rome Discover'd in the Disguise of a Protestant* (1768), contending that Wesley and Rome held belief in the same doctrines of justification. This discourse, a comparison of Wesley's doctrine and Catholic doctrine, asserted: "it is immaterial whether the doctrine of the Church of Rome is propagated and maintained by an Italian Jesuit or an English Jesuit." The author wrote further: "The Jesuit is detected; not by fire and faggot, but by the precious word of God, in which, the truth is made manifest, concerning eternal life in Christ Jesus."[119] Yet Hervey himself did not share the belief that Wesley was a Jesuit as he acquitted Wesley of this charge of being a Jesuit in one of his posthumously published letters.[120] Perhaps Hervey remembered the vow he had made to Wesley in 1739: "but no difference of opinion, no long-continued absence, nothing, I trust in time or through eternity shall put an end to my respectful and honourable regard . . . for dear Mr. Wesley."[121] Later, in 1760, Wesley said: "I am determined to publish nothing against Mr. Hervey unless his answer to my letter is published."[122] The writer of *The Jesuit Detected* avowed that Catholic doctrine would bring the loss of

116. JW, *A Treatise on Justification*, 3–5; see also *JWJ*, November 12, 1764, *Works*, 21:494.

117. JW, *An Answer to All*, 4–36; see also JW to John Newton, April 9, 1765, and JW to John Erskine, April 24, 1765, *Works*, 27:420–25.

118. Hervey, *Eleven Letters*, 122–23, 256.

119. *Jesuit Detected*, 32–33.

120. Hervey, *Eleven Letters*, 122.

121. James Hervey to JW, [August 21, 1739], *Works*, 25:677; see also JW to John Newton, May 14, 1765, *Works*, 27:429, for more on JW's relationship with Hervey.

122. JW to Samuel Furley, December 9, 1760, *Works*, 27:224.

liberty of conscience, in other words, the author accused Wesley of the same tyranny that Wesley had been accused of thirty years previously in Georgia.[123]

Further, Wesley wrote the sermon "The Lord our Righteousness" in response to this controversy with Hervey.[124] He preached it in November 1765. Outler called it a "landmark sermon," for it marked the "end of Wesley's efforts to avoid an open rift with the Calvinists."[125] In the sermon, Wesley agreed with the Calvinists that the righteousness of Christ is imputed to us, but he rejected the distinction Hervey made between active and passive righteousness of Christ. Wesley wrote: "the righteousness of Christ, both his active and passive righteousness, is the meritorious cause of our justification."[126] Wesley's discord with the Calvinists increased throughout the next few years.[127]

Bishop Warburton had proclaimed: "Mr Wesley's enemies are his own fellow members."[128] At times, this was true. Over thirty years of tension between Wesley and Calvinists within and without the Methodist movement exploded in a debate on a statement in the *Minutes* of the Conference of 1770. This is not the place to discuss that quarrel, as it has been well covered by Allan Coppedge, W. Stephen Gunter, and Henry Rack.[129] Nevertheless, it is relevant to focus on the allegations that Wesley's opponents made against him during this time: that he was "papist" and "Jesuitical."

The Methodist Conference had printed a statement in the 1770 *Minutes* asserting that good works were a "condition" of salvation, leading to outcry from those of Calvinist persuasion.[130] This quotation from the *Minutes* establishes the heart of the dispute:

> Is this not 'salvation by works?' Not by the *merit* of works, but by works as a *condition*. What have we then been disputing for these thirty years? I am afraid about words. As to *merit* itself,

123. *Jesuit Detected*, 36–37.

124. Wood, "Atonement," 61; and Outler, "Introductory Comment," *Works*, 1:445.

125. Outler, "Introductory Comment," *Works*, 1:446.

126. JW, "The Lord our Righteousness," *Works*, 1:457; see also Wood, "Atonement," 61.

127. Rack, *Reasonable Enthusiast*, 450–70.

128. Warburton, *Doctrine of Grace*, 1:148.

129. *Works*, 10:379. See Coppedge, *John Wesley in Theological Debate*, 191–254; Gunter, *Limits*, 251–66; and Rack, *Reasonable Enthusiast*, 450–70. For a list of the pamphlets surrounding the 1770 *Minutes* Controversy, see Gunter, *Limits*, 277.

130. Bebbington, *Evangelicalism*, 28.

of which we have been so dreadfully afraid: we are rewarded
according to our works, yea because of our works. How does
this differ from *for the sake of our works*? And how differs this
from *secundum merita operum* [according to the merits of our
works]? As our works *deserve*? Can you split this hair? I doubt,
I cannot.[131]

The problem was that the Calvinists believed that this statement was a
declaration of "salvation by works," something they considered Catholic
doctrine or "Popery," and it resulted in a pamphlet battle.[132]

The Countess of Huntingdon expressed her disapproval when she
wrote to Charles Wesley declaring that the theology in the *Minutes* was
"Popery unmasked."[133] John Wesley said in his letter to her in June 1771,
"I love you well," but still she upheld her theological disagreement.[134]
She expunged Trevecka of anyone who agreed with Wesley in January
1771.[135] Wesley waited over a year to reply saying, "I judged, not only
that silence would be the best answer, but also that which your Ladyship
would be best pleased." By now she had made it known that she had separated from Wesley's movement, and he articulated his pain in the valedic-
tion of the letter, signing, "your ladyship's affectionate but much injured
servant."[136] Unlike many other disputes Wesley had faced, this one came
predominantly from within his circle of friends. This was not the end of
the friendship between himself and the Countess, for an exchange between them in 1776 seemed to display their old affection.[137]

As for the ensuing pamphlet war, one of Lady Huntingdon's preachers, Rowland Hill (1744–1833), wrote against John Wesley. Henry Rack
summarized Hill's issue with Wesley: that Wesley was "reasserting the
Council of Trent's balanced Catholic view of salvation as the product of
co-operative enterprise between the grace of God and the good works

---

131. *Works*, 10:393.

132. [Hill], *Friendly Remarks*, 29.

133. Lady Huntingdon to Charles Wesley, June 8, 1771, MARC DDWes 1/99.

134. JW to Lady Huntington, June 19, 1771, in Telford, 5:259; and Lady Huntingdon
to John Wesley, June 19, 1771, Tyson, *Lady Huntingdon*, 113.

135. Kirkham, "Pamphlet Opposition," 349.

136. John Wesley to Lady Huntingdon, September 14, 1772, in Tyson, *Lady
Huntingdon*, 114.

137. See Lady Huntingdon to JW, September 8, 1776, in Tyson, *Lady Huntingdon*,
115; and JW to Lady Huntingdon, September 15, 1776, in Tyson, *Lady Huntingdon*, 115.

and efforts of man."[138] The editors of the *Gospel Magazine*, a Calvinist publication, agreed with Huntingdon and Hill as they printed a letter that likewise called the 1770 Methodist Conference *Minutes*, "Popery unmasked."[139] Not only were they concerned that Popery was taught, but that the "twenty-nine thousand four hundred and six souls [in Methodist societies] . . . should be so dreadfully seduced from the Protestant doctrine, and deluded into a belief of the doctrines of the mother of harlots–the whore of Babylon–the church of Rome."[140] The *Gospel Magazine* reprinted the *Minutes*, and included a sarcastic "paraphrase" after each section. Surprisingly, after the paraphrases, the editors declared that they did all of this "plainly in love."[141]

Amid the backlash from the *Gospel Magazine*'s articles, in June 1771, Walter Shirley (1725–1786), a cousin to the Countess of Huntingdon, sent out a "circular letter" appealing to those who disapproved of the 1770 *Minutes* to attend the Bristol Conference in August 1771.[142] Wesley defended himself against Shirley in a letter from Dublin in July 1771, but he did not mention any specific charge of "Popery," as he sought to clarify his theology of works.[143]

Wesley's earliest responses to the Calvinists over the 1770 Minutes include *The Question, What Is an Arminian? Answered* and *The Consequence Proved*, which was an edited version of Augustus Toplady's (1740–1778) work of the same name.[144] Only the beginning, the pamphlet war stretched on until it morphed into the controversy over Wesley's *A Calm Address to Our American Colonies* in 1775. Of the 1770 *Minutes* controversy, even Luke Tyerman in his three-volume biography of Wesley declared: "our space renders it impossible to give an outline of Wesley's answers to the charges," although perhaps the charges were not so "reckless" as Tyerman insisted they were.[145] The disagreement between those of Calvinist persuasion and those of Arminian views in the Church

138. [Hill], *Friendly Remarks*, 29; and Rack, *Reasonable Enthusiast*, 458.

139. A Real Protestant, "To the Editors of the Gospel-Magazine," 230–31.

140. "Comment or Paraphrase," 260–76.

141. "Comment or Paraphrase," 270.

142. Shirley's letter is reprinted in *Works*, 22:286n.

143. JW to Several Preachers and Friends, July 10, 1771, in Telford, 5:264; and Gunter, *Limits*, 253.

144. For a summary of Wesley and Toplady's disagreement, see Kirkham, "Pamphlet Opposition," 344–48.

145. Tyerman, *Life of Wesley*, 3:144.

of England was related to the larger disagreement between Arminianism and Calvinism on the Continent.[146] The focus here will center on two specific attacks to which he replied: the ones having to do with his alleged alignment with Catholicism, and those that attacked his catholic spirit.

After examination of the Calvinist critiques of the 1770 *Minutes*, it becomes apparent why John Wesley reprinted *Catholick Spirit* in 1770. Yet if Wesley hoped that his appeal to a catholic spirit would bring about cooperation from the Calvinists, he was mistaken. It seems that the re-printed sermon only gave Richard Hill (1733–1808) more ammunition to renew his attack. It is certain that Hill quoted from the 1770 version as his quotations match the page numbers from that edition rather than the 1755 one. Hill indicated what he considered to be Wesley's inconsisten-cies and then wrote: "no man in the world has ever written more strik-ingly against inconsistency than Mr. Wesley; particularly in his sermon *Catholic Spirit*."[147] Hill continued with a quotation from the sermon be-ginning with: "a Catholic Spirit is not indifference to all opinions."[148] This critique of Wesley may have underlying tones of Hill accusing Wesley of being "Jesuitical" or "papist," even though he did not use the words. Wesley, to Hill, had "no settled, consistent principles" and was for "jum-bling all opinions together." He was near the spirit of "Anti-Christ."[149] In this case, Hill quoted Wesley's *Catholic Spirit* against Wesley, accusing Wesley of doing exactly what Wesley warned others not to do. It seems that Hill was wielding a veiled libel of "crypto-Popery." Anglicans at this time, including Wesley, considered the papacy to be the Antichrist.[150] Many Protestants, not just Anglicans, promoted this belief, beginning with Martin Luther's *Against the Execrable Bull of the Antichrist* (1521).[151] When Wesley responded to this charge, he indicated that most of what Hill called inconsistency had to do with Wesley's reprinting of other people's writings, and thereby, they were not inconsistencies: "These are not myself. . . . If I publish them ten times over, still they are not *myself*.

146. For an overview of the "righteousness" dispute between Calvinists and Arminians, see Clifford, *Atonement and Justification*.

147. Hill, *Review*, 145.

148. Hill, *Review*, 146; and JW, *Catholick Spirit* (1770), 15.

149. Hill, *Review*, 146; and JW, *Catholick Spirit* (1770), 16.

150. See JW, [Note on Rev 17:10], *Explanatory Notes on the New Testament*, 3:316. See also notes on Rev 13:1; 14:8; 17:3–6; 18:2–4, 24.

151. Gregory, "The Making of a Protestant Nation," 309; and Newport, "Revelation 13," 148.

I insist that no man's words but *my own* can ever prove, that I contradict *myself*."[152] However, if Wesley was implying that those who "have no settled, consistent principles" and "jumble opinions" are near the spirit of Antichrist, and if being near the spirit of Antichrist implies a person is a "papist" (as he had stated in his *Notes on the New Testament*), then amidst his appeal to practice a catholic spirit, he had accused some of his listeners of being "papists."[153] For instance, Wesley used these exact words in Catholic Spirit:

> Observe this, you who know not what spirit ye are of, who call yourselves men of a catholic spirit; because your mind is all in a mist; because you have no settled, consistent principles, but are for jumbling all opinions together. Be convinced that you have quite missed your way; you know not where you are. You think you are got into the very spirit of Christ, when in truth you are nearer the spirit of antichrist.[154]

The idea of "jumbling" opinions or doctrines together and having "no settled, consistent principles" were often used in accusatory ways by Protestants against Catholics. For instance, in *The Morning-Exercise against Popery* (1675), the authors accused "papists" of "jumbling the sufferings of saints with the super-abundant satisfaction of Christ."[155] "Popery" and inconsistency went hand in hand according to the anonymous author of *High-Church Doctrine Prov'd to be Popish and Inconsistent*. Wesley's Anglican readers would probably have recognized these code words for "Popery" (jumbling opinions and doctrines together), and thus identified the indirect insult. Thus, the sermon *Catholic Spirit* contains a slur inconsistent with the catholic spirit that Wesley preached.

Hill had labelled Wesley's doctrine of perfection as not only "Popish," but "a mixture of Pelagianism, Semi-Pelagianism, Arminianism, Popery, Mysticism, and Quakerism," to which Wesley replied, "we have not one tittle of proof that this [perfection] is a *popish* doctrine; that it ever was, or is now . . . it has been solemnly condemned by the church of Rome."[156] Wesley did not deny any doctrine on Hill's list except "Popery," which

152. JW, *Some Remarks*, 41, emphasis Wesley's. Reprinted in *Works*, 13:476.

153. For example JW, [Note on Revelation 17:10], *Explanatory Notes on the New Testament*, 3:316.

154. *Works*, 2:93.

155. *Morning Exercise against Popery*, 575.

156. Hill, *Review of all the Doctrines*, 92; and JW, *Some Remarks*, 45.

suggests that Wesley thought "Popery" was a more dangerous claim than any of the other doctrines. Hill's pamphlet had been addressed to John Fletcher (bap. 1729, d. 1785), but Wesley could not resist replying since the allegations were directed towards him.[157] Yet Fletcher wrote much more than Wesley in this controversy, as Fletcher's writings eventually totaled nearly six hundred pages. They were published together posthumously as *Checks to Antinomianism*.[158] Not the first to accuse Wesley of inconsistency, even trickery, Hill joined other voices that dated back to Wesley's time in Georgia.

Critiques for Alleged Trickery, Magic, and Tyranny

To properly evaluate the allegations of trickery, magic, and tyranny towards the Methodists, the focus must hark back to Wesley's time in Georgia. The Georgia Trustees in their Royal Charter (1732) declared in Lockean fashion and the spirit of the Act of Toleration (1689):

> That for ever hereafter there shall be a liberty of conscience allowed in the *worship of* God, to all persons inhabiting or which shall inhabit or be resident within our said Province, and that all such persons, except *Papists*, shall have a free *Exercise of Religion*; so they be contented with the quiet and peaceable enjoyment of the same, not giving offence or scandal to the government.[159]

Wesley, having travelled to Georgia at the invitation of Oglethorpe, angered the colonists with his High Church practices as a priest of the church in Savannah. Allegedly Wesley gave "offence and scandal" to the government because he displayed characteristics and practices of a "papist" and "Jesuit." Wesley "damned all Dissenters," which went directly against "the spirit of toleration and tenderness which the Church of England showed towards them" and received persons suspected of being Catholics.[160] Catholics were banned from the colony, so it makes sense

---

157. For John Fletcher, see Tyerman, *Wesley's Designated Successor*; and Fletcher, "Unexampled Labours." For more on Richard Hill and the Wesleys, see Richard Hill to CW, August 20, 1773, MARC DDPr 1/93.

158. Fletcher, *Checks to Antinomianism*.

159. Tailfer, *True Narrative*, 28–29. See Locke, *Letter Concerning Toleration* in *The Works of John Locke*, 2:244–55.

160. Tailfer, *True Narrative*, 33.

that no one would openly claim to be one.[161] Furthermore, Wesley made use of "all Jesuitical arts," which caused people, "especially women," to divulge to him their secrets.[162]

Wesley had tutored Sophia Hopkey and had spent significant time with her, including a trip from Frederica to Savannah accompanied by a servant. He seemed to be in love with her, and she with him, but Wesley struggled with his commitment to celibacy.[163] A month after Wesley informed Hopkey that he could not marry her before he spent time with the Indians, she became engaged to William Williamson, and married him three weeks later.[164] Wesley refused communion to Mrs. Williamson, which led to legal action being taken against Wesley.

Nonetheless, accusations that Wesley had been too familiar with women reached much further than his failed relationship with Sophia Hopkey Williamson. Escaping the colonies, Wesley may have thought that he had left the scandal behind him. However, Captain Robert Williams printed an affidavit against Wesley in Bristol in 1740, which prompted Wesley to write his own version of what happened in Georgia.[165] The circulation of these documents led to more accusations of Wesley's "Popery" and Jesuitism into the 1740s. This affidavit was attached to a treatise called *The Progress of Methodism in Bristol*, along with a letter from Thomas Christie of Georgia who called Wesley a "base and Jesuitical man."[166]

From the Elizabethan age into the Victorian age, English literature often portrayed Jesuits as villains who would prey on "innocent virgins" and the "strictest matron" would be persuaded to leave behind her integrity.[167] The idea that women were gullible, delicate, and in need of an upright Christian gentleman's protection was one stereo-typical eighteenth-century perception of women. For example, in *The Story of the*

161. Hammond, *JW in America*, 161.

162. Tailfer, *True Narrative*, 34.

163. Hammond, *JW in America*, 171.

164. Hammond, *JW in America*, 172.

165. Impartial Hand, *The Progress of Methodism*.

166. Thomas Christie to Robert Williams, September 18, 1742, reprinted as appendix to Impartial Hand, *The Progress of Methodism*, 60. For more on JW and women see Mack, *Heart Religion*, 144–47.

167. Haydon, "Eighteenth-Century English Anti-Catholicism," 59; and Marotti, "Alienating Catholics," in Mariotti, *Catholicism and Anti-Catholicism*, 1–34. For example, see *The Character of a Jesuit*, 1–2.

Methodist-Lady, or the Injur'd Husband's Revenge. A True History (1752), the author explained that "men of intrigue who are acquainted with all the avenues to, and windings of a female heart' could bring down the most virtuous of women."[168] A 1739 play, *The Mock-Preacher: A Satyrico-Comical-Allegorical Farce*, revealed a similar attitude towards women. The "Mock-Preacher," who sounded suspiciously like Whitefield, convinced a woman to give so much money for his "Georgia Orphan-house" that her husband declared the preacher would "starve us all!"[169] The husband blamed the preacher for his wife's actions, which implied that he believed the preacher had tricked his wife.[170] Furthermore, the skillfully written satirical poem *The Progress of Methodism in Bristol* described women:

> For women are most prone to fall,
> Like *Eve* their mother, first of all,
> Who, can they keep their faults be hidden
> Will eat the *fruit* that is forbidden.[171]

Moreover, early in the movement, a writer in the *Gentlemen's Magazine* saw trickery and deceit in what he called Whitefield's "shocking scheme for confessing the women."[172]

In the societies, it appears that Whitefield was asking women questions such as:

> Are you in love? Do you take more pleasure in any body than in God? Whom do you love just now better than any person in the world? Is not the person an idol? Does he not (esp. in public prayer) steal in between God and your soul? Does any court you? Is there anyone whom you suspect to have any such design? Is there anyone who shows you more respect than to other women? Are you not pleased with that? How do you like him? How do you feel yourself, when he comes, when he stays, when he goes away?[173]

Nonetheless, it may have been Wesley who wrote it, due to the close connection between this and the "Rules of the Band Societies."[174] Kirkham

---

168. *The Story of the Methodist-Lady*, 6.

169. *The Mock-Preacher*, 14, 16–17.

170. For further analysis of the "Mock Preacher," see Lewis, "The Mock Preacher," 179–85.

171. Impartial Hand, *Progress of Methodism*, 20.

172. Maddox, "Earliest Defense," 142.

173. *Compleat Account*, 19; also in *Gentlemen's Magazine* 9 (May 1739), 238–42.

174. "A Method of Confession, drawn up by Mr. Whitefield," 238, reprinted in

implied that this was simply an amended version of Wesley's "Band Rules," but Maddox argued that they were Wesley's rules with a few additions made by Whitefield.[175] No matter who authored them, once printed, they were perceived to be akin to "confessions to priests" that would enable leaders to exploit women, another reason to accuse the Methodists of Jesuitism.

It was a common English opinion that Catholic priests, and especially Jesuits, used trickery and magic to coerce a woman to confess her sins, and then, catching her off guard, in her vulnerability, the priest would succeed in his seduction of her.[176] For example, a famous case emerged in 1732 of the seduction of Marie-Catherine Cadière (b. 1709) by her confessor, Jean-Baptiste Girard (1680–1733), a Jesuit.[177]

Wesley was denounced for "hearing confession" while in Georgia, even before the colonists formally complained against him. Charles Delamotte[178] (c. 1714–1790), a friend of Wesley's, described a situation in Savannah in which Wesley was accused of being a Catholic priest based upon his hearing confession:

> There went a great cry through the streets, 'news concerning the saints' that now there was a proof of the horrid proceedings of that monster Wesley and his crew––Mr. [James] Campbell had committed adultery with Mrs. Mears, and had made confession and had received absolution from you. 'What need have we of further proof of his being a Roman priest, and all his followers Roman Catholics?'[179]

It was most likely the confession and not the absolution that concerned the crowd, as the Book of Common Prayer included absolution.[180] Auricular sacramental confession as practiced by Catholics seemed to be the main concern. A few years later, a letter to William Seward

---

Maddox, "Earliest Defense," 142–44. See also JW, "Rules of the Band Societies," *Works,* 9:77–78.

175. Kirkham, "Pamphlet Opposition," 152; and Maddox, "Earliest Defense," 145.

176. Haydon, *Anticatholicism,* 5. For example, see Fielding, *The Debauchees or the Jesuit Caught*; and *The Adventures of a Jesuit Interspersed.*

177. Haydon, "Anti-Catholicism and Obscene Literature," 202–18.

178. *Works,* 18:136n.

179. Charles Delamotte to JW, February 23, 1738, *Works,* 25:530; and Hammond, *JW in America,* 130.

180. *The Book of Common Prayer* (1662), "Morning Prayer," and "Evening Prayer."

confirmed that the rumors of Wesley's alleged Jesuitism had spread as far as Broadmead, in Bristol:

> Bro Wesley's success you are acquainted of by him, it has made a strange noise, that he hath preached against predestination, especially amongst the Anabaptists they by we in Broadmead, some of them said that he was a Jesuit & a friend to the bringing in of the pretender, because some misunderstood him in his exposition concerning the ordination of ministers, they took it that he condemned all that were not ordained according to the ecclesiastical establishment, when I believe he meant no such thing tho' in truth it seemed to me very intricate, so with it and about Election he had many enemies, but never wants for a large audience, to whom he never scruples speaking his mind Truley [*sic*].[181]

In 1749, Wesley was accused of a subtle form of Jesuitism. People in London had spread rumors that Wesley was a Jesuit. The English seemed convinced that Jesuits were nearly magical in their use of subversive influence and tricky tactics. Wesley wrote in his *Journal*: "Mrs. B[aker] being averred to Mr. M[anning] Himself, that Mr. Wesley was unquestionably a Jesuit.[182] Just such a Jesuit in principle (and desirous to be such in practice) as Sir Nathaniel Barnardiston was."[183] Sir Nathaniel Barnardiston (1588–1653) was a Puritan, not a Jesuit, and a member of the opposition to Charles I.[184]

Not only did the author of *The Progress of Methodism in Bristol* indicate that confessions from women were recorded and reported to Wesley, who acted as a "Pope," but the anonymous author called the class leaders "*spiritual spies*, who inform the principal Teacher of what may be most essential to his *wishes* or his *interest*."[185] Wesley denied he or Whitefield acted as a Pope in letter to the editor of the *Westminster Journal* in

---

181. T. Mitchell to William Seward, May 4, 1739, in MARC GB 133 DDSe 45.

182. David Butler reported that during the Cork Riots, JW was accused of a subtle form of Jesuitism in *Methodists and Papists*, 37. However, this accusation in 1749 seems to have come from the Bakers in London as noted above, and did not happen during the Cork Riots.

183. JW, February 5, 1749, *JWJ, Works*, 20:263. Mrs. Baker was Anne Baker (c. 1724-1796), mother of [Charles] Manning's (1714-1799) wife. Manning was sympathetic to Wesley as he had been at the conferences of 1747 and 1748, *Works*, 20:263n.

184. Greaves, "Barnardiston, Sir Nathaniel (1588-1653)," *ODNB*.

185. Impartial Hand, *Progress of Methodism*, 20-21; and *The Fanatic Saints*, 8.

January 1761, and in "The Large Minutes" in 1770.[186] It is not difficult to perceive that outsiders thought the intimate discussions of love affairs would lead to sexual relationships between the Methodist leaders and the women they were questioning. Nevertheless, there is no evidence that Wesley or Whitefield participated in such, neither is there proof that the society leaders reported "sins" to Wesley. Further, Wesley denied that the societies practiced "Popery" by confession to one another in *A Plain Account of the People Called Methodists*.[187] Nonetheless, Wesley believed that a woman had the right to make decisions about her own spirituality apart from her husband or father, as evident in his extensive correspondence with three women during his Oxford days: Mary Pendarves (later Delany) (1700–1788), Ann Granville, and Sally (Sarah) Kirkham Chapone (1699–1764).[188]

Then again, not all Methodist preachers maintained their integrity. James Wheatley, Methodist preacher, partook in several sexual improprieties with multiple young women in the Bristol and in other regions in the late 1740s.[189] In addition, anti-Methodist writers had to look no further than Wesley's family to find a prime example of unbridled enthusiasm applied to sexual relationship. If any Methodist practiced sophistry and casuistry, it was Westley Hall (1711–1776), brother-in-law of John Wesley. Hall caused chaos in the family when he initiated a romantic triangle by flirting with two of Wesley's sisters, Kezia (1709–1741) and Martha (1706–1791).[190] Hall eventually married Martha, moving to London to work with John and Charles Wesley in 1737.[191] According to Wesley, Hall "fell into a course of adultery, yea, and avowed it in the face of the sun!"[192] The *Gentleman's Magazine* referred to this scandal, publishing an unsigned letter in October 1747 that "for now and then a bastard child was bro't into the world by some of his [Hall's] female

---

186. JW to Editor of the *Westminster Journal*, January 7, 1761, *Works*, 27:236; and "*Large Minutes C and D*, 1770–1771," *Works*, 10:901–2.

187. JW, *A Plain Account of the People Called Methodists*, *Works*, 9:268.

188. See Mary Pendarves to JW, June 16, [1731], *Works*, 25:284; and Hammond, *JW in America*, 173.

189. JW to James Wheatley, June 25, 1751, *Works*, 26:464–45.

190. See CW to Samuel Wesley Jr., July 13, 1734, in CW, *Letters of Charles Wesley*, 39–40.

191. JW to Westley Hall, December 22, 1747, *Works*, 26:269–73.

192. *JWJ*, December 1, 1747, *Works*, 20:200.

devotees."[193] After interviewing the women from Hall's society, Wesley discovered that Hall had started with kissing, claiming it was "Christian fellowship." Hall carried this "affection" further, eventually having sexual affairs with several women. To provide justification for his behavior, he had even instituted laws of polygamy in the society, which showed trickery, and perhaps even tyranny, as his word became "law" in the society and influenced women to become involved with him.[194]

As to why Wesley would encourage the spirituality and leadership of women in a society that generally did not, there are many reasons that go beyond the scope of this book. However, two reasons will be explored here.[195] Using magic to get women to confess, and trickery to confuse them, were not the only reasons some Georgia colonists accused Wesley of Popery and Jesuitism. For not only did he allow women in his societies, in Georgia he seems to have been training "deaconesses" to serve the community, and this angered several men. Wesley's fascination with primitive Christianity had led him to read the *Apostolick Constitutions*, and the *Constitutions* allowed for deaconesses.[196]

Second, his mother's influence on Wesley's perception of women as leaders cannot be underestimated. In the winter of 1711/1712, with John yet a boy of eight, his father heard while attending Church of England convocation that some of his parishioners were choosing to attend Susanna's reading of prayers and sermons in her kitchen over Morning Prayer at the church. He wrote to her, ordering her to end the meetings. Her calm, logical reply stated that she had never planned these meetings, that she had only meant them to be instruction for her children, and parishioners happened to visit at this time. The word spread of Susanna's teaching, and new families started attending the prayer time. In two letters to Samuel Wesley Sr., Susanna argued that these prayer meetings should continue, and that if her husband wished for her to disband them, he must give her a positive command so as to absolve her from guilt.[197] There does not seem to be evidence on whether she continued, but John Wesley thought her words were important enough to transcribe the February 6, 1712

---

193. "Hypocrisy of a Methodist Detected," 531.

194. Gunter, *Limits*, 196.

195. For further examples of Wesley encouraging the leadership of women, see Cracknell and White, *An Introduction to World Methodism*, 217–20.

196. Hammond, *JW in America*, 136–39.

197. Susanna Wesley to Samuel Wesley, Sr., February 5, 25, 1712, in Susanna Wesley, *Complete Writings*, 79–83.

letter in his *Journal* on the day of her death in 1742.[198] Susanna Wesley continued to influence her children's spiritual lives, especially John's, and this is demonstrated in their letters.[199] She died in 1742, and thereby missed much of the conflict her children experienced. As for what her opinion would have been about the American war, the topic of the next section, presumably she would have agreed with her son: that passive obedience to the monarchy was the only answer.[200] John Wesley promoted this, and once again, writing in another pamphlet war that took time away from his preaching.

Critiques of A Calm Address to Our American Colonies

Wesley abridged Samuel Johnson's *Taxation No Tyranny* and published it as *A Calm Address to Our American Colonies* in 1775.[201] He estimated that a few months after he wrote *A Calm Address* "50,000 or 100,000 copies" had been printed.[202] At least twenty reactions to this discourse were published that same year, with a few in the following years until the end of the war in 1783.[203] A few of the key tracts will be addressed in light of their Jesuit allegations towards Wesley. The opposition attacked him for this reason: Wesley advocated the divine right of kings, and that since he had once sympathized with the Americans and changed, he practiced Popery, and was being Jesuitical.[204]

Caleb Evans (1737–1791), a Baptist pastor, accused Wesley of "contemptible sophistry," and the pens of Augustus Toplady and John Fletcher had barely rested from the Minutes controversy before they took them

198. *JWJ*, August 1, 1742, *Works*, 19:284–86.

199. For instance: JW to Susanna Wesley, May 28, 1725, *Works*, 25:162–64; JW to Susanna Wesley, January [28], 1734, *Works*, 25:371–73; and Susanna Wesley to JW, February 14, [1734], *Works*, 25:377–78. See also Wallace, "Some Stated Employment of Your Mind," 354–66.

200. See Susanna Wesley, Journal entry 1709, in Susanna Wesley, *Complete Writings*, 204; and Vickers, *Guide*, 65.

201. See Johnson, *Taxation No Tyranny*; and JW, *A Calm Address to Our American Colonies*.

202. Telford, 6:182n.

203. For a list of the printed responses to *A Calm Address to Our American Colonies*, see Kirkham, "Response of the Critics," 14–15.

204. JW, *Free Thoughts*; and Kirkham, "Response of the Critics," 16.

up again.[205] Toplady lashed out with *An Old Fox Tarr'd and Feather'd*, and Fletcher defending Wesley again, responded with *A Vindication* and *American Patriotism further Confronted*.[206] It is possible that by using the pseudonym "Hanoverian," Toplady was accusing Wesley of being a Jacobite. The pseudonymous author, Patrick Bull, of the satirical *A Wolf in Sheep's Cloathing* supposed that the ghost of a Jesuit had written both Johnson's *Taxation No Tyranny* and Wesley's *A Calm Address*.[207] The author's argument was that Wesley could not have been the author of *A Calm Address* because he had once advocated for the Americans in *Free Thoughts*. However, Wesley had made it clear that he had changed his mind when he read *Taxation*.[208] "Patrick Bull" sarcastically declared: "Mr. Wesley is a loyal subject. He hath subscribed to the thirty-nine articles. He hath taken the oaths of allegiance. Can we then be so absurd as to suppose him the author of a treatise that labours to establish the old fashioned doctrine of hereditary right, or that kings derive their power *jure divinio?*"[209]

William Moore, replying a year later in 1776, likewise accused Wesley of Jesuitism.[210] He proclaimed that Wesley led the Methodists by "deception only" and that "how strange that this quack in both politics, physic, and divinity should always leave himself open to detection."[211] Moore, likewise, believed that Wesley was wrong in advocating the divine right of kings. Allegations of deceit were at the center of this critique. Wesley obviously loudly proclaimed that he was a Protestant, yet these critics saw him as clever and Jesuitical, attempting to deceive by first espousing one idea, and then another.

Nevertheless, Wesley's motive for composing *A Calm Address*, seemed to be in the hope that he might contribute to peace negotiations, using the argument that if the Americans would simply return their allegiance to George III as their divinely appointed king, all would be well. John Fletcher had said, "nothing but reason and Scripture can make the

205. Evans, *A Letter to the Rev. Mr. John Wesley*, 7.

206. See Fletcher, *A Vindication*; Fletcher, *American Patriotism*; and Hanoverian [Toplady], *An Old Fox Tarr'd and Feather'd*.

207. Bull, *Wolf*, 8; and Lyles, "The Hostile Reaction," 9.

208. JW, *A Calm Address*, iii.

209. Bull, *Wolf*, 12.

210. Moore, *Addresses for Blood*, 39.

211. Moore, *Addresses for Blood*, 39–40.

colonies submit to Great Britain."[212] Wesley agreed with Fletcher that the colonies should submit to Great Britain, in other words, advocating passive obedience to the king. As for moving his sympathy away from the American cause, Wesley explained that reading Samuel Johnson's *Taxation No Tyranny* had changed his mind.[213] He expressed his concern over his country entering a war that they would likely lose in a letter to William Legge, Earl of Dartmouth, Secretary of State for the Colonies. In this he declared that "all my prejudices are against the Americans," and then he wrote, "for I am an High Churchman, the son of an High Churchman, bred up from my childhood in the highest notions of passive obedience and non-resistance."[214] This famous statement must be placed in context of the American war, for his insisting on passive obedience and non-resistance was a cry for what many (mostly Whigs and Dissenters) considered "the old ways" in 1775.[215] He did understand the need for liberty, as he remarked: "and yet in spite of all my rooted prejudices, I cannot avoid thinking (if I think at all) that an oppressed people ask for nothing more than their legal rights, and that in the most modest and inoffensive manner which the nature of the thing would allow."[216]

The Americans, however, were past anything "modest and inoffensive" for what had begun in tossing tea and boycotts had led to the Continental Congress (September–October 1774) giving an ultimatum to George III and Parliament for the Intolerable Acts that had to be answered by December 1774. News of the Battle of Lexington and Concord (April 1775) had reached London by May 8, 1775, before Wesley wrote his letter to Dartmouth.[217] War seemed inevitable, and Wesley warned Lord North: "it seems they will not be conquered as easily as was at first imagined. They will probably dispute every inch of the ground, and if they die, they die with sword in hand."[218] It appears, for Wesley, that the reason for this rebellion may have been the turning away from High Church Tory views; for if the Americans had believed in passive obedience and non-resistance, there would be no fighting. This is what he was

212. Fletcher, *American Patriotism*, iii.

213. JW, *A Calm Address*, 2.

214. JW to the Earl of Dartmouth, June 14, 1775, in Telford, 6:156.

215. Ingle, *The British Party System*, 9.

216. Telford, 6:156.

217. "Foreign Intelligence."

218. JW to Lord North, June 15, 1775, in Telford, 6:161.

trying to convince his readers of in *A Calm Address*. Yes, he had changed his mind, but he had good reason. He heard the drums of war and saw the smoke of battle from across the sea, perceiving his responsibility as a religious leader was to talk people out of the bloodshed. In this case, perhaps Wesley thought he was writing in a catholic spirit and in toleration.

Conclusion

This chapter has analyzed accusations of Popery and Jesuitism as it related to John Wesley and the early Methodists. Wesley used the word "Jesuit" to describe the Moravians, and later found himself compartmentalized in like manner. Some bishops, including Lavington and Warburton, attacked Wesley and the Methodists in the 1750s, calling them "papist" and "Jesuitical," and Wesley answered the allegations. Although Wesley had faced criticism for his Arminianism from Calvinists previously, the publishing of the 1770 Conference *Minutes* sparked a pamphlet war with Calvinists that lasted years. Specific allegations about his alleged trickery, use of magic, and tyranny began in Georgia and continued throughout his ministry. Finally, his plea with the Americans to practice passive obedience to the king, and changing his mind about the American situation provoked his opponents to accuse him of Popery and Jesuitism during the American war.

W. Stephen Gunter called Wesley "blind to his own fault!"[219] This is understandable, especially in reference to his break with the Moravians. His perception of them motivated him to declare those who practiced their teaching as "Jesuit['s]." That he used this term in a pejorative way along with his refusal to cooperate when Zinzendorf tried to reason with him, suggests that he had not acted with the catholic spirit of which he had preached. Instead, the Moravian society, in refusing to attack him, showed him what a catholic spirit could truly mean. In accusing the Moravians of Jesuitism, Wesley showed intolerance, the same criticism applied to him by his opponents. Whether he changed his mind towards them is unlikely, even though he visited a Moravian settlement in the Netherlands in 1783 in what seems to have been a spirit of friendship.[220]

Bishop Lavington's angry attack on the Methodists to demonstrate he was not of their number invoked replies from several Methodists.

219. Gunter, *Limits*, 275.
220. *JWJ*, July 17, 1783, *Works*, 23:282.

Wesley, Whitefield, and Vincent Perronet responded with published letters in an attempt to prove their innocence of Lavington's charges of Popery and Jesuitism. Other bishops accused them of the same. Wesley dealt with theological disagreements with Calvinists his entire ministry, but in the 1770s, Calvinists, both Anglicans and dissenters attacked him for his teaching of imparted righteousness. This dispute was not new, it was an oft-used tactic of Calvinists to accuse Arminians of "Popery unmasked," as it seemed to them that imparted righteousness was too close to Catholic doctrine. Richard Hill attacked Wesley not only for his Arminian theology, but for what he called "inconsistency." In this charge, he used Wesley's own sermon, *Catholic Spirit*, and measured him against it, to which Wesley replied. Hill argued that Wesley had changed over the years, but many of Hill's arguments had nothing to do with Wesley's own words, but words he had printed of others, especially in his *Christian Library*.

Finally, when Wesley printed *A Calm Address to Our American Colonies*, his opponents called him "papist" and "Jesuitical," once again for changing his mind. They considered his appeal to the colonists to practice passive obedience a harkening back to Jacobitism, and thus "Popery." Wesley argued in this case that reading Johnson had changed his views, and that his hopes were that his appeal to the Americans might ward off the bloodshed. He was not successful, of course, even though he pled with the Secretary of State not to enter into war.

Overall, it is not surprising that Wesley was accused of Popery and Jesuitism as the terms of derision were oft used by English religious leaders in the eighteenth century. It is also not difficult to comprehend that his opponents accused him of inconsistency. What may be the most challenging aspect of this chapter to grasp is that Wesley himself called the Moravians "Jesuit," which seems a serious departure from his catholic spirit, even though he wrote it in a private letter. This, and his other critiques, led to the permanent separation of the Methodists and Moravians: a rift that has never been restored.

6

The Gordon Riots and a *Catholic Spirit*

NEARLY FIFTY YEARS HAD passed since John Wesley was first accused of leaning towards Catholicism. Wesley and his preachers had faced opposition while attempting to convert Catholics in Ireland. Some Methodist preachers had encountered conscription and prison during the "Forty-five," and Wesley had dealt with multiple allegations that he was a Jacobite and a Jesuit. Nonetheless, in 1778 a new situation arose that would try Wesley: Parliament passed an Act for Catholic Relief.[1] A Protestant Association was set up to challenge the Act, and Wesley was accused of aligning himself with this group. The Protestant Association initiated a petition campaign, and thousands attended the presentation of the London petition to the House of Commons on June 2, 1780.[2] When the Members of Parliament did not respond to the mob's prompting, riots broke out in London. Although Wesley was nowhere near London for the five days of burning and pillaging that were later called the Gordon Riots, he was accused of influencing the riots.[3]

1. 18 Geo. III, c. 60, also called the Papists Act.

2. What began as multiple petitions had been sewn into one long scroll by a tailor before June 2, 1780. See *London Evening Post* 9073, June 1–3, 1780. The handwritten copy of this scroll in the National Archives, UK is eighty-four pages with at least sixty signatures on each page. See TNA, TS 11/388/1212. For simplicity, the Protestant Association petitions sewn together will hereinafter be referred to in this chapter as "the petition."

3. For the Gordon Riots, see Castro, *The Gordon Riots*; Hibbert, *King Mob*; Rudé, "The Gordon Riots," 93–112; Rogers, *Crowd, Culture, and Politics*, 152–75; Randall, *Riotous Assemblies*, 305–24. Haywood and Seed, *The Gordon Riots*; and McCormack, "Supporting Civil Power."

This chapter is a case study of Wesley's view of Catholics, and the Catholic Relief Act of 1778, with a particular focus on the Gordon Riots, providing further evidence that Wesley did not intend for his sermon *Catholic Spirit* to apply to Catholics. Wesley's view of the Catholic Relief Act and the Protestant Association will be examined. Following this, the chapter explores Wesley's relationship with George Gordon (1751–1793), the president of the Protestant Association. Finally, the chapter addresses the accusations that Wesley influenced the riots and analyzes Wesley's responses.

While some biographers have mentioned the Gordon Riots and Wesley's alleged participation, none have provided the detailed assessment of the primary sources necessary to determine the extent of his involvement. John Whitehead (1793) mentioned Wesley's response to the Catholic Relief Act, but made no mention of the riots.[4] Luke Tyerman (1876) covered the riots briefly, revealing his anti-Catholic bias, calling Wesley's arguments about "Popery" "irrefutable" and "damaging to the disloyalty and preposterous assumptions of Popery."[5] John S. Simon (1934) mentioned the Gordon Riots only to indicate that Wesley preached against persecution during the year of the tumults.[6] Henry Rack (1989) addressed the issues surrounding the Catholic Relief Act, saying that Wesley became "involved if not entirely through his own fault in the controversy."[7] Although he discussed the Gordon Riots specifically, David Butler's (1995) coverage is quite brief with a focus on the issue of toleration rather than allegations of Wesley's involvement.[8] Al Truesdale (2005) provided the most detailed study so far of Wesley's alleged involvement with the Protestant Association by examining Wesley's writings: *Popery Calmly Considered*, "Letter to the Printer of the *Public Advertiser*," "Two Letters to the Editors of the *Freeman's Journal*," "Disavowal of Persecuting Papists," and his relevant *Journal* entries. Yet Truesdale did not cite archival material or crucial newspaper articles.[9]

4. Whitefield, *Life of the Rev. John Wesley*, 500–1.

5. Tyerman, *Life and Times*, 3:320.

6. Simon, *John Wesley*, 158.

7. Rack, *Reasonable Enthusiast*, 311.

8. Butler, *Methodists and Papists*, 47–59.

9. Truesdale, "John Wesley," 28–42; JW, *Popery Calmly Considered*, *Works* (Jackson), 10:140–49; JW, "Letter to the Printer of the *Public Advertiser*," *Works* (Jackson), 10:159–61; JW, "First Letter [and Second] to the Editors of the *Freeman's Journal* Dublin," *Works* (Jackson), 10:162–66; and JW, "Disavowal of Persecuting Papists," *Works* (Jackson), 10:173–74.

In order to determine whether the allegations against Wesley were valid, it will be necessary to examine his letters and journals, and those of his brother, Charles. A few key letters that reveal Wesley's views on the events have not been published since 1780–1782.[10] Multiple newspaper accounts, pamphlets, broadsheets, and periodicals provide valuable insight into the events and Wesley's mindset at the time of the passing of the Catholic Relief Act and continuing through the Gordon Riots and their aftermath. The documentary records of the trial of Gordon and the petition itself survive in the National Archives. This chapter is not an attempt to provide an in-depth analysis of the Gordon Riots, but only of Wesley's alleged involvement, and what it reveals about his catholic spirit.

Wesley's Views on the Catholic Relief Act and the Protestant Association

By 1778, anxiety over the passing of the Quebec Act of 1774 had spread through Great Britain.[11] The part of the Act that alarmed many had to do with Catholics receiving freedom to hold public office and enlist in the military. The Oath of Allegiance that an army officer or public servant had to swear, which dated back to the time of Elizabeth I, had been replaced with one that pledged allegiance to George III with no reference to the Church of England or Protestantism.[12] Likewise, the Catholic Relief Act abrogated, subject to the taking of an oath, certain anti-Catholic laws enacted during the reign of Queen Anne.

The Act of 1778 passed through both Houses of Parliament easily. Before it passed, the Catholic clergy had been reluctant to say anything about it, for fear of persecution. Subsequently, Richard Challoner, Catholic Bishop of Debra, author of *Caveat against the Methodists* (1760), and the other Catholic clergy voiced their approval of the Act after it

---

10. The letters yet unpublished are: JW to John Whittingham, July 13, 1780, [broadsheet] MARC MAM JW 5.90; JW to Thomas Rankin, May 29, 1780, MARC, MAM JW 4/49; JW to Brian Bury Collins, June 12, 1780, MARC, MAM JW, 2/54; JW to James Rivington, October 25, 1780, *Royal Gazette* (New York), February 24, 1781; John Whittingham to JW, *Morning Chronicle and London Advertiser* 3500, August 5, 1780; and CW to Sarah Wesley [his daughter], June 8, 1780, MARC DDcw 1/71. The letters from JW are scheduled for publication in *Works*, 29. The letter from CW will be published in CW, *Letters of Charles Wesley*, vol. 2.

11. 14 Geo. III c. 83.

12. Haydon, *Anti-Catholicism*, 164, 193–96, 204.

passed.[13] A bill for Catholic Relief passed in the Irish Parliament later that year.[14] The laws for Scotland had to be altered by the Parliament in London by a separate act because there was no Scottish parliament after 1707. The Scottish Penal Laws predated the Union of 1707. Fears of a papal takeover increased with Spain's declaration of war on Great Britain in June 1779.

The Protestant Association formed first in Scotland in December 1778, and then in England by November 1779, unified with the purpose of getting the Act repealed. George Gordon, M.P. for Ludgershall, Wiltshire, became President.[15] The Protestant Association sought to influence Parliament through a propaganda drive.[16] For example, the Association had published its pamphlet, *An Appeal of the Protestant Association to the People of Great Britain*, on November 5, 1779, the date timed with the observance of the Fifth of November.[17] In the tract, the Association explained why they were against the Catholic Relief Act, for they believed that granting any relief to Catholics would give them power, and in turn undermine toleration and liberty of conscience in Britain.[18] Neither the Protestant Association nor Wesley believed that increased tolerance should be extended to Catholics. Samuel Romilly (1757–1818), Solicitor General (1806–1807), reacted to the Association's pamphlet when he read it months after viewing the riots: "it is extremely ill written: the reasoning such as refutes itself; but the author addresses himself to his readers in a furious declamation, well calculated to work up enthusiasts to very madness."[19]

---

13. Challoner, *Caveat against the Methodists*; for Wesley's reply, see JW to the Editor of *Lloyd's Evening Post*, November 22, 1760, *Works*, 27:215–16. On Challoner and the Catholic Relief Act, see Rupp, *Religion in England*, 196–97. On the correspondence between JW and Challoner, see Butler, *Methodists and Papists*, 70–93.

14. For the Irish bill, see Burns, "The Catholic Relief Act in Ireland, 1778," 181–206.

15. Haydon, "Gordon, George (1751–1793)," *ODNB*. For the formation of the Protestant Association, see Dickinson, *Politics of the People*, 82; and Yates, *Eighteenth-Century Britain*, 42.

16. Haydon, *Anti-Catholicism*, 210.

17. This tract went through three editions in London and one in Dublin. That multiple copies survive in libraries today suggests that it was printed in large quantities, so the influence of the tract would have been far reaching.

18. Protestant Association, *Appeal*, 11.

19. Romilly, *Memoirs*, 100.

Henry Rack indicated that "it is difficult to exonerate Wesley entirely [from responsibility for the riots] because he defended the arguments and the author of the *Appeal* on behalf of the P[rotestant] A[ssociation]."[20] He was correct, as there is no denying that Wesley agreed with the principles advocated in *An Appeal of the Protestant Association to the People of Great Britain* when he wrote "Letter to the Printer of the *Public Advertiser*" on January 21, 1780. It was published in at least five newspapers beginning February 5, 1780, and then as a broadsheet to be distributed more widely.[21] Tyerman called this letter "unanswerable, though obnoxious."[22]

In this letter to the *Public Advertiser*, Wesley remarked that he was writing: "in pursuance of the same kind and benevolent design [as *An Appeal*], namely to preserve our happy constitution." He thought the style of *An Appeal* was "clear, easy, natural, the reasoning, in general, strong and conclusive; the object, or design, kind and benevolent." He explained that he would "endeavour to confirm the substance of that tract, by a few plain arguments."[23] "Confirming the substance" certainly means that he agreed with the core of the Protestant Association's tract. Not only did Wesley write this affirmation of the pamphlet, but a year after the Gordon Riots, he confirmed in response to Arthur O'Leary (1729–1802) that he "wrote three lines in defense of a tract published in London," referring to his "Letter to the Printer of the *Public Advertiser*."[24] This statement clearly demonstrates that Wesley supported the Protestant Association's tract. In the same letter to O'Leary, Wesley insisted that even though he wrote in defense of *An Appeal*, he wrote nothing in the defense of the Protestant Association itself.[25] The evidence indicates that Wesley's self-assessment was correct; he supported the tract, but not the Association as a whole. It is reasonable to assume, however, that some regarded his support of the tract as support for the Association. He recorded in his *Journal* that he thought it was his duty to write a letter warning of the increase

20. Rack, *Reasonable Enthusiast*, 312.

21 See *General Evening Post* 7192, February 5–8, 1780; *London Chronicle* 3616, February 5–8, 1780; *Morning Chronicle and London Advertiser* 3344, February 5, 1780; *Whitehall Evening Post* 5279, February 5–8, 1780; *London Evening Post* 9022, February 3–5, 1780; and *AM* 4, April 1781, 239–42. The broadsheet survives; see MARC MAW.G.339 [a].

22. Tyerman, *Life of Wesley*, 3:318.

23. JW, "Letter to the Printer of the *Public Advertiser*," *Works* (Jackson), 10:159.

24. See JW, "On Popery."

25. JW, "On Popery," 295, 299.

of Popery, but "many were grievously offended. But I cannot help it. I must follow my own conscience."[26] It is reasonable to assume that many would have disagreed with Wesley's interpretation of *An Appeal*, for the author(s) spoke vehemently against Catholicism, and enthusiastically proclaimed the benefits of the Catholic penal laws.[27] In addition to reading *An Appeal*, Wesley likely read *Scotland's Opposition to the Popish Bill: A Collection of All the Declarations and Resolutions . . . for Preventing the Growth of Popery*, as it survives in the library in his house in London.[28]

As Wesley had written "Letter to the Printer of the *Public Advertiser*" in response to *An Appeal of the Protestant Association*, he could have published *Popery Calmly Considered* in response to the Catholic Relief Act, but there is no evidence that he published it in direct response. First published in March 1779, within a year, it went through printings in Dublin and Edinburgh, and at least three London printings.[29] He clearly stated his purpose: "to lay down and examine the doctrines of the church of Rome; secondly to show the natural tendency of a few of those doctrines; with that all the plainness and all the calmness I can."[30] The source material for *Popery* was not original to Wesley; he drew heavily on Bishop of Chichester, John Williams's, *A Catechism Truly Representing the Doctrines and Practices of the Church of Rome with an Answer Thereto* (1686).[31] Wesley had published a slight abridgement of Williams's book in 1756, *A Roman Catechism with a Reply Thereto*, as the threat of French invasion during the Seven Years' War brought fears of "Popery."[32] His main purpose in abridging in 1756 appears to have been to slightly reduce the catechism's length. Wesley's version was printed in a smaller font, but he did not cut much of Williams's text. *Popery Calmly Considered*, therefore, is just a further abridgment of Williams's work. Since the Catholic Relief Act of 1778 granted Catholics the right to serve in the military, it seems to have influenced Wesley to print in *Popery Calmly Considered* the

26. *JWJ*, January 18, 1780, *Works*, 23:159.

27. PA, *Appeal*, 1–23.

28. Maddox, "John Wesley's Reading," 132.

29 Baker, *Union Catalogue*, 24, 152.

30. JW, *Popery Calmly Considered*, *Works* (Jackson), 10:140.

31. Hammond, *JW in America*, 200.

32. [JW], *A Roman Catechism*, and *Works* (Jackson), 10:86–128. JW affirmed that he published *A Roman Catechism* in his *Journal*, December 20, 1768; *Works*, 22:167, although the remaining 1756 publications of *Catechism* have neither Williams's nor Wesley's name on them.

doctrines of the Catholic Church that he thought were most dangerous. Wesley believed that Catholics would use their political power to enforce their doctrines, and that if Protestants did not follow these doctrines, they would be persecuted, or even killed as Jan Hus (1369–1415) had been.[33] At the end of *Popery*, Wesley departed from Williams's words and in his own summary wrote: "And have they not an equal tendency to cause lying and dissimulation among those that are not of their communion; by that Romish principle that Force is to be used in matters of religion."[34] According to Wesley, this appears to have been the most dangerous doctrine of all.

Anglican clergy who read *Popery Calmly Considered* may have recognized Williams's work, as he had been an honoured clergyman.[35] When Williams printed his *Catechism*, it was during the reign of James II amid the king's attempt at Catholic toleration, prior to his "Declaration for Liberty of Conscience" in 1687.[36] Williams, though not yet a bishop, was Prebendary of Rugmere at St. Paul's Cathedral, London.[37]

During the "Forty-five," Anglican bishops instructed their clergy to preach against "Popery." For instance, Archbishop of Canterbury, John Potter (1674–1747), wrote to his clergy during the Rising, imploring them to preach and write about preserving the "happy constitution," specifically against Catholicism.[38] This was a task that Wesley had already embraced when he wrote *A Word in Season: Or, Advice to an Englishman* (1744). In this document Wesley warned of "Popery and slavery," and asked, if Britain had a Catholic king, then "whose life would be safe?"[39] Furthermore, in *A Word to a Protestant* (1746), which Wesley wrote to clarify his view of the differences between Protestants and "papists," he had written: "these grand popish doctrines of merit, idolatry, and persecution, by destroying both faith and love of God and neighbour, tend

---

33. For Wesley's views on Hus, see his "Second Letter to the *Freeman's Journal*" [in response to O'Leary], *Works* (Jackson), 10:170–73.

34. JW, *Popery Calmly Considered, Works* (Jackson), 10:149.

35. Chamberlain, "Williams, John (1633x6–1709)," *ODNB*.

36. Sowerby, *Making Toleration*, 13.

37. Chamberlain, "Williams, John." For the trial of the seven bishops, see Gibson, *James II*.

38. Haydon, "Eighteenth-Century English," 50; and Haydon, *Anti-Catholicism*, 134–35.

39. See JW, *A Word in Season*, 2–3.

to banish true Christianity out of the world."[40] The seventeenth-century perspective that Catholicism was a political danger to the Crown had been re-emphasized during the "Forty-five" in 1745–1746, and not just by Wesley.[41] However, in the late eighteenth century, anti-Catholicism in England had subsided. According to Colin Haydon: "the demise of Jacobitism, and the *de facto* recognition of George III by the papacy after James Edward's death in 1766, put an end to serious political concerns about the papists."[42] Even Anglican clergy, such as Church of Ireland Bishop of Meath, Thomas Lewis O'Beirne (1749–1823), believed the attitude towards Catholicism that Wesley portrayed was outdated.[43] Additionally, William Blackstone (1723–1780), jurist and expositor of English law wrote in 1769 that "our ancestors were mistaken in their plans of compulsion and intolerance [towards Catholics]."[44]

In *Popery Calmly Considered*, Wesley listed disagreements he had had with Catholicism throughout his ministry, such as salvation being subject to the Pope, the Pope as Peter's successor, and worship of saints, angels, and images. Furthermore, Wesley criticized the Catholic Church for forbidding the people to read the Scriptures, yet he did not deny that the Catholic Church was a true church. He said: "[The Church of Rome] it is only one particular branch of the catholic or universal Church of Christ, which is the whole body of believers of Christ, scattered over the whole earth."[45] He condemned the practice of worship in Latin and prayers to the Virgin Mary, and he declared the worship of relics to be idolatry. The celibacy of the priesthood he also disparaged, a view that he had not held throughout his ministry, as it has been argued that it was his own belief in the value of celibacy that, in part, kept him from proposing

40. JW, *A Word to a Protestant*, 3–4.

41. See Jonathan Hawkins, "Imperial '45," 35, for an overview of anti-Catholicism during the "Forty-five." For the process of de-Catholicization and Protestantization in England, see Gregory, "The Making of a Protestant Nation," 314–23.

42. Haydon, "Parliament and Popery," 54.

43. Haydon, *Anti-Catholicism*, 238. See [O'Beirne], *Considerations on the Late Disturbances*.

44. Blackstone, *Commentaries on the Laws of England*, 4:53–54.

45. JW, *Popery Calmly Considered*, *Works* (Jackson), 10:142.

marriage to Sophia Hopkey over forty years previously.[46] Wesley also encouraged the Methodist preachers to be celibate.[47]

In *Popery* and "Letter to the Printer of the *Public Advertiser*," Wesley emphasized his concern with the following issue: namely, that Catholics taught that "no faith is to be kept with heretics," referring to a statement he said was made at the Council of Constance (1414–1418) concerning Jan Hus.[48] Hus, promoting John Wycliffe's (d. 1384) work, was engaged in controversy with the Catholic Church. He agreed to go to the Council of Constance only after receiving a promise of safe conduct from Sigismund, King of Hungary and Croatia and King of the Romans. The promise of safe conduct was only to ensure his travelling to and from the conference, for he was convicted of heresy and burned at the stake on July 6, 1415.[49]

When Catholic priest, Joseph Berington (1743–1827), who would later become active in the movement to pass the next Catholic Relief Act (1791), wrote to Wesley that there had been no decision made at Constance implying that "no faith is to be kept with heretics," he was correct. The statement is absent from the decrees.[50]

Furthermore, in "Letter to the Printer of the *Public Advertiser*," Wesley expressed concern that if given political power, Catholics would be intolerant of anyone who was not Catholic, and that their number would increase.[51] Wesley held the fear that Catholicism had been growing in England. Yet he could not have had accurate knowledge of the number of Catholics in the kingdom, as any information Wesley had on the population of Catholics in England would have been at least a dozen years old.[52] Berington would not publish an informal census of Catholics until December 1780, and there would be another census in

---

46. JW, *Popery Calmly Considered, Works* (Jackson), 10:154; and Hammond, *JW in America*, 171–77.

47. See Abelove, *Evangelist of Desire*, 49–73.

48. JW, *Popery, Works* (Jackson), 10:157; and JW, "Letter to the Printer of the *Public Advertiser*," *Works* (Jackson), 10:160.

49. Fudge, *Jan Hus*, 125.

50. Joseph Berington [also spelled Berrington] to JW, March 31, 1780, in Whitehead, *Life of JW*, 504; and Berington, *State and Behavior*, 151. Berington would later become involved in the movement to pass the Catholic Relief Bill of 1791. For an English translation of the Council of Constance, see "Council of Constance–1414–1418," in Tanner, *Decrees of the Ecumenical Councils*, 1:403–52.

51. See JW, "Letter to the Printer of the *Public Advertiser*," *Works* (Jackson), 10:161.

52. See Worrall, *Returns of Papists*.

1781.[53] Fear, however, can provoke intolerance, and Wesley held the deeply ingrained British anxiety concerning a papal takeover and French invasion.[54] Catholic Spain's declaration of war on Great Britain in 1779 would only have increased Wesley's trepidation. Further, the Calvinist *Gospel Magazine* reported that the Protestant Association sent Wesley unanimous thanks for writing the letter.[55] Although the editors agreed with Wesley on this occasion, this praise might have given Wesley disquiet as the editors of the *Gospel Magazine* had attacked him many times.[56]

Wesley was also concerned about Catholics taking oaths and the possible dispensation of those oaths by a priest or the Pope. He said:

> The power of dispensing with any oath, or vow, is another branch of the spiritual power of the Pope. And all who acknowledge his spiritual power, must acknowledge this. But whoever acknowledges the dispensing power of the Pope, can give no security of his allegiance to any government. Oaths and promises are none; they are light as air; a dispensation makes them null and void.[57]

Wesley wondered how a Catholic could love anyone outside of the Catholic Church if they believed that all were condemned to an after-life of eternal torment except their own members. The spirit of *Popery Calmly Considered* and "Letter to the Printer of the *Public Advertiser*" was of concern that if given any political power, Catholics would be intolerant of Protestants.[58] John Locke was probably one of several sources from which Wesley would have drawn this view. For instance, in a *Letter Concerning Toleration*, Locke said: "That church can have no right to be tolerated by the Magistrate, which is constituted upon such a bottom,

---

53. Berington, *State and Behavior*, 159–61. Berington's report did not cover Ireland or Scotland.

54. For JW's fear of the French, see *JWJ*, February 15, 1744, *Works*, 20:9; *JWJ*, April 5, 1756, *Works*, 21:48; *JWJ*, November 28, 1759, *Works*, 21:235; JW, *A Word in Season*; and JW, *A Compassionate Address*. In 1779, Spain, a Catholic country, declared war on Great Britain and attempted invasion, and Britain was still at war with America, who had allied with France.

55. JW, "A Letter from John Wesley," 86–89.

56. One of the reasons John Wesley began the *Arminian Magazine* was to counter the *Gospel Magazine*'s doctrines, which Wesley claimed "are intended to shew that *God is* not *loving to every man*, and that *his mercy is* not *over all his works*; and consequently, that *Christ did* not *die for all* . . . but for one in ten, for the Elect only." *AM* 1 (1778), 1.

57. JW, "Letter to the Printer of the *Public Advertiser*," *Works* (Jackson)10:160.

58. JW, *Popery Calmly Considered*, *Works* (Jackson), 10:155–56; and JW, "Letter to the Printer of the *Public Advertiser*," *Works* (Jackson), 10:160–61.

that all those who enter into it, do thereby, *ipso facto*, deliver themselves up to the Protection and Service of another Prince."[59] Because of their loyalty to the Pope in Rome, a foreign "prince," this statement from Locke became a prevalent argument used against the toleration of Catholics.[60]

Although Locke taught that groups or individuals who did not believe in toleration of others should not be tolerated, he did write that a Catholic might be tolerated who embraced tolerant principles and renounced allegiance to the Pope.[61] Wesley disagreed somewhat with Locke, for he believed that a Catholic would not normally be tolerant.[62]

Nevertheless, challenged by Catholics in his interpretation of their doctrine and practices, Wesley continued to insist that he was correct. After having defended himself against monasticism, Jacobitism, Jesuitism, and Popery, it is understandable that Wesley continued with the same attitude towards Catholicism that he had been expressing since the 1730s. However, his viewpoint displayed in *Popery Calmly Considered* and "Letter to the Printer of the *Public Advertiser*" suggests that Wesley allowed his fears of possible papal persecution to dominate his response to the Catholic Relief Act of 1778 long after much of Britain had relinquished that dread. This anxiety kept Wesley from practicing a catholic spirit towards the oppressed Catholics during this time.

Further evidence that Wesley aligned with the Protestant Association is to be found in the *Gazetteer and Daily Advertiser* which reported that a meeting was held in Newcastle upon Tyne on February 12, 1780 for establishing a Protestant Association: "to act with other Associations in Great Britain for a petition to Parliament for the repealing of the late Popish bill." "A letter was received from Mr. Wesley, warmly approving of the measure."[63] The letter was probably sent to the national organization of the Protestant Association rather than the Newcastle branch as the latter was meeting to establish a branch at this time. However, the letter to which the Protestant Association referred does not seem to be "Letter to the Printer of the *Public Advertiser*," nor has it survived. It appears that Wesley's approval was for the association to work for the repeal of the Catholic Relief Bill. The Protestant Association met in Southwark, and

59. Locke, *Letter Concerning Toleration*, 47.

60. Sowerby, *Making Toleration*, 256–57.

61. Locke, *Letter Concerning Toleration*, 45, 47, 146, 194.

62. JW, "Letter to the Printer of the *Public Advertiser*," *Works* (Jackson), 10:161.

63. This was reported in *Gazetteer and New Daily Advertiser* 15915, February 15, 1780.

five days later it was resolved "that the secretary transmit the thanks of this association to the Rev. John Wesley for his excellent letters."[64] If the secretary did so, this letter has not survived.

In April 1780, Lord Robert Gregory (c. 1729–1810), Member of the House of Commons for Rochester, presented a petition to Parliament asking for a repeal of the Catholic Relief Bill. Gordon seconded the motion for the repeal, bewailing that so few clergy had signed the petition.[65] Gordon then read the declaration against tolerance of Popery, written in 1626 and signed by Archbishop James Ussher (1581–1656) and eleven other Irish prelates.[66] Sir Charles Turner (c. 1727–1783), M.P. for York, replied: "A Protestant did not plough the ground better than a Papist, nor a Papist better than a Protestant—if Catholics conformed to the laws of the country—they had a right to every possible indulgence."[67] As the *Northampton Mercury* reported, this did not stop Gordon:

> It was his [Gordon's] belief that a massacre in Ireland was in agitation, and he justified his belief by reading a letter from Father O'Leary to the Rev. Mr. Wesley, published in an Irish newspaper: This letter contained a rebuke to Mr. Wesley, as having endeavoured to sow the Thorn of Sedition, and stir up the Protestants to massacres similar to those imputed to the Papists.[68]

The letter to which Gordon referred was one O'Leary had written to Wesley, published in *Public Register, or the Freeman's Journal* of Dublin in March 1780.[69] Additionally, this is the only mention of Wesley in the Parliamentary Minutes at least for the years of 1778–1782. It seems that Gordon and Wesley had not yet met, as John had written to Charles

64. "Protestant Association," *London Evening Post*; also printed in *St. James's Chronicle or the British Evening Post*.

65. See "Parliament," *Northampton Mercury*, 2.

66. For a reprint of the declaration see, Ford *James Ussher*, 146.

67. Cobbett, *Parliamentary History*, 21:387.

68. A group called the Right boys, similar to the Whiteboys, had started some protests in Ireland in 1780, see Bartlett, *Ireland*, 202. For the quotation from Gordon, see "Parliament," *Northampton Mercury*, 2; also printed in *London Chronicle*; *St. James's Chronicle or the British Evening Post*; and *Morning Chronicle and London Advertiser*.

69. Arthur O'Leary to JW, February 28, 1780, in *The Public Register, or; the Freeman's Journal* (Dublin), [March 1780]; reprinted in *Walker's Hibernian Magazine, or Compendium of Entertaining Knowledge*, April 1780, 186–90.

Wesley during the riots, saying that it was good that he had accepted none of Gordon's invitations.[70]

The Protestant Association Petition and the Gordon Riots

At the Protestant Association meeting on May 29, 1780, Gordon moved a resolution: "that the whole body of the Protestant Association do attend St. George's Fields, on Friday next, at ten o'clock in the morning to accompany his Lordship [Gordon] to the House of Commons on the delivery of the Protestant Petition."[71] The resolution carried unanimously.[72] Wesley could not have been at the meeting as he wrote a letter from Newcastle upon Tyne that day.[73] Horace Walpole (1717–1797), fourth Earl of Orford, political writer and historian, in a letter, sarcastically alleged that Gordon "had set himself up as head of the Methodists" in June 1780.[74] There is no evidence that Gordon was ever a Methodist.

As directed, the people had assembled with Gordon on June 2. The Association, concerned that Catholics would interfere, had distributed a handbill proclaiming that they expected many "Papists would assemble to breed [a] riot."[75] Many of the dissidents targeted members of Parliament trying to reach the House, especially the M.P.s whom they thought had been connected to the passing of the Catholic Relief Act. They flipped the carriages of William Markham (1719–1807), Archbishop of York, and William Murray (1705–1793), Lord Mansfield, Chief Justice of the King's Bench. Twice the mob tried to shove its way into the House of Commons. Lord North (1732–1792), Prime Minister, arrived and pledged his word to the Protestant Association that he would support their cause. Gordon insisted that the petition be addressed and came out to address the crowd thrice. General Henry Seymour Conway (1719–1795) reprimanded Gordon publicly, telling him that he disgraced his family and if "anybody was killed he should not escape."[76] About nine o'clock that evening

70. JW to CW, June 8, 1780, in MARC DDWes 3/51, and in Telford 7:21–22.

71. See Gordon, "Protestant Association"; PA, *Defense,* 5.

72. PA, *Defense,* 5.

73. JW to Lancelot Harrison, May 29, 1780, in Ker, "Two Unpublished Wesley Letters," 46.

74. Horace Walpole to Mary Berry, June 23, 1791, in Walpole, *Correspondence,* 11:296–97.

75. "The Monthly Chronologer, " 283.

76. Walpole, *Journal,* 2:404.

Charles Stanhope, Lord Mahon (1753–1816), convinced the crowd to disperse. Parliament debated the repeal of the Catholic Relief Act, but after six hours voted to adjourn. This was likely due to the intensified atmosphere as the crowd broke into the lobby.[77]

The riots continued for days. The mob ransacked the Catholic chapel for the Bavarian ambassador on June 3 and destroyed the Sardinian envoy's chapel in Lincoln Fields.[78] Although there were Catholic chapels built in Britain in the late seventeenth-century, Catholic worship was technically illegal until the Catholic Relief Act of 1791.[79] Embassies were permitted to have in-house chapels, and often they drew other members of their faith to worship.[80] Also on June 3, Gordon issued a public proclamation denouncing the violence. Most of the buildings in the city had "No Popery" chalked on the outside walls.[81] Finally, the king acted, called an emergency Privy Council, and declared martial law. Fifteen thousand soldiers mustered to London, fired on the crowds, and the violence ended.[82] The *London Quarterly* observed the irony of a riot in the name of religion: "It is much to be lamented that in the name of religion, which should ever be conducted with meekness and lenity, such extreme acts of violence as those we are going to record should have been committed."[83] In all, 285 deaths were reported due to the riots, and 200 were wounded. The riots inflicted over £200,000 worth of damage (the rough equivalent of £12.5 million today), and the mob burned 100 buildings.[84]

Wesley recorded that he preached in Aycliffe on June 1, over 250 miles from London. He made no entries on June 2, but June 3 he preached in Northallerton, 225 miles from London.[85] Charles Wesley, however, was in London during the riots, for he had written several letters from London. For instance, on June 8, he wrote to his daughter. He

77. Haywood, *Gordon Riots*, 4–5.

78. Hibbert, *King Mob*, 79; de Castro, *Gordon Riots*, 55; Haydon, *Anti-Catholicism*, 204–5; and Norman, *Roman Catholicism in England*, 46.

79. 31 George III, c. 32.

80. Hughes, "Catholicism in the South of England," 473–75.

81. Haywood, *Gordon Riots*, 4.

82. "Monthly Chronologer," 289; see also McCormack, "Supporting Civil Power," 27–41; and George III, *By the King*.

83. "Monthly Chronologer," 284.

84. "Monthly Chronologer," 339.

85. *Works*, 23:174–5; see also JW to Thomas Rankin, May 29, 1780, in MARC MA.JW.4.49, and in Telford, 7:20.

assured Sally that they were all well, and that his wife had taken the boys to "your aunt's" and had remained awake to guard them. His apprehension showed when he wrote: "matters here are in a dreadful situation."[86] Likewise, Charles wrote to John Wesley on the same day that "the floods have risen, and lifted up their voice. Last night the mobs were parading, and putting us in bodily fear."[87] Additionally, Charles had heard that some had asked why he had not marched with the petitioners, for they had asked, "What then? Does he not stand up for the Protestant cause?"[88] He wrote on June 5, 1780 when he breakfasted with Methodist preachers John Pawson (1737–1806), Thomas Coke (1747–1814), and John Atlay (b. 1736), book steward, that Atlay had been kept awake the entire night by a bonfire in Moorfields. Atlay feared for the survival of the City Road Methodist chapel. Charles assured John Wesley that he had gathered the preachers at the chapel, prayed, and charged them to keep the peace.[89] The rioters never turned on the chapel, so it survived. Likewise, Lady Huntingdon's chapel at Spa Fields sustained no damage.[90]

After the riots, it was alleged that Wesley founded, led, and defended the Protestant Association. Soon after the riots, David Williams (1738–1816), former Presbyterian minister, and later founder of the Literary Fund, claimed that along with Scottish Presbyterians, English Methodists were "Gordon's principal supporters," "who are of the same intolerant complexion."[91] Nearly sixty years later, writing to the Wesleyan Methodists in Manchester in 1839, Daniel O'Connell (1775–1847), campaigner for Irish independence and Catholic emancipation, asserted that Wesley had been "one of the principal founders of the Protestant Association."[92] Colin Haydon thought it significant that Wesley did not join the Protestant Association, and surmised that it may have been because he feared the fanaticism of the group.[93] As late as 2005, Al Truesdale indicated that, after the riots, Wesley spoke in defense of the Protestant

86. CW to Sarah Wesley [his daughter], June 8, 1780, MARC DDcw 1/71.
87. CW to JW, June 8, 1780, in Jackson, *Life of Charles Wesley*, 2:320.
88. Telford, 7:21; see also Nockles, "'Emissaries of Babylon,'" 15–16.
89. CW to JW, June 8, 1780, in Telford, 7:22.
90. Jones et al., *Elect Methodists*, 170.
91. [Williams], *Plan of Association*, 10.
92. O'Connell, *Letters*, 5, 16–17.
93. Haydon, *Anti-Catholicism*, 238.

Association.[94] Wesley wrote in defense of the Protestant Association tract, but he never joined, nor did he promote the Protestant Association.

The Protestant Association attempted to gain support by getting signatures to repeal the Catholic Relief Act. Some alleged that Methodists signed the petition. For example, Thomas Lewis O'Beirne wrote two weeks after the riots: "the Protestant Petition was an instrument originating from Methodist preachers. And majority of signers were drawn from frequenters of followers of John Wesley."[95] Likewise, O'Beirne commented on the signers:

> Among the forty thousand who are said to have subscribed to it, do we find more than *one* archdeacon, reprobated in this by all his brethren, and a few, *very few* of the inferior clergy, notorious for Methodism, with Westley at their head? The rest are taken from the very dregs of the people, from the frequenters of tabernacles, and nightly conventicles, and from the fanatic followers of Westley and others like him, and from the scum of the Scotch fanatics, whom that nation has thrown out in such numbers upon this country.[96]

Perhaps O'Beirne had heard that an archdeacon had signed the petition. As for claiming that the Methodists signed the petitions, it seems unlikely that he could have known. The petitions had been held by the Protestant Association, and once put together were taken to the House of Commons. They remained in the custody of Parliament as evidence for the trials that ensued. O'Beirne could not have read them.

Eugene Black (1936) claimed that the Protestant Association increased in power when it reached London because of support from "Methodists, enthusiasts, and small segments of the regular clergy."[97] His only citation for Methodist involvement is the transcript of Gordon's trial, which is puzzling, because the transcript does not mention the Methodists.[98] Without substantial evidence, Black asserted that the Methodists and the Protestant Association worked together. John English

94. Truesdale, "Inspiration for a Catholic Mob?," 36.

95. [O'Beirne], *Considerations*, 4. Extract printed in *London Courant and Westminster Chronicle*, June 24, 1780, and in *General Evening Post* 7230, July 1–4, 1780. See also Black, *The Association*, 161.

96. [O'Beirne], *Considerations*, 13; and O'Beirne, *Short History*.

97. Black, *Association*, 151.

98. Black, *Association*, 151; Court of King's Bench, *The Trial of George Gordon*, 13; and Court of King's Bench, *The Proceedings at Large on the Trial of George Gordon*.

(1995) and John Seed (2012) wrote that Wesley "seemed" to have signed the Protestant Association petition.[99] However, Seed's only source for this claim is Henry Rack, who in *Reasonable Enthusiast*, did not state that Wesley signed the petition. Instead, Rack said that Wesley had a "controversial connection with the Protestant Association and the Gordon Riots."[100]

John A. Vickers (1995) stated that Charles Wesley did not sign the petition, but claimed John Wesley did sign it, saying: "but his brother [John Wesley] did sign and probably encouraged other London Methodists to do so," yet he indicated that his source was John English, and not the petition itself.[101] There is a manuscript in the National Archives of the United Kingdom that is a handwritten copy of the petition that Gordon dropped on the floor of the House of Commons. Judging by the differences in handwriting, the copy was made by at least four scribes. Since it is a copy and not the original, comparison of signatures is futile. There is one signature that could be interpreted as "John Wesley," however careful comparison between the letters "m" and "w" and the letters "e" and "o" in this signature to the same letters in other names by the same scribe reveal that the signature reads "Mosely" and not "Wesley."[102] Wesley never said whether he signed the petition. The evidence concerning Charles Wesley signing the petition is much clearer as he wrote to his daughter a week after the riots, clarifying that he had not signed it.[103]

Wesley and George Gordon

After Gordon was arrested, and imprisoned in the Tower, he asked Wesley to visit him.[104] Between Gordon's invitation and Wesley's visit to him, Wesley preached on November 5 at the City Road Chapel. The description of the sermon in his *Journal* read: "supposing the Papists to be heretics, schismatics, wicked men, enemies to us all and to our church and nation,

99. English, "Wesley and the Rights of Conscience," 362; and Seed, "Fall of Romish Babylon," 75.

100. Seed, "Fall of Romish Babylon," 75, and Rack, *Reasonable Enthusiast*, 310.

101. Vickers, Review of *Methodists and Papists*, 119; and English, "Wesley and the Rights of Conscience," 362.

102. TNA TS 11/388/1212.

103. CW to Sarah Wesley [his daughter], June 12, 1780, MARC DDcw 7/42.

104. JW to Brian Bury Collins, January 3, 1781, in MARC MAW.JW.2.55, and in Telford 7:46–47.

yet we ought not to persecute, to kill, hurt, or grieve them, but barely to prevent their doing hurt."[105] It appears that Wesley thought the penal laws were in place to prevent Catholics from persecuting Protestants. It seems that he believed that true persecution was physical persecution, although he never gave a clear definition of what he thought entailed persecution of Catholics.[106] His view can be interpreted, however, from his letter to the *Freeman's Journal* of March 31, 1780 in which he said:

> Would I then wish the Roman Catholics to be persecuted? I never said or hinted at any such thing. I abhor the thought: it is foreign to all I have preached and wrote for these fifty years. But I would wish the Romanists in England (I had no others in view) to be treated still with the same lenity that they have been these sixty years; to be allowed both civil and religious liberty, but not permitted to undermine ours. I wish them to stand just as they did before the late Act was passed; not to be persecuted or hurt themselves; but gently restrained from hurting their neighbours.[107]

This "gentle restraint" most likely referred to the penal laws. Wesley saw them as keeping the Catholics from doing harm, and this he thought was necessary.

Since November 5 was the remembrance of the Gunpowder Treason plot, perhaps the congregation would have expected a sermon against "Popery." Although Wesley had always discouraged physical persecution of Catholics, that he mentioned it in this sermon may have been because he felt unease due to the allegations that he had influenced the riots.[108] Nehemiah Curnock remarked that this sermon may have been influenced by Gordon's requests for Wesley to visit him.[109] Ward agreed: "it undoubtedly betrays uneasiness at the contribution to which his preaching and publishing had made to the Gordon riots."[110]

If Wesley was uneasy, it did not stop him from writing to the Secretary of State, Lord Stormont (David Murray, 1727–1796), in December 1780 reporting that Gordon desired to speak to him but that

105. *JWJ*, November 5, 1780, *Works*, 23:188–89.

106. Rack, "Man of Reason and Religion?," 10.

107. JW to the *Freeman's Journal*, March 31, 1780, *Works* (Jackson), 10:173.

108. Wesley preached on Luke 9:55, but the title of the sermon is unknown, *Works*, 23:188n.

109. JW, *Journal*, 6:299n.

110. *Works*, 23:189n.

he had no inclination to visit him.[111] Wesley divulged to Lord Stormont: "I think verily, your Lordship knows my Sentiments too well, to apprehend any ill consequence of my conversing with Lord George: especially as I should be very willing to communicate to your Lordship, whatever [passed?] in our conversation."[112] Certainly it was not out of character for Wesley to visit someone in prison. It is puzzling that he would risk a scandal by visiting Gordon in prison when he knew that people were already aligning him with the Protestant Association and accusing him of inciting the riots. These words to Lord Stormont provide a possible clue concerning the reason that Wesley would risk his reputation to call upon Gordon. Perhaps he was attempting to use the request for a visit to clear his name of accusations that he was aligned with Gordon, as he promised to report what Gordon said to Lord Stormont, yet this would not have been reported to the public to satisfy them. Regrettably, no letter from Wesley to Stormont reporting on the visit survives.

Although Wesley seems not to have published that he was going to visit Gordon, at least four newspapers reported:

> Mr. John Wesley, on application to the Secretaries of State for a warrant to visit Lord G. Gordon in the Tower, obtained that favour on Tuesday last for one visit only. One hour was the prescribed bounds of the permission, and a Warder at the same time was appointed to stay in the room with them, and to report the subject of their conversation to the Governor.[113]

This provides evidence that the public knew of Wesley's visit, which could certainly have aided in the allegations that Wesley was aligned with Gordon. Although he wrote about his visit of December 19, 1780 in his *Journal*, it would not be published until 1786. He described their exchange:

> I spent an hour with him at his apartment in the Tower. Our conversation turned upon Popery and religion. He seemed to be well acquainted with the Bible and had abundance of other books, enough to furnish a study. I was agreeably surprised to find he did not complain of any person or thing, and cannot but

111. JW to David Murray (1727–1796), Seventh Viscount Stormont, Secretary of State, December 15, 1780, in Baker, "Wesley and Gordon," 45.

112. Baker, "Wesley and Gordon," 45.

113. *Public Advertiser* 14417, December 23, 1780; *General Evening Post* 7305, December 21–23, 1780; *London Evening Post* 9162, December 21–23, 1780; and *Gazetteer and Daily Advertiser* 16196, December 25, 1780.

hope his confinement will take a right turn and prove a lasting blessing to him.[114]

A year later, he further remarked on the visit in a letter to Brian Bury Collins (1754–1807):

> In our whole conversation I did not observe that he had the least anger or resentment to anyone. He appeared to be in a very desirable spirit, entirely calm and composed. He seemed to be much acquainted with the Scripture, both as to the letter and the sense of it. Our conversation turned first upon Popery, and then upon experimental religion. I am in great hopes this affliction will be sanctified to him as a means of bringing him nearer to God. The theory of religion he certainly has. May God give him the living experience of it![115]

This letter does not seem to have been published during Wesley's lifetime.

Ten days after his visit, Wesley wrote in his *Journal*, December 29, 1780: "I saw the indictment of the Grand Jury against Lord George Gordon. I stood aghast! What a shocking insult upon common sense! But it is the usual *form*. The more is the shame. Why will not Parliament remove this scandal from our nation?"[116] Wesley obviously did not agree with Gordon's indictment, and thought the fact that Gordon had been arrested was a scandal.

Since his journal for 1780 was not published until 1786, and since the letter to Collins appears to be the only other account Wesley wrote of the visit, the public would have been left to speculate as to what transpired in the conversation between Gordon and Wesley. They also would not have known what Wesley thought of the indictment until 1786. This certainly could have contributed to accusations of Wesley's alignment with Gordon and causes one to wonder why Wesley would publish these words about Gordon six years after the fact. It is notable that, on the day of Gordon's indictment, Wesley wrote the preface to the letter collection called "On Popery" that he would later publish in the *Arminian*

---

114. JW, *An Extract* (1786), 42. See also *Works*, 23:189–90.

115. JW to Brian Bury Collins, January 3, 1781, MARC MAW.JW.2.55; the first publication of the letter seems to have been in "Wesley Letters," 161–62. See also Telford 7:46–47.

116. *Works*, 23:190.

Magazine.[117] Yet "On Popery" revealed nothing about Wesley's view of Gordon.

The trial of Gordon took place February 5, 1781 at the bar of the Court of the King's Bench.[118] Gordon was on trial for high treason, according to the Treason Act of 1351, "for intending to levy war against the king."[119] After less than half an hour, the jury declared Gordon "Not Guilty."[120] There seems to be no record of Wesley's perception of the jury's declaration. Significantly, not one person who was associated with Gordon was ever "convicted, tried, or even apprehended on suspicion" concerning the riots.[121]

In 1789 Wesley asked one of his preachers to visit Gordon in prison, who was incarcerated this time for defaming Queen Marie Antoinette (1755-1793) of France and the French ambassador, Jean-Balthazar d'Adhémar (1736-1790).[122] Peard Dickinson (1758-1802) visited the imprisoned Gordon in Newgate, and reported back to Wesley.[123] Dickinson wrote of visiting Gordon because Wesley wanted to know Gordon's "religious opinions" and hoped that the reports of Gordon's religious opinions were "ill grounded." Wesley was likely concerned that Gordon had converted to Judaism.[124] Dickinson said of the visit: "having expressed much respect for Mr. Wesley's character, and approbation of the good that he had done in the nation, he began to speak with frankness, and desired me to inform him, that he believed the Scriptures of the Old and New Testament to be of divine original." Gordon informed Dickinson of his conversion to a type of Judaism that embraced Jesus as Messiah; and Dickinson indicated that as they were leaving Gordon "desired me to give his compliments to Mr. Wesley, and tell him that he should be happy to see him."[125] There is no record that Wesley visited Gordon again, neither did Dickinson reveal what he told Wesley about the visit.

117. JW, "On Popery," 295.

118. "Kalender of Prisoners to be Tried," TNA TS KB 33/81/4.

119. "The King against Lord George Gordon," TNA KB 33/27/50; and 25 Edw. 3, stat. 5.

120. Hostettler, *Thomas Erskine*, 42.

121. Haydon, *Anti-Catholicism*, 239, see also Howel, *Complete Collection of State Trials*, 21:557.

122. Watson, *Life of Lord George Gordon*, 80–83.

123. Dickinson, *Memoirs*, 64–65.

124. See Haydon, "Gordon, George (1751-1793)," *ODNB*.

125. Dickinson, *Memoirs*, 65, 67.

Despite the efforts of Gordon and the Protestant Association, Parliament never repealed or modified the Catholic Relief Act of 1778. The act was debated a second time on June 20, 1780. That debate ended only with the statement "that leave be given that a bill be proposed to keep Catholics from teaching Protestant children."[126] This bill was presented to the Commons by Sir George Savile (1726–1784) on June 23. It passed with amendments in the Commons on June 28. It was debated in the House of Lords on June 28, and finally defeated.[127] Wesley would insist in 1782 that Catholics "enjoyed a full toleration. I wish them to enjoy the same toleration still; neither more nor less."[128] This statement demonstrates that Wesley believed that Catholics were tolerated even under the penal laws. The Act of Toleration of 1689 had not provided toleration to Catholics. A 1791 Act allowed Catholics freedom to worship with priests who had registered. They were allowed to build their own schools, but no Protestants could be admitted to the schools. A Catholic could now practice law.[129] The Catholic Relief Act of 1829 allowed Catholics to sit as members of Parliament, vote, and hold most, but not all, government offices.[130]

Allegations against Wesley

After the Gordon Riots, Wesley was accused of aligning with the Protestant Association and influencing the riots.[131] Wesley was accused of influencing them by both Catholic and Protestant writers. It was alleged that he "raised the cry against Popery," "stirred up Protestants to persecute Catholics," "inflamed the masses against Catholics," and was "chief author of the riots."[132] Following the Gordon Riots, two of Wesley's opponents, James Barnard and Samuel Romilly, accused him of

126. Haydon, "Parliament," 58; and Cobbett, *History*, 21:702, 714.

127. Cobbett, *History*, 21:715, 726, and 766.

128. JW, "Disavowal," 199.

129. 31 George III, c. 32.

130. 10 George IV, c. 7.

131. Husenbeth, *Life of Milner*, 21.

132. See Romilly, *Memoirs*, 1:84; Barnard, *Challoner*, 135; John Whittingham to JW, in *Morning Chronicle and London Advertiser* 3500, August 5, 1780; Husenbeth, *Life of Milner*, 21; and Palgrave, "A Slander upon John Wesley," 383–86. See also Black, *The Association*, 157.

anti-Catholicism. James Barnard, who was Richard Challoner's biographer, remarked on the Methodists:

> The field preachers inveighed with the utmost vengeance against Popery: and it may be reasonably concluded, that they were no less strenuous against it in their meetings, than they were in the fields. They formed in their own imaginations, a most horrid picture both of its tenets, and of the practices of its professors, and endeavoured to represent, and imprint the same idea in the minds of their deluded hearers. They falsely asserted it to be an Article of the Faith of the church of Rome that it was in the power of the Pope to depose Kings; and that it was another Article of their faith, that no faith is to be kept with heretics.[133]

Barnard asserted that the field preachers printed their words against Popery in pamphlets, but he did not name or cite any specific works, by Wesley or any other Methodists. Likewise, Romilly, an eyewitness to the riots, and supporter of Catholic emancipation, later recalled: "the Methodists, the followers of Wesley, and the sectaries of Whitefield were the first, if not to raise, at least to join the cry against Popery." Romilly, in agreement with Barnard, alleged that Wesley "magnify[ied] the terrors of the people, by painting to their imagination in the most glaring colours of all horrors of Popery, or could infuse among them a mistaken zeal and a dangerous spirit of fanaticism."[134]

Although it must be taken into consideration that Joseph Berington was not an entirely typical or representative voice of the Catholic communion as a whole, he asserted in *The State and Behavior of English Catholics* (1780), written as an attempt to clarify what Catholics believed, that "we do not hold that the Pope has the power to dispense with oaths."[135] Similarly, Arthur O'Leary insisted that "the history of Europe proclaims aloud that Catholics are not passive engines of the Pope."[136] This was written in reply to Wesley's statement that since Catholics could receive absolution from a priest for any sin committed, they could never be trusted.[137] On absolution, Berington said: "God alone interiorly absolves: the priest

---

133. Barnard, *Life of Challoner*, 162–63; for more on the Methodist preachers and anti-Catholicism, see Haydon, "Eighteenth-Century English," 134.

134. Romilly, *Memoirs*, 1:84.

135. Berington, *State and Behavior*, 151.

136. O'Leary, "Remarks on Mr. Wesley's," in *Miscellaneous Tracts*, 248.

137. JW, "Letter to the Printer of the *Public Advertiser*," *Works* (Jackson), 10:160.

only does it exteriorly."[138] Yet Wesley insisted: "I have known thousands of Roman Catholics in Ireland: but I never knew one who understood it thus."[139]

Did Wesley's views change much in thirty years? Perhaps not, for although *Letter to a Roman Catholic* has been heralded as a monumental ecumenical document, as stated in chapter three, the context and motive behind Wesley's writing of it does not align with this conclusion. When the historical context of the *Letter to a Roman Catholic* was examined, it was suggested that Wesley wrote the *Letter* to influence Catholics to stop rioting and listen to Methodist preaching. After writing the *Letter*, Wesley preached evangelical conversion to Catholics, for Wesley believed the only way they could learn to practice a catholic spirit was to experience "New Birth."

Out of all the criticism of Wesley after the Gordon Riots, the O'Leary/Wesley dispute holds the most "extraordinary historiographical legacy."[140] O'Leary, although he had not yet met Wesley, accused Wesley of authoring a letter that he did not write. Wesley denied his authorship in answer to O'Leary: "The second of the letters is not mine. I never saw it before."[141] O'Leary published his correspondence with Wesley as *Mr. O'Leary's Remarks on the Rev. John Wesley's Letters in Defense of the Protestant Association to Which Are Prefixed Mr. Wesley's Letters* (1780) in both a Dublin and a London edition. The first letter was Wesley's "Letter to the Printer of the *Public Advertiser*," after which O'Leary's reply was affixed. The next document in the publication was "Defence of the Protestant Association," after which O'Leary printed his reply. The "Defence" was what O'Leary called Wesley's "second letter," which Wesley denied writing. Yet when O'Leary published his *Miscellaneous Tracts* (1781), the "Defense of the Protestant Association" still listed Wesley as the author. *Miscellaneous Tracts* was reprinted four times in Wesley's lifetime, and in 1797, 1821, and 1832.

Tyerman declared that attributing authorship of the *Defense* to Wesley was a "popish deception, intended, no doubt, to cast upon Wesley the odium incurred by the Protestant Association during the Gordon

---

138. See also Berington, *State and Behavior*, 151.

139. JW to Joseph Berington, February 24, 1780, in Doughty, "John Wesley's Letters to Mr. Berington," 42.

140. Hempton, *Methodism and Politics*, 34.

141. See JW, "On Popery," 295.

riots."[142] No one seems to have any idea who the author might have been. Writing in 1840, George Cubitt (1792–1850), Wesleyan minister, said that O'Leary was the only one who attributed it to Wesley. He correctly indicated that "neither O'Leary or any of the papists of the day made any attempt to authenticate this fabricated document." Cubitt thought that whoever had placed the "ridiculous cover" with Wesley's named attached, was "guilty of forgery."[143] According to Cubitt, it appears that O'Leary assumed Wesley's authorship because the author had the initials "J. W.," but it is unknown where O'Leary acquired the *Defense.* Cubitt declared that it "bears no resemblance whatever to Mr. Wesley's style of thought and expression." Upon comparison of this document with Wesley's writings of the same year, this may be a reasonable conclusion. Cubitt also surmised that O'Leary could have written it himself to slander Wesley.[144] However, there is no hard evidence that indicates it came from O'Leary's pen. There were at least seven Methodist preachers with the initials "J. W." active in 1781 who could have written it, including Dr. John Whitehead (1740–1804), but it seems unlikely that a Methodist would have written it as Wesley insisted that he told his preachers to have nothing to do with the riots. Therefore, the authorship of the *Defense of the Protestant Association* remains unknown.

The evidence strongly suggests that O'Leary greatly exaggerated Wesley's influence on and possible participation in the Protestant Association. It is for this reason that, in 1781, Wesley published his two letters to O'Leary in the *Arminian Magazine* that had been previously been printed in the *Freeman's Journal.*[145] Wesley may have published his responses to O'Leary to deny that he wrote *Defense,* but the charge that he wrote it has endured. John Milner (1752–1826) [Catholic] Vicar Apostolic of the Midland District, writing in 1800, asserted that Wesley wrote *Defense.*[146] After all of their tumultuous conversation, Wesley seemed surprised that when he met O'Leary in Dublin seven years later, O'Leary was not: "the stiff queer man I expected."[147]

142. Tyerman, *Life of Wesley,* 3:322n.

143. Cubitt, *Strictures,* 52, 72.

144. Cubitt, *Strictures,* 52, 57, and 56.

145. JW, "On Popery," 295–300; and JW, "On Popery," 352–60

146. Milner, *Letters to a Prebendary,* 211.

147. *JWJ,* May 12, 1787, *Works,* 24:25; England, *Life of O'Leary,* 87–88; and Southey, *Life of Wesley,* 2:389–90. Both O'Leary and Berrington wrote essays on tolerance after the Gordon Riots. See O'Leary, "An Essay on Toleration," 315–29; and Berrington, *State and Behavior,* 139–86.

Wesley answered O'Leary's claim that "Queen Elizabeth and James roasted heretics in Smithfield," saying "in what year, I doubt the fact."[148] John Coffey claimed that no Catholic was attacked by a mob and killed for his or her faith in Elizabethan England, but affirmed that Elizabeth I "executed almost 200 Catholics."[149] The reason that Wesley could overlook this is that Elizabeth had Catholics condemned for treason, rather than burned for heresy.[150] The Catholic Church still holds the view of O'Leary, as the *New Catholic Encyclopaedia* claims 189 martyrs under the reign of Elizabeth I.[151]

Thomas England, Arthur O'Leary's biographer, said in 1822 that it would appear that during the Gordon Riots Wesley wanted "the extermination of Popery by use of force."[152] Likewise, Barnard posited that the Methodists sought to stir up Protestants to persecute Catholics "to the utmost of their power; as if they thought that by *killing them they should render a service to God*."[153] Similarly, John Whittingham (c. 1722–?), Coventry nurseryman and Catholic apologist, writing in response to "Letter to the Printer of the *Public Advertiser*," accused Wesley of "a design to inflame the masses against Roman Catholics."[154] Whittingham said:

> The weak remark with which Mr. Wesley concludes, prove [*sic*] to me that he is not tied by either truth, justice or mercy, and so I shall leave him to repent of the opposition which he and his friends have raised against the Bill in favour of Roman Catholics, it being begun in malice, and ended in such outrage that no meek teachers can vindicate their proceedings. The pretence of religion has only aggravated the guilt of sedition, and offended thousands.[155]

In addition to Whittingham's remarks, a ditty published shortly after the riots as the caption to the print of a riot scene said this:

148. JW, "On Popery," 354.

149. Coffey, *Persecution and Toleration*, 102.

150. Middleton, *Martyrdom*, 103.

151. Culkin, "England and the Catholic Church," 5:247.

152. England, *Life of O'Leary*, 83–84.

153. Barnard, *Challoner*, 135.

154. John Whittingham to JW, *Morning Chronicle and London Advertiser* 3500, August 5, 1780. For more on Whittingham, see Barbour, "John Whittingham," 8–25.

155. John Whittingham to JW, *Morning Chronicle and London Advertiser* 3500, August 5, 1780.

> Religious strife is raised to life,
> By canting whining John;
> No Popery he loud doth cry,
> To the deluded throng.[156]

The print titled "Fanaticism Revived" portrays a Church of England priest with arms outstretched, preaching in front of a burning building with several people listening. There are torn books in the picture, and people are carrying dishes and candlesticks as if they are looting. The print implies that the priest in the picture is "John." It is not clear whether this was meant to be John Wesley.

In 1807, John Milner declared Wesley to be the "chief author" of the riots.[157] Additionally, Daniel O'Connell insisted that Wesley was "an intolerant bigot, who blew the flame of religious animosity until it burst into a conflagration in the capital [sic] of this great empire."[158] Yet Wesley denied that he had anything to do with the riots, and had pronounced that the Methodists had not participated when he wrote to James Rivington (1724–1802), publisher of the *Royal Gazette*, on October 25, 1780. Apparently, a letter had been published in New York about the Gordon Riots that reported that the Methodists and Dissenters were "secretly blowing up the flame." Wesley wrote that the Dissenters could answer for themselves, but he would answer for the Methodists, saying: "all of them who are connected with me fear God and honour the King and not one of them was any otherwise concerned in the late tumults than in doing all they possibly could to suppress them."[159] Wesley did not encourage the preachers to join in the riots, but his anti-Catholic writings still may have influenced the preachers to preach against "Popery."

The *Gentleman's Magazine* editors agreed with Wesley that the Protestant Association should not be held responsible for the riots. Their reason was that nothing in the Association's meetings showed a plot to "rob the Bank and burn the city." They blamed the rioting on the fact that "no proper police exists in this country," and "if there had been any

156. Haydon, *Anti-Catholicism*, 65. The June 1780 etching is found in the British Museum, B. M., D. P. D., 5, 685.

157. John Milner to Unknown, June 29, 1807, in Milner, *An Inquiry*, 16. Husenbeth, *Life of Milner*, 21; see also Palgrave, "Slander upon John Wesley," 383–86.

158. Daniel O'Connell to the Wesleyan Methodists, August 15, 1839, in O'Connell, *Letters*, 24.

159. John Wesley to James Rivington, Publisher, October 25, 1780, in *Royal Gazette* (New York), February 24, 1781.

ringleaders of note, even behind the curtain, the trials of those who have been condemned as most active in the riot would certainly have led to a discovery." Instead they found that "blind and ignorant fury, inflamed by drunkenness, and seconded by the interested views of thieves and house-breakers has, in fact been the cause of the whole commotion."[160] Charles Wesley left no question of his perception of the Protestant Association. He labelled them: "an army of Associators, of rebels, regicides, and traitors."[161] This suggests that John Wesley disagreed with his brother over the responsibility that the Protestant Association had for the riots. Charles Wesley's poem "The Protestant Association in the Midst of the Tumults" indicated the paradox of his enemies accusing him of being "Papist" when he wrote against Catholics:

> Or list beneath a madman's sign.
> Old Wesley too to Papist's kind,
> who wrote against them for a blind,
> Himself a papist still in heart,
> He and his followers shall smart.
> No one of his fraternity
> We here beneath our standard see,
> To which the whole regiments resort
> Both form the Lock and Tottenham-court [Whitefield's chapel].[162]

Ralph Reed called Charles Wesley's "The Protestant Association written in the Midst of the Tumults:"

> One of the most remarkable statements in defense of the English social order in the history of eighteenth-century Methodism. [Charles] Wesley equated social revolution with national suicide, popular radicalism with Satanic intrigue, and King George with Christ as an instrument of Divine wrath. His rhetoric made almost no distinctions between civil and religious duty.[163]

Reed rightly indicated that it is "difficult to imagine a people with this kind of psychic response to deprivation and suffering as a breeding

---

160. "Particular Detail of the Late Riotous Tumults," 369.

161. CW, "The Protestant Association," in CW and JW, *Poetical Works*, 8:440.

162. CW, "Protestant Association," 8:458.

163. Reed, "From Riots to Revivalism," 180.

ground for revolution, for the Methodist theology of suffering left no room for provoking revolution."[164]

Charles may have included a theology of suffering in his hymns, but he also gave advice to the city of London: "do, what so few of you have done, poor, guilty worms, your Maker fear, and then ye *must* your king revere."[165] Charles's argument is that of a Tory: all would have been well in the city of London if only people had revered the king.

John Wesley published "A Disavowal of Persecuting Papists" in the *Arminian Magazine* in 1782, probably because of the accusations against him.[166] In this document, he declared: "I set out early in life with an utter abhorrence of persecution in every form, and a full conviction that every man has a right to worship God according to his own conscience." This statement further indicates that Wesley did not regard the penal laws as amounting to persecution. He asserted that he believed he knew some Catholics "who sincerely love both God and their neighbour, and who steadily endeavour to do to everyone as they wish to do unto them."[167] Wesley demonstrated a catholic spirit by speaking against physical persecution of Catholics.[168] He understood that Catholics believed the penal laws were a form of persecution, but he did not agree with this view.

Conclusion

Keith Thomas has observed that many "systems of belief pose a resilience which makes them virtually immune to external argument. Once the initial premises are accepted, no subsequent discovery will shake the believer's faith, for he can explain it away in terms of the existing system."[169] This appears to have been the case with Wesley after the Catholic Relief Act of 1780.

It is certain that Wesley's two writings, "Letter to the Printer of the *Public Advertiser*" and *Popery Calmly Considered* became a part of the anti-Catholic Relief Act propaganda, even if Wesley did not intend it.

164. CW, "Protestant Association," 8:450–78.

165. CW, "Protestant Association," 8:469, 475.

166. JW, "Disavowal," 198–99; see also *Works* (Jackson), 10:173–75.

167. JW, "Disavowal," 199.

168. Heitzenrater, *People Called Methodists*, 305.

169. Haydon, "Eighteenth-Century English," 60, quoting Thomas, *Religion and the Decline of Magic*, 250–51.

This could have contributed to the hysteria concerning Catholics, yet he was reiterating one strand of post-Reformation Anglican perception of Catholicism. Wesley held the view that the penal laws had their place and did not change his mind even though some Catholics informed him that they viewed them as being oppressive. It is quite clear that Wesley did not directly encourage the Methodists to participate in the riots, and his letter to Whittingham clarified that he held no support for the "rabble."

Although Wesley never said so, it seems reasonable to presume that he did not sign the Protestant Association petition. He did say that he did not join the Protestant Association. There is no hard evidence that he wrote in defense of the Protestant Association after the riots; only that he approved of their publication *An Appeal of the Protestant Association*, and of their efforts to have the Catholic Relief Act repealed legally. He was nowhere near London during the riots nor had he encouraged any of his preachers to participate in them or even in the march to Parliament to deliver the petition. There is no proof that any Methodists participated in the march or the riots. Charles Wesley's statement that he gathered the preachers to pray and keep the peace enforces his brother's claim that the Methodist preachers had not been encouraged to riot. Wesley's visit to Gordon was enigmatic considering that he knew it could further the rumors that he had influenced the riots. He never gave a full explanation for why he did it. It makes sense that his visit would cause some to think that he was allied with Gordon. It does not appear that Wesley considered Gordon guilty for the riots; and Gordon was declared "not guilty" by the Court of the King's Bench.

After the Gordon Riots, it was alleged that Wesley influenced them. It was said that he "raised the cry against Popery," "stirred up Protestants to persecute Catholics," "inflamed the masses against Catholics," and that he was "chief author of the riots."[170] Was Wesley guilty of these things? After examining *Popery Calmly Considered* and "Letter to the Printer of the *Public Advertiser*," it is understandable that he was accused of "rais[ing] the cry" by displaying Catholicism in a way that would provoke fear.[171] It is true that Hus was executed, but bringing it up at the time of the Catholic Relief Act would certainly cause Protestant anxiety to rise.

170. Romilly, *Memoirs*, 1:84; Barnard, *Challoner*, 135; John Whittingham to JW, *Morning Chronicle and London Advertiser* 3500, August 5, 1780; and Husenbeth, *Life of Milner*, 21.

171. JW, *Popery Calmly Considered*, Works (Jackson), 10:140–58; and "Letter to the Printer of the *Public Advertiser*," Works (Jackson), 10:159–61.

Advocating for the penal laws to stay in place was arguably promoting bigotry, but Wesley did not see it this way.[172] Contemporary Catholics such as Berington and O'Leary disagreed with him as they taught that Catholicism had progressed from the fifteenth- and sixteenth-century stories that Wesley told.[173]

"Disavowal of Persecuting Papists" demonstrated his nonviolent stance, but only confirmed his anti-Catholicism as he still insisted that the Catholic Relief Act was not in the best interest of Britain.[174] Wesley may have been guilty "raising the cry against Popery," but of influencing Protestants to physically persecute Catholics, he was certainly not guilty.[175] Wesley seems to have shown no empathy to Catholics for the injustice of the penal laws despite the Methodists having experienced opposition for decades. His fears, not a catholic spirit, are what dominated the writings examined in this chapter.

172. Samuel Johnson defined bigotry as "blind zeal; prejudice; unreasonable warmth in favour of party or opinions." See Johnson, *Dictionary*, 1: s.v. "Bigotry."

173. Berington, *State and Behavior*, 17, 28, 36, 117, 166, 179.

174. JW, "Disavowal," *Works* (Jackson), 10:174–75.

175. Barnard, *Life of Challoner*, 162–63.

7

A *Catholic Spirit*
and Catholic Devotional Material

THIS CHAPTER WILL EXPLORE Wesley's use of Catholic devotional authors by examining his publications, recommendations, and critiques of Catholic devotional literature. Wesley asserted:

> I know that many of these [Catholics] in former ages were good men, (as Thomas á Kempis, Francis Sales, and the Marquis de Renty,) but that many of them are so at this day. I believe I know some Roman Catholics who sincerely love both God and their neighbour, and who steadily endeavour to do unto everyone as they wish him to do unto them.[1]

This chapter takes into account that although Wesley criticized the Catholic Church, he often recommended that Methodists read Catholic devotional literature. This chapter argues that Wesley criticized the Catholic devotional resources he recommended, yet he showed a catholic spirit by using and recommending them.

This chapter falls into four sections: first an overview of Wesley as publisher will be provided. The second section introduces the Catholic devotional authors Wesley used. The third section examines Wesley's disagreements with Catholic devotional writers. The fourth and final section explores positive influences of the Catholic devotional authors on Wesley's life and thought.

In *Methodists and Papists*, David Butler gave a brief review of Wesley's use of these sources, but he focused on á Kempis and did not

---

1. JW, "Disavowal," 198.

thoroughly discuss the other works.[2] Eamon Duffy included a brief section on Wesley's use of Catholic devotional sources in his essay, "Wesley and the Counter Reformation."[3] Further, Isabel Rivers explored Wesley's publications of Catholic devotional material in *Vanity Fair and the Celestial City*.[4] The primary sources used in this paper include John Wesley's sermons, journals, letters, and most importantly, his abridged publications of the Catholic devotional sources.

"When talking about sanctification and perfection, Wesley plainly drew much more on Catholic than Protestant sources."[5] Some say that John and Charles Wesley drew on Catholic sources early, before 1738 when they experienced evangelical conversion, and not later. However, the Wesleys used Catholic sources throughout their writing careers, especially for the theology of sanctification. Additionally, David Hempton agreed that John Wesley drew on á Kempis, de Sales, De Renty, and Fénelon for his doctrine of sanctification.[6] Nevertheless, throughout their lives, the Wesleys continued to "believe in the sanctity of catholic authors" that they used.[7]

Although this study agrees that it was ecumenical of Wesley to use, recommend, and publish Catholic devotional material, it is important to understand that he still criticized the authors. In spite of admiring the authors, he often told his listeners why he disagreed with their lifestyles, especially the mysticism that led to quietism. On the other hand, the pragmatic Wesley found helpful advice for the life of piety from multiple sources. He could take the good with the bad, and when he thought his followers may not be able to discern the chaff from the wheat, he abridged.

As always, Wesley was way more concerned that a person experience a personal relationship with Christ than he was with the label they carried. For instance, less than a year before he died, he said to his nephew, Charles's son, Samuel, "I care not a rush for your being called a Papist or a Protestant. But I am grieved at your being an heathen. Certain

---

2. Butler, *Methodists and Papists*, 141–58.

3. Duffy, "Wesley and the Counter Reformation," 1–19.

4. Rivers, *Vanity Fair*, 164–74.

5. Rack, *Reasonable Enthusiast*, 156.

6. Hempton, *Methodism and Politics*, 31.

7. Heitzenrater, *The Poor and the People Called Methodist*, 48.

it is that the general religion of Protestants and Catholics is no better than refined heathenism."[8]

John Wesley as Publisher

Wesley made classical texts of spiritual direction available to ordinary people, and it is well known that Wesley expected the Methodists to be a reading people.[9] He expected every Methodist to read, but raised the bar even higher with his preachers. In one of the last letters of his life, he wrote: "It cannot be that the people should grow in grace unless they give themselves to reading. A reading people will always be a knowing people."[10] Even in his value of books, we find á Kempis an influence, for á Kempis said: "We ought to read plain and devout books, as willingly as high and profound ones."[11]

"To control the book supply and literacy practices of a whole religious community was to control the language with which they engaged the world. To bring written texts to the lives of the poor was a work of both the mind and the spirit."[12] Wesley sought to make reading an affordable pastime; this was one of the reasons he abridged and published so many books. Isabel Rivers noted that John Wesley was "editor, author or publisher of more works than any other single figure in eighteenth-century Britain."[13] He published around 3500 texts. However, outside of Methodist studies, his contributions to literature are not well understood.[14] "John Wesley's press, at the time of his death, was the owner of approximately 351 titles, and 254,512 book volumes worth nearly £4,000."[15]

Yet, why did Wesley use and promote Catholic devotional books when he was a Protestant? When the Protestants began writing, they competed with a well-established foundation of Catholic devotionals. These materialized in Anglicized versions in the seventeenth and

---

8. JW to Samuel Wesley (his nephew), April 29, 1790, in Telford, 8:218.

9. Rivers, "Editor and Publisher," 150.

10. JW to George Holder, November 8, 1790, in Telford, 8:247.

11. JW, *Christian's Pattern*, 11.

12. Burton, *Spiritual Literacy*, 261.

13. Rivers, "Editor and Publisher," 145.

14. Cunha, *Practical Divinity*, 4.

15. Burton, *Spiritual Literacy*, 235. For the transcription of the book inventory taken at JW's death (stored in the MARC), see Burton, *Spiritual Literacy*, 315–39.

eighteenth centuries. While the some of the books provided models for private devotions, others were created to be used not by laity, but by the priesthood.[16] Methodists appreciated Catholic devotional writers because of their "emphasis on inward religion, perfection, and union with the divine, interests they shared with some high churchmen and Nonjurors as well as with some continental Protestants."[17] However, Wesley wished to form a body of literature not only for his preachers, but for the average Methodist disciple.

Therefore, Wesley was not the only one who reshaped Catholic books for Protestant use, there was an established tradition of Protestants tailoring beloved Catholic works for their purposes. It seems that eighteenth-century editors reshaped earlier works to conform to the qualifications of their denominations. For example, "Protestants reshaped Catholic books; Arminians reshaped books by Calvinists; heterodox Unitarians reshaped books by orthodox Trinitarians."[18] A portion of Wesley's challenge was to create a vocabulary of Methodism, one that granted him the ability to express theological ideas, and that influenced his readers to have the words to express their own experience.[19] By abridging and republishing Catholic devotional books, Wesley joined with a long line of Protestants modifying previous works to meet their own viewpoints.

When the Methodists were not reading, it concerned Wesley, for he said: "The Societies are not half supplied with books, not even with Kempis, 'Instructions for Children,' and *Primitive Physick*, which ought to be in every house."[20] According to Wesley, every Methodist house should also have access to *Extract of the Christian's Pattern* by Thomas á Kempis, *Primitive Physick*; *Hymns and Spiritual Songs, Intended for Use of Real Christians of All Denominations*; *Collection of Hymns, for the Use of the People Called Methodist*; and *Pocket Hymn Book, for the Use of Christians of All Denominations*.[21]

16. Cunha, *Practical Divinity*, 24.

17. Rivers, *Vanity Fair*, 165.

18. Rivers, "Editor and Publisher," 146.

19. Cunha, *Practical Divinity*, 37.

20. "Large Minutes 1753–1763," *Works*, 10:867.

21. Norris, *Financing*, 171.

The Catholic Devotional Authors Wesley Used

Isabel Rivers provided a list of the Catholic works Wesley published in her book, *Vanity Fair*.[22] Out of these, the most widely used by Wesley was *The Christian's Pattern* by Thomas á Kempis.[23] Wesley read á Kempis with the Oxford Methodists and repeatedly in Georgia.[24] From his reading it in 1725, to his death, it heavily influenced him. Wesley published an abridged version of á Kempis between his father's death and his leaving for Georgia. Charles Rivington, a High Church friend with Nonjuror sympathies published it. Rivington had published John Wesley's father, Samuel's, book on Job and his *Advice to a Young Clergyman*.[25]

The Christian Pattern "illustrated his lifelong desire to make classical texts of spiritual direction accessible to ordinary people."[26] Henry Moore, in the *Life of the Reverend John Wesley*, wrote of Wesley, "He was dissatisfied with Dean Stanhope's translation [of Kempis], and determined to give a full view of self-denying purity of his favorite guide."[27] His publication of Kempis was for his students at Oxford.[28] As stated above, he later published *A Companion for the Altar: Extracted from Thomas á Kempis* in 1742. It was a brief, twenty-four-page booklet that people could use as they prayed. Amazingly, the estimated sales to the year 1800 of John Wesley's abridgement of á Kempis, are forty thousand.[29]

Additionally, Wesley recommended á Kempis to his correspondents.[30] For example, to his niece, Sarah, he wrote: "And now when the worst of these [temptations] occur, you may answer with pious Kempis, 'Go, go thou unclean spirit. These are not my thoughts but thine, and thou shalt answer for them in God.'"[31]

---

22. Rivers, *Vanity Fair*, 167. "Wesley first published extracts from Guyon and Fénelon in his abridgement of Heylin's *Devotional Tracts* in *A Christian Library* XXXVIII (1754)." Rivers, *Vanity Fair*, 172.

23. Hammond, "Imitating Christ," 207.

24. Hammond, "Imitating Christ," 206–7.

25. *Homes, Haunts, and Friends*, 42

26. Burton, *Spiritual Literacy*, 249.

27. Moore, *Life of JW*, 2:401; Burton, *Spiritual Literacy*, 249.

28. Rivers, "Editor and Publisher," 150.

29. Norris, *Financing*, 171.

30. Rack, *Reasonable Enthusiast*, 420.

31. JW to Sarah Wesley (his niece), March 31, 1781, in Telford, 7:54

Wesley recommended á Kempis along with Gaston Jean Baptiste de Renty (1611–1649) to "Men of Reason and Religion" in 1745.[32] De Renty read á Kempis and "converted," and wished to become a Carthusian hermit.[33] His parents were against this, and persuaded him to enter public service. Yet in 1638, he left his career behind and gave himself to ascetic piety. Wesley abridged de Renty's life from an English translation of 1658. He started it in about 1729, and was still working on it on way home from America 1738. His finished the final abridgement in 1741, reducing it from 358 pages to 67.[34]

Wesley discovered Gregory Lopez (1542–1596), an obscure Spanish mystic, in Francisco Losa's *Holy Life of Gregory Lopez, A Spanish Hermite in the West Indies* (1618, trans. 1675). He abridged and published this in 1755 in *A Christian Library*.[35] Lopez travelled to Mexico, arriving in 1562, forming a hermitage in the wilderness of Amajac. He traveled and preached while living an ascetic lifestyle. He spent his last seven years near Santa Fe, where he eventually died. Albert Outler indicated how Lopez's example influenced Wesley. His voyage to Mexico paralleled Wesley's voyage to Georgia. Like Wesley, Lopez sought after holy living, stressed self-denial, identified with the poor, practiced "primitive physick," and equated holiness with happiness. Although Wesley called him: "That good and wise (though much mistaken) man," he also printed Lopez's abridged life in *Arminian Magazine* in 1780.[36] "Lopez and de Renty stood side by side in John Wesley's view as models of practical godliness."[37]

Lopez influenced Madame Jeanne Guyon (1648–1717), French Catholic mystic and writer. She became an important leader in seventeenth-century France's theological debates because she advocated for Quietism, the belief that spiritual perfection could be attained. At sixteen she married an older man who died by the time she was twenty-eight, leaving her with three children. Her husband left her wealth, and with this she served God through helping the poor, writing, and telling others

32. JW, *A Farther Appeal*, 66.

33. JW, *De Renty*, 3–4, 45, and *Works*, 2:375–76.

34. JW, *Journal*, *Works*, 18:208; and Butler, *Methodists and Papists*, 139.

35. Outler, *Works*, 2:375n2; JW, *Christian Library*, 50:337–406.

36. Ward and Heitzenrater, *Works*, 19:294n73; and JW, *Journal*, August 31, 1742, *Works*, 19:294.

37. Ward and Heitzenrater, *Works*, 19:294n73.

of the love of God. The Catholic Church disagreed with her Quietism, and eventually imprisoned her.[38] Wesley often recommended her writings.

Additionally, Wesley read Quietist François de Sales (1567–1622), Bishop of Geneva's *Introduction to the Devout Life*.[39] Anglican Bishop of Exeter, condemned Wesley's use of de Sales, saying of de Sales: "He is the Methodist's bosom friend."[40] To this Wesley retorted: "I believe he is in Abraham's bosom, but he is 'no bosom friend of the Methodists.'"[41] Vincent Perronet's (one of Wesley's preachers) response to Lavington's accusation about Wesley's use of Catholic writings was: "if the Methodists had in mind to imitate the popish fanatics, they have done it very poorly."[42] Perronet's attitude, reflected in his letter, seems to align with Wesley's view of Catholic writings.[43] Like Wesley, Perronet was practical. If a Catholic writer provided him with instruction and inspiration, he would not hold Catholicism against the author. De Sales was popular outside of the Methodist use, for his *Introduction to the Devout Life* went through 100 editions before 1740.[44]

Wesley also read Juan de Castaniza (c. 1536–1599), a Spanish Benedictine. His mother owned the English translation of Castaniza's book by Richard Lucas. It has now been attributed to Lorenzo Scupoli, a Spanish Theatine.[45] Furthermore, Wesley recommended, John of Avila (1500–1569) in a letter to his nephew, Samuel in 1789.[46] He also read Francis Xavier (1506–1552). Yet, at the time of Wesley's death, only Ignatius, á Kempis, and Clementina survived in his library to represent the Catholic tradition.[47]

38. James, *Complete Madame Guyon.*

39. de Sales, *Introduction;* and JW, *A Second Letter, Works,* 11:425–26.

40. [Lavington], *Enthusiasm,* 1:131.

41. JW, *A Second Letter, Works,* 11:426.

42. Perronet, *Some Remarks,* 10.

43. Perronet, *Some Remarks,* 16.

44. Ward, *Protestant Evangelical Awakening,* 44

45. *Works,* 3:506.

46. JW to Samuel Wesley [his nephew], September 16, 1789, in Telford 8:171.

47. Burton, *Spiritual Literacy,* 241.

Wesley's Disagreements with Catholic Devotional Authors

Wesley wrote to Lady Maxwell, a Scottish noblewoman, in 1764: "I want you to be all a Christian; such a Christian as the Marquis de Renty, or Gregory Lopez was."[48] He considered de Renty and Lopez "real Christians." However, a Catholic author could have "real Christianity" but be wrong on his or her opinions. In Wesley's sermon, "On the Trinity," he asserted:

> Persons may be quite right in their opinions, and yet have no religion at all. And on the other hand, persons may be truly religious who hold many wrong opinions. Can anyone possibly doubt this while there are Romanists in the world? For who can deny, not only that many of them formerly have been religious (as á Kempis, Gregory Lopez, and the Marquis de Renty), but that many of them even at this day are real, inward Christians? And yet what a heap of erroneous opinions do they hold, delivered by tradition from their fathers![49]

This aligns with Wesley's assertion in his sermon *Catholic Spirit* that one can have erroneous opinions yet be a real Christian. Opinions were not as important as a person's heart being right. If a person's heart was right with God, if they walked by faith, and if they believed in the Lord Jesus Christ, then Wesley said, "Give me thine hand."[50] This meant he could work with the person; that he could accept the person as a brother or sister in Christ. This helps us to understand why he could be against many Catholic doctrines but instruct his preachers and people to read Catholic devotional literature. Of course, if he found serious theological errors among the Catholic writers, he would edit their words or leave them out completely in his abridgements when he republished them.

Furthermore, in the same sermon, "On the Trinity," Wesley pointed out he disagreed with de Sales and Castaniza, saying they did not comprehend the nature of justification. This is how he phrased it:

> On the other hand, how many writers of the Romish Church (as Francis Sales and Juan de Castaniza in particular) have wrote strongly and scripturally on sanctification; who nevertheless were unacquainted with the nature of justification. Insomuch that the whole body of their divines at the Council of Trent in their *Catechisms ad Parochos* totally confound sanctification

48. JW to Lady Maxwell, September 22, 1764, *Works*, 27:388.
49. JW, "On the Trinity," *Works*, 2:374–75.
50. JW, "Catholic Spirit," *Works*, 2:87–88.

and justification together. But it has pleased God to give the Methodists a full and clear knowledge of each, and the wide difference between them.[51]

Another disagreement had to do with the claim that Christians should be miserable in the world. This, especially, was in the writings of á Kempis. Wesley could not agree that God sent us into the world to be "perpetually miserable in it." If so, pursuing happiness would be a sin. Wesley said á Kempis said: "all mirth is vain and useless, if not sinful."[52] But the Psalmist tells us to be joyful, especially the sixty-eighth Psalm.[53] He asked for his mother's thoughts upon this, which she replied.[54]

Susanna agreed with her son on this point, she said: "I was about to say, blasphemous–suggestion, that God by an irreversible decree hath determined any man to be miserable in the world. His intentions, as himself, are holy, just, and good, and all the miseries incident to men here or hereafter proceed from themselves." Restoring humans to the happiness experienced in Adam is done in our redemption by Jesus Christ. Endeavouring after happiness by gratifying bodily appetites is wrong. Further, Susanna wrote:

> I take Kempis to have been an honest, weak man, that had more zeal than knowledge, by his condemned all mirth or pleasure as sinful or useless, in opposition to so many direct and plain texts of Scripture. Would you judge the lawfulness or unlawfulness of pleasure, of the innocence or malignity of actions?[55]

Additionally, according to Wesley, Saint Jure's *Life of de Renty* left too many weak things in the book casting "the shade of superstition and folly over one of the brightest patterns of heavenly wisdom." Wesley shortened the book, showing de Renty as a model of Christian perfection.[56] He left out de Renty's specific Catholic practices and his distaste for the world.[57]

Although Wesley often recommended her writings, he held strong reservations concerning Madame Guyon. He asserted:

---

51. JW, "On God's Vineyard," *Works*, 3:305–6.

52. Hammond, "Imitating Christ," 205.

53. JW to Susanna Wesley, May 28, 1725, *Works*, 25:162–64.

54. Susanna Wesley to JW, June 8, 1725, *Works*, 25:164–67.

55. Susanna Wesley to JW, June 8, 1725, *Works*, 25:164–67.

56. JW, *Journal*, January 6, 1738, *Works*, 18:208

57. JW, *Journal*, January 6, 1738, *Works*, 18:208

I believe Madame Guyon was in several mistakes, speculate and practical too. Yet I would not more dare to call her than her friend, Archbishop Fénelon, 'a distracted enthusiast.' She was undoubtedly a woman of a very uncommon understanding and of excellent piety. Nor was she any more 'a lunatic' than she was an heretic.[58]

She brought suffering unto herself by bodily austerities, which Wesley called "unscriptural."[59] However, Wesley was criticized at Oxford for austerities. William Morgan, a student at Oxford, had been a member of the Oxford Methodists, and allegedly died because of the "ascetic excesses" of the group.[60] At least, his father accused the Wesleys of such. This prompted a long letter from Wesley to Richard Morgan, William's father, defending the group.[61] Additionally, related to suffering, Wesley disagreed with Guyon that only suffering would purify a person. He said:

Hence rose that capital mistake, which runs thro' all her writings, That God never does, never can purify a soul, but by inward or outward suffering. Utterly false! Never was there a more purified soul that the apostle John. And which of the apostles suffered less? Yea, or all the primitive Christians? Therefore, all she says on this head, 'darkness, desertion, privation,' and the like, is fundamentally wrong.[62]

Wesley also thought that Guyon did not take Scripture seriously enough as he wrote of her:

The grand source of all her mistakes was this, The not being guided by the written word. She did not take the Scripture for the rule of her actions: at most, it was but the secondary rule. Inward impressions, which she called inspirations, were her primary rule. The written word was not a lantern to her feet, a light in all her paths.[63]

As for Francis Xavier, he may have influenced Wesley in the vegetarian diet in which he engaged while in Georgia.[64] Further, Xavier may

58. *Works*, 22:245–46.

59. JW, *Madam Guion*, vii.

60. Rack, *Reasonable Enthusiast*, 83.

61. JW to Richard Morgan Sr., October [19], 1732, *Works*, 25:335–44.

62. JW, *Madam Guion*, vii.

63. JW, *Madam Guion*, vi.

64. Hammond, *JW in America*, 48.

have influenced Wesley's missionary vision.[65] Later, Wesley accused him of not teaching real Christianity to converts.[66]

Wesley wrote of mystics in 1738:

> whose noble descriptions of union with God and internal religion made everything else appear mean, flat, and insipid. But in truth they made good works appear so, yeah, and faith itself, and what no? These gave me an entire new view of religion, nothing like any I had had before But alas! It was nothing like that religion which Christ and his apostles lived and taught.[67]

Nonetheless, the greatest disagreement Wesley had with Catholic devotional authors had to do with mysticism and quietism. One of the reasons Wesley became more critical of Guyon later in life was that the Quakers held her in great importance.[68] "He contradicted Madame Guyon's quietism, the understanding of 'pure love' that meant to her the abandonment of the search for one's salvation in favour of stillness before God."[69] Yet "rejection of mystical writers was not wholesale after 1738 as Wesley needed some aspects of their teaching to back up his own thought."[70] Later Wesley claimed to Richard Hill "he was never in the way of mysticism."[71] Additionally, Wesley left out of the books in *A Christian Library* what he considered "too mystical."[72]

Wesley and the mystics held that a private devotional life was important for Christians. Prayer was of utmost importance.[73] However, Wesley disagreed with the mystics on the matter of solitude. He believed it could get in the way living a life of good works. This became one of the main reasons Wesley disagreed with them, and why he preferred the practical mystics.[74] John and Charles Wesley's Preface to *Hymns and Sacred Poems* of 1739 gave this explanation:

---

65. Hammond, *JW in America*, 74.
66. Butler, *Methodists and Papists*, 136; and Telford, 5:121–22.
67. Second Theological Memorandum, January 25, 1738, *Works*, 18:213.
68. Rivers, *Vanity Fair*, 172.
69. Butler, *Methodists and Papists*, 147.
70. Butler, *Methodists and Papists*, 147.
71. Butler, *Methodists and Papists*, 147; *Works* (Jackson), 10:403.
72. JW, *Christian Library*, 1:iii.
73. Lowery, *Salvaging*, 125.
74. Lowery, *Salvaging*, 125–26.

Some verse, it may be observed, in the following Collection, were wrote upon the scheme of the Mystic Divines. And these, it is owned, we had once in great veneration, as the best explainers of the gospel of Christ. But we are now convinced, that we therein greatly erred, not knowing the Scriptures, neither the power of God. And because this is an error which many serious minds are sooner or later exposed to, and which indeed most easily besets those who seek the Lord Jesus in sincerity, we believe ourselves indispensably obliged, in the presence of God, and angels, and men, to declare wherein we apprehend those writers not to teach "the truth as it is in Jesus."[75]

John English stated: "Wesley did not realize the extent of his indebtedness to the mystical tradition."[76] He rejected mysticism based upon "solitude, Pelagianism, sanctification before justification, and quietism that depreciates the means of grace, especially before Scripture, prayer, and the Sacraments."[77] However, English insisted that Wesley did not recognize a lot of what is called "mysticism" "because he operated with a limited concept of the term."[78]

Writing to his brother, Samuel, John Wesley mused in 1736: "I think the rock on which I had the nearest made shipwreck of the faith was in the writings of the mystics, under which term I comprehend all, and only those, who slight any of the means of grace."[79] Furthermore, he admonished: "These men [mystics] have renounced their reason and understanding; else they could not be guided by a divine light. They seek no clear or particular knowledge of anything, but only an obscure general knowledge which is far better. They know it is mercenary to look for a reward from God, and inconsistent with perfect love."[80]

Outler said that Wesley put de Renty, Sales, and Guyon in this group, because Wesley said "All other enemies of Christianity are triflers; the mystics are the most dangerous of all its enemies. They stab it in the vitals, and its most serious professors are most likely to fall by them. May I praise him who snatched me out of this fire likewise, by warning all

---

75. JW and CW, Preface to *Hymns and Sacred Poems* (1739), in *Works* (Jackson), 14:319.

76. English, "Francis Rous," 4.

77. Lowery, *Salvaging*, 126; and English, "Francis Rous," 33.

78. English, "Francis Rous," 33.

79. JW to Samuel Wesley Jr., November 3, 1736, *Works*, 25:487.

80. JW to Samuel Wesley Jr., November 3, 1736, *Works*, 25:488.

others that it is set on fire of hell."[81] Further, George Croft Cell stated that Wesley had four critiques of mysticism. First, it took away from an emphasis on Christian fellowship. Second, solitude can lead to retreat from the world, and third, it undervalues reason in religion. Finally, sometimes union with God is described in sexual terms.[82]

Madame Guyon and her disciple Fénelon were admired for their commitment to God, but Wesley disagreed with their view of revelation. He believed they relied too heavily on their own personal impulses. Guyon "subjugated Scripture to inward impressions." She read Scripture to teach, not to learn.[83] Guyon taught that when one "fully entered into oneself" that one would sense the presence of God. "Hence, being 'calmly united to God' in love gives one the devotion to contemplate 'every divine mystery.'"[84] Essentially, it was not quietistic mysticism that was attractive to Wesley, but the focus on loving God and others that emphasized the role of insight and responsibility without dismissing God's work in one's life.[85]

Positive Influences of Catholic Devotional Authors on Wesley's Life and Thought

Although Wesley disagreed with Catholic authors, he made many positive comments about them. *A Christian's Pattern* by á Kempis "was central to Wesley's own spiritual development, drawing him toward inward Christianity and outward holiness."[86] Á Kempis was the first on Wesley's list of books recommended for every house. Burton indicated Wesley meant every house, not just every literate house.[87] Not just Wesley who valued it, *A Christian's Pattern* "went through 188 editions in Latin and the vernacular languages in the sixteenth century and, 444 in the seventeenth century."[88]

81. *Works*, 18:213; Outler, *John Wesley*, 46n.
82. Lowery, *Salvaging*, 126; Cell, *Rediscovery of John Wesley*, 125–29.
83. Lowery, *Salvaging*, 144.
84. Lowery, *Salvaging*, 144. Chadwick, *Madame Jeanne Guyon*, 46.
85. Lowery, *Salvaging*, 147.
86. Burton, *Spiritual Literacy*, 249.
87. Burton, *Spiritual Literacy*, 251; and "Minutes of Several Conversations," *Works* (Jackson), 8:319.
88. Ward, *Protestant Evangelical Awakening*, 48.

Wesley revealed his appreciation for á Kempis in the preface to his abridgement: "The style of this treatise is the most plain, simple and un-adorned that can be conceived; yet such is the strength, spirit and weight of every sentence, that is scarce possible, without injury to the sense, to add or diminish anything."[89] Further, he commented: "And herein greatly resembles the holy scriptures, that, under the plainest words, there is a di-vine, hidden virtue, continually flowing into the soul of a pious and atten-tive reader, and by the blessing of God, transforming it into his image."[90] This demonstrates that he valued the work for its timeless message. He valued "plain words," and that it was like the Scriptures.

It is evident that à Kempis work influenced his view of holiness, for further in the preface he stated: "The scope of this treatise is, that perfection which every Christian is bound to aspire to." He underscored the belief in holy love: "Now altho' the whole essence of this consists in love, which unites the soul to God." This love implied humility, self-renunciation, unreserved resignation. This brought "a union of our will with the divine," it "makes the Christian one spirit with God; a great part of it describes these tempers, whereby he that loves God is made partaker of the divine nature."[91] Wesley admonished the reader to "expect no soft-ening here; no mincing of evangelical truths." He ended with a phrase he often used: "That since *but one thing is needful*, on that alone thou are to fix thy single eye, namely, to love the Lord thy God with all thy heart, and with all thy soul, and with all thy mind, and with all thy strength."[92]

Next to à Kempis, Wesley's next favorite Catholic author seemed to be de Renty. For instance, he commented when he ended the abridge-ment of de Renty's life:

> O that such a life should be related by such a historian! Who by inserting all, if not more than all the weak things that holy man ever said or did, by his commendation of almost every action or word which either deserved or needed it not, and by his injudi-cious manner of relating many others which were indeed highly commendable; has cast the shade of superstition and folly over one of the brightest patterns of heavenly wisdom.[93]

89. JW, *The Christian's Pattern*, lx.

90. JW, *The Christian's Pattern*, lx

91. JW, *The Christian's Pattern*, x.

92. JW, *The Christian's Pattern*, xxvi. Emphasis mine.

93. JW, *Journal*, January 6, 1738, *Works*, 18:208.

This extract is short, sixty-seven pages. It seems that de Renty also influenced Wesley's life at Oxford and Georgia. For in Oxford and Georgia he practiced self-denial, and in the story of de Renty's life, there is a chapter on self-denial and mortification. De Renty only ate one meal a day.[94] He was grieved that his friends were "feasters." He spent the night in a chair or in his coat and boots and visited the prisoners.[95] He was in possession of riches but disengaged from them. Like Wesley, de Renty wore plain clothes.[96] Further, Wesley said of de Renty: "He was dead to riches," and, "He was dead to his own will, which he had perfectly resigned in conformity to the will of God."[97]

In addition to de Renty's life, the *Life of Gregory Lopez* could have influenced Wesley's vegetarian diet in Georgia.[98] "Evidence from Wesley's reading on the Simmons suggests that he modelled his missionary vision to an extent after the ascetical Roman Catholic models of Francis Xavier (1506–1552) and Gregario López (1542–1596)."[99] Sleeping rough, on the floor, may have been influenced by López.[100]

How Wesley thought Christians should experience physical pain and suffering may have been influenced by de Renty, for Wesley wrote:

> An eminent instance of this kind of deliverance is that which occurs in the life of that excellent man, the Marquis de Renty. When he was in a violent fit of rheumatism, a friend asked him, "Sir, are you in much pain?" he answered: "My pains are extreme; but through the mercy of God I give myself up, not to them, but to him."[101]

Wesley's view of how people should approach the death of a loved one may have been formed by de Renty. De Renty's wife died and this was his remark:

> I cannot but say that this trial affects me in the most tender part. I am exquisitely sensible of my loss. I feel more than it is possible to express. And yet I am so satisfied that the will of God is

94. JW, *An Extract*, 14.

95. JW, *An Extract*, 15.

96. JW, *An Extract*, 17.

97. JW, *An Extract*, 18, 21.

98. Hammond, *JW in America*, 48–49.

99. Hammond, *JW in America*, 74.

100. Hammond, *JW in America*, 133.

101. JW, "On Temptation," *Works*, 3:66–67.

done, and not the will of a vile sinner, that were it not for giving offence to others I could dance and sing!"[102]

Wesley used this as an example that Christians could escape temptation.[103] Apparently the temptation was to show sadness.

Further, one of de Renty's children died in 1641 and he "spoke not one word, nor shewed the least sign of disturbance: his affection to the child yielding to his absolute conformity to the will of God."[104] This became Wesley's expectation for people who lost children to death. In 1791 he wrote to Adam Clarke who had just lost a daughter, "You startle me when you talk of grieving so much for the death of an infant. This was certainly a proof of inordinate affection; and if you love them all thus all your children will die. How did Mr. de Renty behave when he supposed his wife to be dying? This is the pattern for a Christian."[105]

De Renty learned to "let blood" and do "several parts of surgery." He knew how to compound medicines and consulted a physician in administering the compounds. The sick would seek him; he was seen surrounded by them. This may have influenced Wesley's interest in medicine, for one of Wesley's best sellers was *Primitive Physick*.[106] It went through twenty editions, somewhere around forty thousand copies before his death.[107] Wesley understood salvation in a holistic way. That is why he provided such books as *Primitive Physick*. Wesley encouraged his followers to believe God could heal physically and spiritually.

John Wesley's great-grandfather, Bartholomew Wesley, who was ejected with the Puritan ministers forced out of their positions during the Restoration of Charles II in 1662, gave medical advice as part of his ministry. After ejection, he supported himself as a physician.[108] Wesley articulated his views on helping others with health matters by saying:

> Will you condemn a man who, having some little skill in physic and a tender compassion for those who are sick or dying all around him, cures many of those, without a fee or reward, whom the doctor could not cure? . . . Will you object that he

102. JW, "On Temptation," *Works*, 3:166–67
103. JW, "On Temptation," *Works*, 3:166–67
104. JW, *De Renty*, 35.
105. JW to Adam Clarke, January 3, 1791, in Telford 8:253.
106. JW, *Primitive Physick*.
107. Donat and Maddox, "Introduction," *Works*, 32:20
108. Donat and Maddox, "Introduction," *Works*, 32:7.

is no physician, nor has any author to practise? I cannot come into your opinion. I think he is a physician who heals . . . And that every many has authority to save the life of a dying man. But if you only mean he has no authority to take fees, I contend not–for he takes none at all.[109]

Though Wesley appreciated physicians, and used them himself, he offered free medical advice until he died. He understood that most people could not afford to pay a physician, and there were not enough physicians to attend the population.[110]

Notwithstanding, partial precedents can be found for Societies in de Renty.[111] For de Renty went to St. Anthony's Gate and brought newly arrived people to his home where he served them food and instructed them in the "chief points of Christianity."[112] Bishop Lavington guessed that Wesley had left "unaltered the offensively Catholic parts" in the life of de Renty. But Wesley "replied that he had paired away the trash, but was forced to leave some bits of popery in, to show that de Renty really was a Catholic."[113]

In admiring Madame Guyon (1648–1717) for John Wesley said of her, "How few such instances do we find of exalted love to God, and our neighbor; of genuine humility; of invincible meekness and unbounded resignation."[114] What's more, Wesley wrote: "Such another life as that of the celebrated Madam Guion, I doubt whether the world ever saw. I am sure, I never did: I have seen many worse: and I have seen few better. But I never saw one either ancient or modern, which contained so wonderful a mixture."[115] Furthermore, he wrote: "So that upon the whole, I know not whether we may not search many centuries to find another woman who was such a pattern of true holiness."[116]

109. JW, *Letter to a Clergyman*, May 4, 1748, *Works*, 9:248–49.

110. Donat and Maddox, "Introduction," *Works*, 32:40.

111. Rack, *Reasonable Enthusiast*, 120.

112. JW, *De Renty*, 42.

113. Butler, *Methodists and Papists*, 139.

114. JW, *Madam Guion*, vii; and Rivers, *Vanity Fair*, 172; Madame Guyon, *Devotional Tracts Concerning the Presence of God, and Other Religious Subjects*. Heylin not identified as author or translator but Isabel Rivers states they are identified as Heylin's by John Byrom and Wesley identifies them as Heylin's in the 1746 *Minutes*, in *Works*, 10:180.

115. JW, *Madam Guion*, viii.

116. JW, *Madam Guion*, viii.

Wesley also admired Francis Xavier, whom he called a martyr. He said in 1772,

> I was never more struck than with a picture of a man lying upon straw with this inscription, 'The true effigy of Francis Xavier, the apostle to the Indies, forsaken of all men, and dying in a cottage.' Here was a martyrdom, I had almost said more glorious than that of St. Paul or St. Peter![117]

Conclusion

This chapter has attempted to demonstrate that Wesley used and recommended Catholic devotional resources. He often criticized Catholic works, but he also published many abridged versions. Even though he valued the Catholic mystics at the beginning of his ministry, he later disagreed with them, especially their Quietism. He valued Catholic writers because he was more concerned with their practical advice of piety than he was that they were Catholic.

The Catholic writer he recommended the most was Thomas á Kempis. He wished for every Methodist household to have a copy of his abridgement of *The Christian's Pattern*. Other writers including de Renty and de Sales, he abridged and published and recommended, but disagreed with on occasion. He drew on some of the Catholic sources for his views on holiness and sanctification. Wesley demonstrated his catholic spirit by using the devotional resources. However, he disagreed with many aspects of Catholic doctrine and made it quite clear.

117. JW to Hannah Ball, May 30, 1772, in Telford, 5:320.

8

Conclusion

THIS BOOK IS A historical investigation of John Wesley's relationship with Catholicism, examining the limits to which Wesley, as an evangelical Protestant, practiced his ideal of a catholic spirit. It has been a claim of this book that Wesley's sermon *Catholic Spirit* was not aimed at Catholics or Catholicism. It has been argued by scholars that he proposed principles of religious tolerance in the sermon. In contrast to the assertions of some scholars, this study has argued that Wesley did not expect these principles to bring about unity between Protestants and Catholics. Wesley remained wedded to the anti-Catholicism that was prevalent in eighteenth-century England.

Although it is tempting to designate *Catholic Spirit* and *Letter to a Roman Catholic* as an attempt to promote unity between Catholics and Protestants, this was not Wesley's original purpose. The desire among biographers for Wesley to be saintly has perhaps influenced some scholars to view these writings as ecumenically progressive.[1] By measuring *Catholic Spirit* and *Letter to a Roman Catholic* alongside Wesley's critical writings on Catholicism, Wesley's anti-Catholic proclivities have been revealed.

This book has attempted to provide a critical analysis of Wesley that is faithful to the primary sources both inside and outside of Methodism. The examination of Wesley and his views of Catholicism is timely because a thorough historical study of Wesley and Catholicism has not heretofore been attempted. Additionally, historical case studies in this

---

1. See Gunter, *Limits*, 9; and Wynkoop, "John Wesley," 5–14.

book have provided a fresh perspective concerning Wesley's interaction with Catholicism.

This book has followed up on Henry Rack's assertion that Wesley's relationship with Catholicism needs more study.[2] Wesley wrote far more about the "evils of popery" than he did about the possibility for Protestants and Catholics to peacefully coexist. From Wesley's first known writing concerning Catholicism, a letter to an unknown Catholic (1735), to his last known document about "popery," "Disavowal of Persecuting Papists" (1782), he took issue with the Catholic Church.[3] His main disagreements included the supremacy of the Pope, that Catholics were denied access to the Bible, that Catholics added to Scripture, and that they were denied liberty of conscience. Further, Wesley maintained that if granted political power, Catholics would physically persecute Protestants.

Wesley's *Letter to a Roman Catholic* is the exception and not the rule concerning his writings on Catholicism.[4] Explaining the inconsistencies between *Letter to a Roman Catholic* and the rest of Wesley's writings on Catholicism has been part of the task of this book. His pragmatism convinced him of the need to write a document that would hopefully create space for the Methodists to preach in Ireland, but Wesley never accepted that Catholicism was "true religion." Only Protestantism could qualify as "true religion," and the Church of England had the best form of that "true religion."

In the case of *Letter to a Roman Catholic*, Wesley was motivated by the need to convince Catholics to relax their concern enough to allow him and the preachers to proclaim the message of New Birth. That he wrote *A Short Method of Converting all the Roman Catholics of Ireland* (1752) only three years later is often ignored by those who claim *Letter to a Roman Catholic* was Wesley's plea for Methodists and Catholics to work together in unity.[5] *A Short Method* displays Wesley's true intentions in Ireland: preaching the New Birth in Christ and forming people into societies. He asked Catholics not to change their religion but to practice it. By this he meant for them to practice primitive Christianity; not Catholicism. According to Wesley, the Catholic Church as an institution did not meet the standards of the primitive church, for he believed that Constantine

2. Rack, *Reasonable Enthusiast*, 558.

3. *JWJ*, August 20, 1739, *Works*, 10:91–2; and *Works* (Jackson), 10:173–74.

4. JW, *Letter to a Roman Catholic*, *Works* (Jackson), 10:80–86.

5. For instance: Schwenk, *Catholic Spirit*, 3; Crutcher, *John Wesley*, 168–9; and Burrows, "Wesley the Catholic."

and medieval Catholicism had corrupted the church. Although Wesley stated that he thought the Church of England was closest to the primitive church, he never made it clear whether he intended Catholic converts to join the Established Church. In Ireland, when Catholics "renounced popery" in Methodist societies, it is unclear whether they were encouraged to communicate with the Church of Ireland.

Accused of Jacobitism while at Oxford, Wesley's family background, his comments about the Hanoverians, and the Methodists' austere lifestyles may have influenced his opponents to apply this reproach against Wesley himself. Additionally, his mother may have kept her Jacobite leanings all of her life. This book has demonstrated that despite the accusation, Wesley was not a Jacobite. However, the turmoil concerning Jacobitism may have been one of the many conflicts that influenced Wesley to write *Catholic Spirit*, and influenced his anti-Catholicism.

No sooner had the Crown defeated the Jacobites than Wesley answered a plea to come and preach in Dublin. After a productive two weeks with many added to the society, Charles Wesley arrived to find the Methodists under physical attack. For at least four years the societies in Dublin and Cork faced occasions of mob violence, to the point where George Whitefield engaged the law on behalf of the Methodists and through the Lent Assizes put an end to most of the violence in Cork.

Wesley criticized the Moravians for their "Jesuitical ways."[6] His opposition to the Moravians led to a lasting breach between the Methodists and Moravians, even after the Moravians tried to demonstrate a catholic spirit to Wesley. In this case, using "Jesuitical" as a slur against the Moravians was just one of the ways Wesley did not display a catholic spirit towards them, even after Charles Wesley and Count Zinzendorf tried to reason with him.

Over the course of Wesley's ministry, his opponents accused him of popery and Jesuitism. His Anglican antagonists, including George Lavington and William Warburton, challenged him for displaying enthusiasm which they believed led to "popery." They accused him of glorying in persecution and field preaching as Ignatius of Loyola had done. That Wesley proclaimed the importance of receiving assurance of salvation provoked episcopal criticism as Loyola had done the same (although in very different ways).

6. *JWJ*, November 28, 1750, *Works*, 20:371.

Calvinists reproached Wesley for Jesuitism because they believed the 1770 Conference minutes taught imparted righteousness. This led them to accuse Wesley of practicing trickery, magic, and tyranny. Wesley reprinted *Catholic Spirit* in 1770 during this conflict; and Richard Hill, a Calvinist Anglican, attacked the sermon *Catholic Spirit* directly. However, Wesley's response seemed only to magnify Hill's criticism of him. In this case, Wesley seems to have tried to practice a catholic spirit.

Allegations of magic, trickery, and tyranny commenced in Georgia when some colonists accused Wesley of damning Dissenters and displaying the characteristics of a Jesuit priest. "Popery" and Jesuitism, many believed, was a threat to Protestantism in Great Britain and the colonies. Wesley's insistence on strict practices of primitive Christianity caused some to proclaim that he was a Jesuit. That he allegedly claimed to be a Protestant yet practiced "papist" principles led some to label him "Jesuitical" as well.

Wesley's relationship with women led some to denounce him for Jesuitical ways as it was believed that Catholic priests, especially Jesuits, would take women captive by outsmarting and tricking them into confession, and that the priests would eventually seduce the women. Wesley's relationship with Sophia Hopkey and the allegations that he and Whitefield required women to confess to them in society meetings provoked these rumors. Susanna Wesley must be considered as an influence on Wesley believing that women could have their own spiritual lives apart from the men in authority over them.

After Wesley wrote *A Calm Address to Our American Colonies* (1775), Wesley was again accused of Jesuitism. Caleb Evans and William Moore criticized him for sophistry and deceit. These allegations emerged because Wesley had changed his mind towards the American cause after reading Samuel Johnson's *Taxation No Tyranny*. The opposition to Wesley alleged that he advocated passive obedience, which they believed might signify a hankering after Jacobitism and Catholicism.

The Catholic Relief Act of 1778 provided a challenge that the Methodists had not yet faced: being accused of anti-Catholicism. Wesley's *Popery Calmly Considered*, "Letter to the Printer of the *Public Advertiser*," and correspondence with Catholics and Anglicans concerning his response to the Act led many to blame him for influencing the Gordon Riots. That Wesley visited Gordon in prison probably increased the rumors against him. Even after being accused of encouraging the riots, Wesley refused to modify his anti-Catholic attitude, although he insisted that Catholics not be physically persecuted; he likely considered the penal laws a "gentle restraint."[7] Wesley did not consider the penal laws to be persecution. His writings in the years following the Catholic Relief Act of 1778 further demonstrate his anti-Catholicism.

Wesley likely believed that this "gentle restraint" was a type of toleration since Catholics were not physically persecuted. John Locke taught that those who did not tolerate did not deserve to be tolerated, but that a Catholic who held tolerant principles and denied allegiance to the Pope might be tolerated.[8] Wesley was influenced by Locke, but it seems that Wesley believed a Catholic was not likely to be tolerant.[9] Since he thought they could not be tolerant, Wesley insisted that Catholics did not deserve any more toleration than what he believed they had received already. He did not wish for the penal laws to be lifted or altered in any way. This would keep Great Britain safe from "popery."

Although he criticized the Catholic church, Wesley recommended and published Catholic devotional authors throughout his life. He recommended several authors including Thomas á Kempis, Madame Guyon, the Marquis de Renty, Francis Xavier, and Gregory Lopez. Even though he suggested many of his followers read these authors, he also criticized them. When he published their writings, he abridged them.

This book has agreed with W. Stephen Gunter's claim that sometimes Wesley was "blind to his own fault."[10] Gunter implies that a possible explanation for Wesley's "blindness" is that "the success of the revival would have been thwarted if Wesley had not so steadfastly pursued his goals."[11] Wesley measured the success of the revival by his statement on the purpose of Methodism: "to reform the nation, more particularly the church, and to spread Christian holiness over the land."[12] Wesley's work in Ireland, and everywhere else, was consistent with this aim. Connected to this, Wesley did not believe it impossible for a Catholic to experience holiness, but he thought it would be quite difficult since he believed they would not hear "true religion" preached. That he believed Catholics did not normally have access to Scripture provided certitude that Catholics

---

7. JW to the *Freeman's Journal*, March 31, 1780, *Works* (Jackson), 10:173.

8. Locke, *Letter concerning Toleration*, 45, 47, 146, 194.

9. JW, "Letter to the Printer of the *Public Advertiser*," *Works* (Jackson), 10:161.

10. Gunter, *Limits*, 275.

11. Gunter, *Limits*, 275.

12. *The Large Minutes A and B*, *Works*, 10:845.

would rarely experience the New Birth. As he did to all people in Britain and Ireland, Wesley preached evangelical conversion to Catholics.

In common with one strand of post-Reformation perceptions of Catholicism, Wesley allowed his fears of possible papal persecution to dominate his view of Catholics and Catholicism throughout his life. His trepidation kept him from practicing a catholic spirit with Catholics. His empathy was lacking despite the Methodists having experienced persecution for years. Though Catholics tried to reason with him, his ears remained closed to their concerns.

Wesley continuously argued that Catholicism was theologically and politically dangerous. This anti-Catholicism commonly persisted in Methodism to the time of Vatican II. Perhaps if Wesley had practiced the principles he set forth in *Catholic Spirit*, and had focused on the similarities he laid out in *Letter to a Roman Catholic*, his nineteenth-century heirs may have found it more difficult to justify Methodist anti-Catholicism, and his twentieth and twenty-first century heirs could have hailed him as an ecumenical pioneer with greater accuracy.

Appendix 1

Wesley's Use of the Phrase *Catholic Spirit,* Chronologically, in Order of Publication

1750

Catholic Spirit.
Works, 2:81–95.

1751

A Second Letter to the Author of The Enthusiasm of Methodists and Papists, Compar'd.
[Quoting Lavington] "We may see in Mr Wesley's writings that he was once a *strict churchman,* but gradually put on a more catholic spirit, tending at length to Roman Catholic . . . He rejects any design to convert others *from any communion*; and *consequently, not from popery.*"
Works, 11:422–23.

1753

The Complete English Dictionary, Explaining Most of Those Hard Words, Which Are Found in the Best English Writers. By a Lover of Good English and Common Sense.
Definition: "Catholic Spirit: universal love."

1753

Hymns and Spiritual Songs, Intended for the Use of Christians of All Denominations Published by John and Charles Wesley, 1753.
Preface
"The ease and happiness that attend, the unspeakable advantages that flow from a truly catholic spirit, a spirit of universal love (which is the very reverse of bigotry) one would imagine one might recommend this amiable temper to every person of cool reflection."
Works, 7:736.

July 3, 1756

JW to James Clark
"Catholic love is [a] catholic spirit."
Works, 27:39.

June 18, 1757

JW to Dorothy Furly
"You may profitably converse with even those honourable Christians if you watch and pray that they do not infect you 1) with mystical notions, which stand in full opposition to plain old Bible divinity, or 2) with their odd, senseless jargon of a *Catholic Spirit,* whereby they have themselves suffered a great loss."
Works, 27:88.

November 22, 1769

JW to Miss Bishop
"It is exceedingly strange. I should really wonder (if I could wonder at any weakness of human nature) that so good a woman as —, and one who particularly piques herself on her catholic spirit, should be guilty of such narrowness of spirit."
Telford, 5:162.

November 18, 1770

"On the Death of George Whitefield."

"He longed to see all who had 'tasted of the good word' of a truly catholic spirit–a word little understood, and still less experienced by many who have it frequently in their mouth. Who is he that answers this character? Who is a man of 'catholic spirit?'"

"He is a man of a truly catholic spirit who bears all these continuously upon his heart; who having an unspeakable tenderness for their persons, and an earnest desire of their welfare, does not cease to commend them to God in prayer, as well as to plead their cause before men; who speaks comfortably to them, and labours by all his words to strengthen their hands in God."

Works, 2:344.

September 9, 1772

Some Remarks on Mr. Hill's Review of all the Doctrines.
    [Hill criticized Wesley's sermon, *Catholic Spirit*, and Wesley replied.]
Works (Jackson), 10:374–414.

February 13, 1782

Of Attending the Church
    "Lastly. Whenever this happens, is it through prejudice, or rational piety? Is it through bigotry, or a catholic spirit?"
Works (Jackson), 13:247.

July 13, 1788

Thoughts upon a Late Phenomenon
    "Is there any other society in Great Britain or Ireland that is so remote from bigotry? That is so truly of a Catholic spirit? So ready to admit all serious persons without disturbance? Where then is there such a society in Europe? In the habitable world? I know none. Let any man show it me that can. Till then let no one talk of the bigotry of the Methodists."
Works, 9:537.

Appendix 2

The Gordon Riots and a *Catholic Spirit*

Chronology of Primary Sources

This appendix provides a chronology of the publication of the primary sources used in chapter of six of this book.

January 13, 1774, The Quebec Act of 1774 (14 Geo. III c. 83).

June 14, 1775, John Wesley to the Earl of Dartmouth, Telford, 7:156.

May 25, 1778, The Catholic Relief Act of 1778 (18 Geo. III, c. 60) passed in House of Commons May 18, 1778, became law May 25, 1778.

September 5–7, 1778, Charles Wesley to Sarah Wesley, MARC DDcw 7/36.

1779, Protestant Association, *An Appeal by the Protestant Association to the People of Great Britain Concerning the Probable Tendency of the Late Act of Parliament in Favour of the Papists.* London: Pasham, 1779.

1779, John Wesley, *Popery Calmly Considered*. London: Hawes, 1779; Dublin: Whitestone, 1770; Edinburgh, 1779; 2nd ed., London: Hawes, 1779; 3rd ed., London: Hawes, 1779; London: Cordeux, 1812. Broadsheets, six times as late as 1800.

August 1779, Methodist Conference, *Works*, 10:492.

January 21, 1780, John Wesley to the Printer of the *Public Advertiser*, Broadsheet (1780), MARC MAW G.339 [a]; *AM* 4 (1781) 23–42; *Public Advertiser* (February 5), 2, says "Mr Wesley's letter, desired and promised for this day's paper, being printed in another morning paper, is now omitted."

January 21, 1780, "A Letter from John Wesley," *Gospel Magazine* 7 (1780) 86–89.

February 3–5, 1780, reprint of "John Wesley's Letter to the Printer of the *Public Advertiser*," *London Evening Post* 9022.

February 5, 1780, reprint of "John Wesley's Letter to the Printer of the *Public Advertiser*," *Morning Chronicle and London Advertiser* 3344.

February 5–8, 1780, reprint of "John Wesley's Letter to the Printer of the *Public Advertiser*," *London Chronicle* 3616.

February 5–8, 1780, reprint of "John Wesley's Letter to the Printer of the *Public Advertiser*," *Whitehall Evening Post* 5279.

February 5–8, 1780, reprint of "John Wesley's Letter to the Printer of the *Public Advertiser*," *General Evening Post*.

February 10, 1780, reprint of "John Wesley's *Letter to the Printer of the Public Advertiser*," *Bristol Gazette*.

February [10?], 1780, "Comments on a Letter from John Wesley," *Gospel Magazine* 7 (1780) 80.

February 11, 1780, John Wesley to Joseph Berrington, W. L. Doughty, "John Wesley's Letters to Mr. Berrington, 1780," *PWHS* 26 (1947) 41.

February 11, 1780, John Wesley to Joseph Berrington, *PWHS* 26 (1947) 41.

February 12, 1780, reprint of "John Wesley's Letter to the Printer of the *Public Advertiser*," Felix Farley's *Bristol Journal.*

February [12-15?], 1780, reprint of "John Wesley's Letter to the Printer of the *Public Advertiser*," *Scots Magazine,* 60–61.

February 15, 1780, "Report of Protestant Association's approval of John Wesley's Letter," *Gazetteer and New Daily Advertiser* 15915.

February 19–22, 1780, "Protestant Association," *London Evening Post* 9029.

February 19–22, 1780, "Protestant Association," *St. James's Chronicle or the British Evening Post* (London) 2956.

February 24, 1780, JW to Joseph Berington, *PWHS* 26 (1947) 41–42.

February 28, 1780, Arthur O'Leary, *Remarks on the Foregoing Letter and Defence Addressed to the Conductors of the Free Press,* letters 1 and 2.

March 23, 1780, John Wesley to the Editors of *Freeman's Journal*, in "On Popery," *AM* 4 (1781) 296–300.

March 31, 1780, John Wesley to the Editors of *Freeman's Journal*, [*Freeman's Journal* does not appear to have printed this according to Wesley *Works* project]; printed in *Walker's Hibernation Magazine* (1780) 428–31; and as "On Popery II," *AM* 4 (1781) 353–60.

March 31, 1780, Joseph Berington [also spelled Berrington] to Papist Compar'd. London: W. Strahan, 1749. John Whitehead, *The Life of the Rev. John Wesley, M.A.* 2 vols. London: Couchman, 1796, 2:504.

[March 1780] Arthur O'Leary, *Rejoinder to Mr. Wesley's Reply*, [extract of Locke's letter on Toleration sent to O'Leary with John Wesley's reply].

[March? 1780], Protestant Association, *An Appeal from the Protestant Association to the People of Great Britain, Concerning the Probable Tendency of the Late Act of Parliament in Favour of the Papists.* London, 1780.

April 11-13, 1780, "Parliament," *London Chronicle* 3644.

April 11-13, 1780, "Parliament," *St. James's Chronicle or the British Evening Post* 2978.

April 12, 1780, "Parliament," *Morning Chronicle and London Advertiser* 3401.

April 17, 1780, "Parliament," *Northampton Mercury* 6, 2.

May 27–30, 1780, "Protestant Association" [advertisement], *London Evening Post* 9701.

May 29, 1780, "Meeting of the Protestant Association," *Public Advertiser* 14239.

May 29, 1780, John Wesley to Thomas Rankin, MARC MA.JW.4.49.

May 29, 1780, John Wesley to Lancelot Harrison, 29 May 1780, R. Ernest Ker, "Two Unpublished Wesley Letters," *PWHS* 32 (1959) 46.

July 1–4, 1780, extract of [Thomas Lewis O'Beirne], *Considerations on the Late Disturbances by a Consistent Whig* (1780), printed in *General Evening Post* 7230.

June 2, 1780, "Protestant Association Petition," TNA TS 11/388/1212.

June 2–3, 1780, *London Evening Post* 9073.

June 6, 1780, "By the King, A Proclamation," *London Gazette* 12089.

June 7, 1780, George III, *By the King: A Proclamation*. London: Eyre and Strahan, 1780.

June 8, 1780, Charles Wesley to John Wesley, Telford, 7:21.

June 8, 1780, Charles Wesley to Sarah Wesley, MARC DDcw 1/71.

June 8, 1780, John Wesley to Charles Wesley, MARC DDWes 3/51.

June 12, 1780, Charles Wesley to Sarah Wesley [his daughter], MARC DDcw 7/42.

June 24, 1780, Charles Wesley to Sarah Wesley [his wife], MARC DDcw 7/68.

June 24, 1780, [Thomas Lewis O'Beirne], *Considerations on the Late Disturbances, by a Consistent Whig*, 2nd ed. London: Almon, 1780, extract printed in *London Courant and Westminster Chronicle* (June 24, 1780) and in *General Evening Post* 7230 (July 1–4, 1780).

June 1780, "The Monthly Chronologer," *The London Magazine: Or Gentleman's Monthly Intelligencer* 49, 269–84.

July 10, 1780, "Kalender of Prisoners to be Tried," TNA TS KB 33/81/4.

July 1780, "Trial [Gordon's] Notes," TNA KB 33/24/55.

[July 1780], Plea of George Gordon, TNA KB 33.

[July 1780], Joseph Berington, *The State and Behaviour of English Catholics, from the Reformation to the Year 1780, with a View of Their Present Number, Wealth, Character, &c.* London: Faulder, 1780.

July 13, 1780, John Wesley to John Whittingham, [broadsheet] MARC MAM, JW 5.90 [a].

August 5, 1780, John Whittingham to John Wesley, *Morning Chronicle and London Advertiser* 3500.

August 1780, "Particular Detail of the Late Riotous Tumults," *Gentleman's Magazine* 50, 369.

October 25, 1780, John Wesley to James Rivington, Publisher, reprinted *Royal Gazette* [New York] (February 24, 1781), 3.

November 13, 1780, "Erskine Assigned to Lord Gordon," TNA KB 33.

December 6, 1780, Arthur O'Leary, *Mr. O'Leary's Remarks on John Wesley's Letters in Defence of the Protestant Associations in England to Which Are Prefixed Mr. Wesley's Letters.* Dublin: McDonnel 1780.

December 15, 1780, John Wesley to David Murray, Seventh Viscount Stormont, Secretary of State, Frank Baker, "John Wesley and Lord George Gordon," *PWHS* 26 (1947) 45.

December 21–23, 1780, "John Wesley Granted Permission to Visit Lord Gordon," *General Evening Post* 7305.

December 21–23, 1780, "John Wesley Granted Permission to Visit Lord Gordon," *London Evening Post* 9162.

December 23, 1780, "John Wesley Granted Permission to Visit Lord Gordon," *Public Advertiser* 14417.

December 25, 1780, "John Wesley Granted Permission to Visit Lord Gordon," *Gazeteer and Daily Advertiser* 16196.

December 29, 1780, "Lord Gordon's Indictment," TNA KB/33.

December 29, 1780, John Wesley, *Journal* entry on Gordon's indictment, *Works*, 23:190.

December 29, 1780, "On Popery," Two Letters to the Editors of the *Freeman's Journal*, republished *AM* 4 (1781) 295.

1780, Thomas Holcroft, *Plain and Succinct Narrative of the Late Riots and Disturbances in the Cities of London and Westminster, and Borough of Southwark.* London, 1780.

1780, [David Williams], *A Plan of Association on Constitutional Principles by Which the Outrage of Mobs, and the Necessity of a Military Government Will Be Prevented.* London: Kearsley, 1780.

1780, [Anonymous], *Scotland's Opposition to the Popish Bill: A Collection of All the Declarations and Resolutions . . . for Preventing the Growth of Popery,* 3rd ed. Edinburgh: Paterson, 1780.

1780, Charles Wesley, "The Protestant Association in the Midst of the Tumults" [reprinted in JW and CW, *The Poetical Works of John and Charles Wesley: Reprinted from the Originals, with the Last Corrections by the Authors; Together with the Poems of Charles Wesley Not Before Published,* edited by G. Osborn, 13 vols. London: Wesleyan-Methodist Conference, 1870–1872, 8:440–78].

February 5, 1781, "The King against Lord George Gordon, form of trial," TNA KB 33/27/50.

February 1781, Court of King's Bench, *The Trial of George Gordon, Esquire, Commonly Called Lord George Gordon, for High Treason, at the Bar of the King's Bench, on Monday February 5th, 1781, Taken in Shorthand by Joseph Gurney,* 3rd ed. London: Kearsley, 1781.

February 1781, *The Proceedings at Large on the Trial of George Gordon, Esquire, Commonly Called Lord George Gordon, for High Treason, in the Court of the King's Bench . . .* shorthand writing of William Blanchard. London, [1781].

February 24, 1780, JW to Joseph Berington, *PWHS* 26 (1947) 42.

April 1781, Reprint of "John Wesley to the Printer of the *Public Advertiser*," *AM* 4 (1781) 239–42.

June 3, 1781, JW to Brian Bury Collins, MARC MAW.JW.2.55.

June 1781, Reprint of "John Wesley to Editors of *Freeman's Journal*" as "On Popery I," *AM* 4 (1781) 295–300.

1781, Arthur O'Leary, *Mr. O'Leary's Remarks on the Rev. John Wesley's Letters in Defence of the Protestant Association to Which Are Prefixed Mr. Wesley's Letters.* Dublin: McDonnell, 1781; 2nd ed. Dublin: Chambers, 1781.

1781, Arthur O'Leary, *Miscellaneous Tracts: By the Rev. Arthur O'Leary Containing A Defence of the Divinity of Christ . . . Loyalty Asserted . . . An Address to the Common People of Ireland . . . Remarks on a Letter Written by Mr. Wesley, and a Defence of the Protestant Association . . . Rejoinder to Mr. Wesley's Reply to the Above Remarks. Essay on Toleration.* Dublin: McDonnel, 1781.

January 22, 1782, *Six Miscellaneous Tracts by the Rev. Arthur O'Leary . . . in Which Are Introduced Mr. Wesley's Letter, and a Defence of the Protestant Association.* London: Keating, 1782.

March 18, 1782, John Wesley, "Disavowal of Persecuting Papists," *AM* 5 (1782) 197–99.

1782, Arthur O'Leary, *Mr. O'Leary's Remarks on the Rev. John Wesley's Letters in Defence of the Protestant Association to Which Are Prefixed Mr. Wesley's Letters*, 3rd ed. enlarged and corrected. London: Revell, 1782.

May 17, 1787, John Wesley meets Arthur O'Leary, *JWJ, Works*, 24:25.

September 22, 1787, Lord Mansfield to Charles Wesley, MARC DD/ Wes 1/98.

March 1791, The Catholic Relief Act of 1791 (31 Geo. III, c. 32).

June 23, 1791, Horace Walpole to Mary Berry, Horace Walpole, *Horace Walpole's Correspondence*, edited by W. S. Lewis. 48 vols. New Haven: Yale University Press, 1937–83, 11:296–97.

1793, James Barnard, *The Life of the Venerable and Right Reverend Richard Challoner, D. D. Bishop of Debra*. Dublin: Fitzpatrick, 1793.

1795, Robert Watson, *The Life of Lord George Gordon: With a Philosophical Review of his Conduct*. London: Symonds and Eaton, 1795.

1797, Arthur O'Leary, *Mr. O'Leary's Remarks on the Rev. John Wesley's Letters in Defence of the Protestant Association to Which Are Prefixed Mr. Wesley's Letters*, 3rd ed. Dublin: McDonnell, 1797.

1800, John Milner, *Letters to a Prebentary: Being an Answer to Reflections on Popery, by the Rev. J. Sturges*. Winchester: Robbins, 1800.

1803, Peard Dickinson, *Memoirs of the Life of Peard Dickinson . . .* revised by Joseph Benson. London: The Conference-Office at Finsbury Square, 1803, 64–65.

1821, Arthur O'Leary, *Mr. O'Leary's Remarks on the Rev. John Wesley's Letters in Defence of the Protestant Association to Which Are Prefixed Mr. Wesley's Letters*, 3rd ed. New York: Walker, 1821.

March 23, 1829, The Catholic Relief Act of 1829 (10 George IV, c. 7).

1832, Arthur O'Leary, *Essays and Tracts of Arthur O'Leary to Which Is Introduced His Correspondence with John Wesley.* Lewistown: Bell & Sons, 1832.

August 15, 1839, Daniel O'Connell to the Wesleyan Methodists of Manchester, *Letters of Daniel O'Connell, Esquire, to the Ministers and Office-Bearers of the Wesleyan-Methodist Societies in Manchester.* Langston, Canada: MacDonnell, 1839–42.

1840, George Cubitt, *Strictures on Mr. O'Connell's Letter to the Wesleyan Methodists.* London: Mason, 1840.

1841, Samuel Romilly, *Memoirs of the Life of Samuel Romilly: Written by Himself with a Selection of His Correspondence Edited by His Sons,* 3rd ed. 2 vols. London: Murray, 1841.

Bibliography

Manuscripts

British Museum

Etching of the Gordon Riots (June 1780)
D.P.D., 5.685, at http://www.britishmuseum.org/collectionimages/
AN00074/AN00074445_001_l.jpg.

Methodist Archives and Research Centre, John Rylands Library,
Manchester

Charles Wesley Papers
Correspondence of Charles Wesley
DDCW/1-2, 7
Notebooks and Manuscript Items
DDCW/8–10, 8–13

Early Preachers Collection
DDPr 1/93
DDSe 45

Letters to John Wesley Box
MAW.JW.2.55
MAW.JW.5.90

Wesley Family Papers
Letters of Samuel Wesley
DDWF/1
Wesley Family Letters
DDWES/1, 3, 38

The National Archives of the United Kingdom, London

"Erskine Assigned to Lord Gordon," TNA KB 33.

"Kalender of Prisoners to be Tried," TNA TS KB 33/81/4.

"The King against Lord George Gordon, Form of Trial," TNA KB 33/27/50.

Protestant Association Petition, June 2, 1780, TNA TS 11/388/1212.

Printed Primary Sources

A. B. *Ward's Downfall: Or, the Plot Detected.* A poem. London, 1734.

Annesley, Samuel. *How We May Be Universally and Exactly Conscientious: An Extract from a Sermon Preached at Cripplegate.* London, 1767.

The Adventures of a Jesuit Interspersed with Several Remarkable Characters and Scenes in Real Life. 2 vols. London: Bigg, 1771.

Ballantyne, George. *A Vindication of the Hereditary Right of His Present Majesty, King George II to the Crown of Great Britain, &c. Most Humbly Inscrib'd to His Royal Highness Frederick Augustus, Prince of Wales, &c. By George Ballantyne, Esq.; Being a Full Answer to All the Arguments of the Nonjurors, and Others Disaffected to the Present Happy Establishment, in Their Own Way, and upon Their Own Principles.* London, 1743.

Barnard, James. *The Life and Times of Richard Challoner, D.D., Bishop of Debra Collected from his Writings from Authentick Records, and from Near Twenty Years of Personal Acquaintance with Him.* London: Coghlan, 1784.

Baxter, Richard. *The Autobiography of Richard Baxter; Being the* Reliquiae Baxterianae *Abridged from the Folio.* Edited by J. M. Lloyd Thomas. London: Dent, 1974.

———. *Gildus Silvianius: The Reformed Pastor; Showing the Nature of Pastoral Work; especially in Private Instruction and Catechizing; with an Open Confession to Our Open Sins Prepared for a Day of Humiliation Kept at Worcester 4 December 1655.* London: White, 1657.

———. *Of Catholick Unity, or the Only Way to Bring Us All to Be of One Religion.* London: R. W., 1660.

————. *The Practical Works of Richard Baxter.* Edited by William Orme. 23 vols. London: Duncan, 1830.

————. *The Reformed Pastor.* Abridged by Samuel Palmer. London: Buckland, 1766.

Beckerlegge, Oliver A. *John Wesley's Writings on Roman Catholicism.* London: Protestant Truth Society, 1993.

————, ed. *The Lavington Correspondence: Being Letters to the Author of* The Enthusiasm of Methodists and Papists Compar'd. North Lodge: Wesley Historical Society, 1980.

————. "A Letter of George Whitefield," *PWHS* 33 (1962) 109–10.

Bennis, Elizabeth. *Christian Correspondence: Being a Collection of Letters, Written by the Late Rev. John Wesley and Several Methodist Preachers in Connexion with Him, to the Late Mrs. Eliza Bennis, with Her Answers: Chiefly Explaining and Enforcing the Doctrine of Sanctification.* Philadelphia: Graves, 1809.

————. *The Journal of Elizabeth Bennis.* Edited by Rosemary Raughter. Dublin: Columba, 2007.

Berington, Joseph. *The State and Behaviour of English Catholics, from the Reformation to the Year 1780, with a View of Their Present Number, Wealth, Character, &c.* London: Faulder, 1780.

Berkeley, George. *Passive Obedience or the Christian Doctrine of Not Resisting the Supreme Power, Proved and Vindicated Upon the Principles of Law of Nature, in a Discourse Deliver'd at the College-Chapel.* Dublin: Dickson, 1712.

————. *A Word to the Wise: or an Exhortation to the Roman Catholic Clergy of Ireland by a Member of the Established Church.* n. p., 1749.

Bindon, David. *An Abstract of the Number of Protestant and Popish Families in the Several Counties and Provinces of Ireland, Taken from the Returns Made by the Hearthmoney Collectors, to the Hearthmoney Office in Dublin, in the Years 1732 and 1733. Those Being Reckon'd Protestant and Popish Families, Where the Heads of Families are Either Protestants or Papists. With Observations.* Dublin: Rhames, 1736.

The Book of Common Prayer and Administration of the Sacraments, and other Rites and Ceremonies of the Church according to the Use of the Church of England Together with the Psalter or Psalms of David Pointed as They are to be Sung or Said in Churches. Cambridge: Hayes, [1662] 1701.

Brown, Peter. *The Procedure, Extent, and Limits of Human Understanding.* 3rd ed. London: Innys and Manby, 1737.

Bugg, Francis. *The Quakers Infallibility Shaken All to Pieces, or the Sinful Pretence to a Sinless Perfection.* London, 1711.

Bull, Patrick. *A Wolf in Sheep's Cloathing, or an Old Jesuit Unmasked, Containing an Account of the Wonderful Apparition of Father Petre's Ghost in the Form of the Rev. John Wesley with Some Conjectures Concerning the Secret Causes that Moved Him to Appear at this Very Critical Juncture.* Dublin, 1775.

Byrom, John. *The Private Journal and Literary Remains of John Byrom.* Edited by Richard Parkinson. Vol. 2, part 2. Manchester: Chetham Society, 1854.

Calvin, John. *Commentary on a Harmony of the Evangelists, Matthew, Mark, and Luke.* Translated by William Pringle. 2 vols. Edinburgh: Calvin Translation Society, 1845.

Cave, William. *Primitive Christianity, or the Religion of the Antient Christians, in the First Ages of the Gospel.* 7th ed. London: Midwinter and Cowse, 1714.

Challoner, Richard. *The Catholick Christian Instructed in the Sacraments, Sacrifice, Ceremonies, and Observances of the Church by Way of Question and Answer.* London, 1737.

———. *A Caveat Against the Methodists: Shewing How Unsafe It Is for Any Christian to Join Himself to their Society, or Adhere to Their Teachers.* London: Cooper, 1760.

———. *The Grounds of the Old Religion: Or Some General Arguments. In Favour of the Catholic, Apostolick, Roman Communion, Collected from Both Ancient and Modern Controvertists, and Modestly Proposed to the Consideration of His Countrymen.* Augusta, 1742.

The Character of a Jesuit. London: Newton, 1681.

The Character of the Late Dr. Samuel Annesley: By Way of Elegy: with a Preface Written by One of His Hearers. London: Whitlock, 1697.

[Cobbe, Charles]. *A Charge Given by the Vicar-General of Dublin, on the Triennial Visitation of that Province: In the Year 1760. Published at the Request of the Clergy.* Dublin: Faulkner, 1760.

"A Comment or Paraphrase on the Extract of the Minutes of the Rev. Mr. Wesley &c." *The Gospel-Magazine* 66 (June 1771) 260–76.

A Compleat Account of the Conduct of the Eminent Enthusiast Mr. Whitefield. London: Corbett, 1739.

[Court of the King's Bench]. *The Proceedings at Large on the Trial of George Gordon, Esquire, Commonly Called Lord George Gordon, for High Treason, in the Court of the King's Bench, Westminster: Before the Right Hon. William, Earl of Mansfield, Lord Chief Justice, Edward Willes, Esq.; Sir William Henry Ashurts, Knt. Sir Francis Buller, Knt. on Monday and Tuesday, February the 5th and 6th, 1781. Carefully Compiled from the Short-hand Writing of William Blanchard, and Revised by the Several Counsels Concerned.* London, [1781].

———. *The Trial of George Gordon, Esquire, Commonly Called Lord George Gordon, for High Treason, at the Bar of the King's Bench, on Monday February 5th, 1781, Taken in Shorthand by Joseph Gurney.* 3rd ed. London: Kearsley, 1781.

"Council of Constance–1414–1418." In *Decrees of the Ecumenical Councils*, edited by Norman P. Tanner, SJ. 2 vols. London: Sheed & Ward, 1990.

de Sales, François. *Introduction à la vie Dévote, par François de Sales, Evesque & Prelat de Geneve.* Avignon: Lyon, 1619.

Denzinger, H., and C. Bannwart, eds. *Enchiridion Symbolorum, Definitionum et Declarationum.* Frieburg-im-Breisgau: Herder, 1922.

Dickinson, Peard. *Memoirs of the Life of the Rev. Peard Dickinson. In Which the Dispensations of Providence and Grace, towards Individuals, Are Exemplified, in Some Remarkable Instances Written by Himself and Revised and Corrected by Joseph Benson.* London: Conference Office, 1803.

Doughty, W. L. "John Wesley's Letters to Mr. Berington, 1780." *PWHS* 26 (1947) 38–45.

Evans, Caleb. *A Letter to the Rev. Mr. John Wesley, Occasioned by His Calm Address to the American Colonies.* New ed. London: Dilly, 1775.

A Faithful Warning to the Followers of the Rev. Mr. John Wesley Shewing the Falsehood, Calumny, and Art, Made Use of in That Gentleman's Societies, to Deceive the Ignorance and Unwary in the Things of God. London: Buckland & others, 1774.

The Fanatic Saints, or Bedlamites Inspired: A Satire. London: Bew, 1778.

Fielding, Henry. *The Debauchees: Or the Jesuit Caught. A Comedy.* London: Watts, 1746.

Fletcher, John. *American Patriotism Further Confronted with Reason, Scripture: Being Observations on the Dangerous Politics Taught by the Rev. Mr. Evans and the Rev. Dr. Price with a Scriptural Plea for the Revolted Colonies.* Shrewsbury: Edpowes, 1776.

———. *Checks to Antinomianism.* 2 vols. London: Mason, 1829.

———. *A Vindication of the Rev. Mr. Wesley's 'Calm Address to our American Colonies' in Some Letters to Caleb Evans.* Dublin: Whitestone, 1776.

Fleury, Claude. *The Manners of the Antient Christians.* Edited by John Wesley. 5th ed. London: Paramore, 1791.

"Foreign Intelligence." *Morning Post* and *Daily Advertiser*, May 8, 1775.

Foxe, John. *Actes and Monuments of these Latter and Perillous Days, Touching Matters of the Church* London: Day, 1563.

———. *The Book of Martyrs: Containing an Account of the Sufferings and Death of the Protestants in the Reign of Queen Mary the First Illustrated . . . Revised and Corrected by an Impartial Hand.* London: Hart and Lewis, 1732.

———. *The Book of Martyrs or the History of the Church from the Beginning of Christianity to the Conclusion of the Reign of Queen Mary.* 2 vols. London: Lewis, 1747–48; London: Fuller, 1760–61.

———. *The Book of Martyrs.* Revised by the Revd Mr. [Martin] Madan. London, 1776; London, 1784.

———. *Papas Confutatas or The Pope Confuted: The Holy and Apostolique Church Confuting the Pope. The First Action.* Translated by James Bell. London: Dawson, 1580.

———. *A Select History of the Lives and Sufferings of the Principal English Protestant Martyrs: Chiefly of Those Executed in the Bloody Reign of Queen Mary Carefully Extracted from Fox and Other Writers: Being Designed as Cheap and Useful Book for Protestant Families of All Denominations.* London: Gardner, 1746.

———. *The Unabridged Acts and Monuments Online or TAMO (1576 edition).* Sheffield: HRI Online, 2011. http//www.johnfoxe.org.

Frey, Andre. *A True and Authentic Account of Andrew Frey. Containing the Occasion of His Coming among the Herrnhuters or Moravians, His Observations on Their Conference, Casting Lots, Marriages, Festivals, Merriments, Celibrations of Birth-Days, Impious Doctrines, and Fanatical Practices Abuse of Charitable Contributions and Linnen Images, Ostentatious Profuseness, and Rumour Against Any Who in the Least Differ from Them; and the Reasons for Which He Left Them; Together with the Motive for Publishing This Account.* Translated from the German. London: Robinson, 1753.

George III. *By the King: A Proclamation. Gentlemen's Magazine* (1785).

Gibson, Edmund. *Observations upon the Conduct and Behaviour of a Certain Sect, Usually Distinguished by the Name of Methodists. Gospel Magazine* (1771; 1780).

Gordon, George. "Protestant Association." *London Evening Post* 9071, May 27–30, 1780.

Hampson, John. *Memoirs of the Late Rev. John Wesley, A.M. with a Review of His Life and Writings, and a History of Methodism, from Its Commencement in 1729 to the Present Time.* 3 vols. London: Sunderland, 1791.

Henry VIII. *Assertio Septem Sacramentorium or The Defence of the Seven Sacraments, Against Martin Luther.* Dublin: Griffin, 1800.

Hervey, James. *Eleven Letters from the Late Rev. Mr. James Hervey to the Rev. Mr. John Wesley; Containing an Answer to that Gentleman's Remarks on Theron and Aspasio. Published from the Author's Manuscript, Left in Possession of His Brother W. Hervey. With a Preface, Shewing the Reason of Their Being Now Printed.* London: Rivington, 1765.

———. *Theron and Aspasio: Or a Series of Dialogues and Letters on the Most Important and Interesting Subjects.* 3 vols. London: Rivington, 1755.

Hickes, George. *A Discourse to Prove that the Strongest Temptations are Conquerable by Christians or A Sober Defence of Nature and Grace, Against the Cavils, and Excuses of Loose Inconsiderate Men: In a Sermon Preach'd Before the Right Honourable the Lord Mayor of London, and Court of Aldermen, the 14th of January 1676/7.* 3rd ed. London: Churchill, 1713.

Higden, William. *A View of the English Constitution with Respect to the Sovereign Authority of the Prince, and Allegiance of the Subject in Vindication of the Lawfulness of Taking Oaths to Her Majesty to Which is Added a Defence by Way of Reply of Answers That Have Been Made to It.* London: Keble, 1710.

Hill, Richard. *Review of all the Doctrines Taught by the Rev. Mr. John Wesley: Containing a Full and Particular Answer to a Book Entitled, "A Second Check to Antinomianism." In Six Letters to the Author of That Book.* London: Dilly, 1772.

[Hill, Rowland]. *Friendly Remarks Occasioned by the Spirit and Doctrines Contained in the Rev. Mr Fletcher's Vindication, and More Particularly in His Second Check to Antinomianism: To Which is Added, a Postscript, Occasioned by His Third Check. In a Letter to the Author.* London: Dilly, 1772.

The History and Proceedings of the House of Commons from the Restoration to the Present Time. 14 vols. London: Chandler, 1743.

Horneck, Anthony. *The Happy Ascetick, or the Best Exercise: To Which is Added, A Letter to a Person of Quality, Concerning the Holy Lives of Primitive Christians.* 6th ed. corrected. London: Chapman, [1724].

Howel, T. B. *A Complete Collection of State Trials and Proceedings for High Treason and Other Crimes and Misdemeanors: From the Earliest Period to the Year 1783: With Notes and Other illustrations.* 34 vols. London: Hansard, 1814.

Hume, David. *Essays, Moral and Political.* Edinburgh: Fleming and Alison, 1741.

"Hypocrisy of a Methodist Detected." *Gentlemen's Magazine* 12 (1747) 531.

An Impartial Hand. *An Essay Containing Evident Proofs Against the Methodists, from Certain Aspects of Their Secret Practices, That Their Religion is an Artful Introduction of Popery in Directly in Support of It.* London, [1745].

Ingham, Benjamin. *Diary of an Oxford Methodist, Benjamin Ingham 1733–1734.* Edited by Richard P. Heitzenrater. Durham: Duke University Press, 1985.

Jackson, Thomas, ed. *The Lives of Early Methodist Preachers Chiefly Written by Themselves.* 12 vols. London: Wesleyan Conference, 1871.

James I et al. *The Gunpowder-Treason: With a Discourse of the Manner of its Discovery; and a Perfect Relation of the Proceedings against Those Horrid Conspirators; wherein is Contained their Examinations, tryals, and Condemnations, Likewise King James's Speech to Both Houses of Parliament, on that Occasion; Now re-printed. A Preface Touching that Horrid Conspiracy, by the Right Reverend Father in God. Thomas [Barlow] Lord Bishop of Lincoln. And by Way of Appendix. Several Papers or Letters of Sir Everard Digby, Chiefly Relating to the Gun-powder Plot, Never before Printed Likewise.* London: Newcomb and Hills, 1679.

The Jesuit Detected or the Church of Rome Discover'd in the Disguise of a Protestant under the Character of All That is Material in the Rev. Mr. Hervey's Eleven Letters to John Wesley. London: Johnson, 1763.

John against Wesley: A Dialogue on the Imputation of Christ's Righteousness under the Character of All that is Material in the Rev. Mr. Hervey's Eleven Letters to John Wesley. London: Dilly, [1765].

Johnson, Samuel. *A Dictionary of the English Language: In Which the Words are Deduced from Their Originals and Illustrated in their Different Significations by Examples from the Best Writers.* 2nd ed. 2 vols. London: Strahan, 1755–56.

———. *Taxation No Tyranny: An Answer to the Resolutions and Address to the American Congress.* London: Cadell, 1775.

à Kempis, Thomas. *The Christian's Pattern: Or, a Treatise of the Imitation of Christ by Thomas à Kempis.* Translated by John Wesley. London: Rivington, 1735.

Ker, R. Ernest. "Two Unpublished Wesley Letters." *PWHS* 32 (1959) 45–47.

Law, William. *A Serious Call to a Devout and Holy Life.* London: Innys, 1729.

Latimer, John. *The Annals of Bristol in the Eighteenth Century.* Bristol: Butler & Tanner, 1893.

[Lavington, George]. *The Enthusiasm of Methodists and Papists Compar'd.* 3 parts. London: Knapton, 1749–52.

———. *The Moravians Compared and Detected.* London: Knapton, 1755.

Lenfant, James [Jacques L'Enfant]. *History of the Council of Constance.* Translated from the new ed. 2 vols. London: Bettersworth, Rivington, and others, 1730.

Leo X. *Exsurge Domine: Condemning the Errors of Martin Luther.* Encyclical Letter. June 15, 1520.

Lewis, John, ed. *The Weekly History, or, An Account of the Most Remarkable Particulars Relating to the Present Progress of the Gospel.* London: Lewis, 1741–42.

Luther, Martin. *Luther's Works.* Edited by Jaroslav Pelikan. 44 vols. St. Louis: Concordia, 1957–86.

Locke, John. *An Essay Concerning Human Understanding.* Edited by Peter H. Nidditch. Oxford: Oxford University Press, 1975.

———. *Letter Concerning Toleration.* London: Churchill, 1689.

———. *The Works of John Locke.* 2nd ed. 3 vols. London: Churchill, 1714.

Lyttelton, George. *A Letter to the Tories.* London: Say, 1747.

Madame Guyon. *Devotional Tracts Concerning the Presence of God, and Other Religious Subjects.* Translated from the French. London: Downing, 1724.

Madan, Martin. *Letters on Thelyphtor: With an Occasional Prologue and Epilogue by the Author.* London: Dodsley, 1782.

Manning, Robert. "The Catholic Devotion to the Blessed Virgin." In *The Moral Entertainments on the Most Important Practical Truths of the Christian Religion,* 3 vols. London: Meighan, 1742.

Milner, John. *The End of Religious Controversy in a Friendly Correspondence between a Religious Society of Protestants and a Catholic Divine Addressed to Bp. Burgess, in Answer to His Protestant's Catechism.* 8 vols. London: Keating, Brown and Co., 1818.

———. *An Inquiry into Certain Vulgar Opinions Concerning the Catholic Inhabitants and the Antiquities of Ireland.* 2nd ed. London: Keating, Brown, and Co., 1810.

———. *Letters to a Prebentary: Being an Answer to Reflections on Popery, by the Rev. J. Sturges.* Winchester: Robbins, 1800.

The Mock-Preacher: A Satyrico-Comical-Allegorical Farce. London: Corbett, [1739].

"The Monthly Chronologer." *The London Magazine: Or Gentleman's Monthly Intelligencer* 49 (1780) 283–84, 339.

Morgan, James. *The Life and Death of Mr. Thomas Walsh.* London: Cock, 1762.

Moore, Henry. *The Life of the Rev. John Wesley.* 2 vols. New York: Bangs and Emory, 1824–25.

Moore, Henry, and Thomas Coke. *The Life of the Rev. John Wesley, A.M. Including an Account of the Great Revival of Religion, in Europe and America, of Which He Was the First and Chief Instrument.* 2nd ed. London: Paramore, 1792.

Moore, William. *The Addresses for Blood and Devastation, and the Addressers Exposed; Together with Idolatrous Worship of Kings and Tyrants and the Americans Justified by Several Precedents from Scripture, in Their Resistance to the Depredations and Lawless Violence of an English King, and His Bribed Servile Parliament with May Serve as an Answer to Taxation No Tyranny. Wesley's Calm Address c&c.* London: Shaw, 1776.

Morning Exercise against Popery and the Principle Errors of the Church of Rome. London: Maxwell, 1675.

Murray, John. *The Life of the Rev. John Murray, Preacher of Universal Salvation Written by Himself.* Boston: Monroe and Francis, 1816.

Nelson, John. *The Case of John Nelson: Written by Himself.* London, 1745.

Nelson, Robert. *A Companion for the Festivals and Fasts of the Church of England with Collects and Prayers for Each Solemnity.* London: W. B., 1704.

Newman, John Henry. *Apologia Pro Vita Sua.* London: Dent & Sons, 1864.

[O'Beirne, Thomas Lewis]. *Considerations on the Late Disturbances, by a Consistent Whig.* 2nd ed. London: Almon, 1780.

———. *A Short History of the Last Session of Parliament.* London: Almon and Debrett, 1780.

O'Connell, Daniel. *Letters of Daniel O'Connell, Esquire, to the Ministers and Office-Bearers of the Wesleyan-Methodist Societies in Manchester.* Langston: MacDonnell, 1842.

O'Leary, Arthur. *Essays and Tracts of Arthur O'Leary: To Which is Introduced His Correspondence with John Wesley.* Lewistown: Bell & Sons, 1832.

———. *Miscellaneous Tracts by the Rev. Arthur O'Leary Containing I. A Defence of the Divinity of Christ, and the Immortality of the Soul: In Answer to the Author of a Work Lately Published in Cork, Entitled 'Thoughts on Nature and Religion.' Revised and Corrected. II. Asserted, or a Vindication of the Oath of Allegiance: With an Impartial Inquiry into the Pope's Temporal Power, and the Claims of the Stuarts to the English Throne; Proving That They Are Both Equally Groundless. III. An Address to the Common People of Ireland, on Occasion of an Apprehended Invasion by the French and Spaniards, in July 1779, when the United Fleets of Bourbon Appeared in the Channel. IV. Remarks on a Letter Written by Mr. Wesley, and the Defence of the Protestant Associations; Tending to Prove That a Man's Speculative Opinions Ought Not to Deprive Him of the Rights of Civil Society. In Which Are Introduced The Rev. John Wesley's Letter, and the Defence of the Protestant Association.* Dublin: McDonnel, 1781. 2nd ed. Dublin: Chambers, 1781.s

———. *Mr. O'Leary's Remarks on the Rev. Mr. Wesley's Letters, in Defence of the Protestant Associations in England, to Which Are Prefixed Wesley's Letters.* London: Coglan, 1780.

Ousely, Gideon. "Another Olda Podrida." *The National Magazine Devoted to Literature, Art, and Religion* 6 (1855) 515.

Outler, Albert, ed. *John Wesley*. New York: Oxford University Press, 1964.

Ozello, Oliver, and the Philosophical Society. *An Account of the Rise, Progress, and Nature of Methodism in Corke with the Suffering of Its Professors, and Some Proposals for Preventing Any Further Troubles, and Augmenting the General Fund. In a Letter to the Rev. John Wesley, M.A., Fellow of Lincoln College*. Cork, 1749.

"Parliament." *Northampton Mercury*, April 17, 1780.

———. *London Chronicle*, April 11–13, 1780.

———. *St. James's Chronicle or the British Evening Post*, April 11–13, 1780.

———. *Morning Chronicle and London Advertiser*, April 12, 1780.

Parsons, Robert. *A Treatise Tending to Mitigation towards Catholicke-Subjects in England*. St. Omer, 1607.

"Particular Detail of the Late Riotous Tumults." *Gentlemen's Magazine*, August, 1780.

Perkins, William. *A Discourse of Conscience: Wherein Is Set Downe the Nature, Properties and Differences Thereof, As Also the Way to Get and Keepe Good Conscience*. Cambridge: Legate, 1596.

Perronet, Vin[cent]. *Some Remarks on a Late Anonymous Piece, Intitled the Enthusiasm of Methodist and Papist Compar'd: In a Letter to the Author*. London: Roberts, 1749.

The Progress of Methodism in Bristol: Or the Methodist Unmask'd. Wherein the Doctrines, Discipline, Policy, Divisions, and Successes of That Novel Sect are Fully Detected, and Properly Display'd, in Hudibrastick Verse. Bristol: Watts, 1743.

"Protestant Association." *London Evening Post*, February 19–21, 1780.

———. *St. James's Chronicle or the British Evening Post*, February 19–22, 1780.

Protestant Association. *An Appeal from the Protestant Association to the People of Great Britain*. London: Pashan, 1779.

———. *A Defence of the Protestant Association, or an Attempt to Show That the Fifty Thousand Petitioners to Parliament, Assembled under the Direction of Their President Lord George Gordon, Were Not Chargable with the Outrages in the City of London, June 1780. Including Two Letters to the Right Honourable Lord L-gh-h, Occasioned by His Speech to the Jury of S-y, Appointed for the Trial of the Rioters*. Glasgow, 1780.

Raithby, John, ed. *Statutes of the Realm*. 7 vols. London, 1819.

Reeves, Jonathan. *An Affectionate Address to the Inhabitants of the City of Corke*. Corke: Harrison, 1747.

"Register of Books, April 1735." *Gentleman's Magazine* 6 (1735) 222.

The Rev. John Wesley's Letter Concerning The Civil Principles of Roman Catholics, Also a Defence of the Protestant Association. n. p., n. d.

[Richardson, Samuel]. *The Oxford Methodists: Being Some Account of a Society of Young Gentlemen: Setting Forth Their Rise, Views, and Designs. With Some Occasional Remarks on A Letter Inserted in* Fog's Journal *of December 9th, Relating to Them*. London: Richardson, 1733.

Roddie, Robin. "Register of Irish Methodist Preachers." Belfast: Methodist Historical Society in Ireland. https://methodisthistoryireland.org/people/ministers/.

Romilly, Samuel. *Memoirs of the Life of Samuel Romilly: Written by Himself with a Selection of His Correspondence Edited by His Sons*. 2 vols. 3rd ed. London: Murray, 1841.

Rutty, John. *A Spiritual Diary and Soliloquies by John Rutty, M.D., Late of Dublin.* Dublin: Phillips, 1796.

Sedgwick, Romney, ed. *The House of Commons 1715–1754.* 2 vols. London: Her Majesty's Stationary Office, 1970.

Sherlock, William. *A Preservative against Popery. In Two Parts. I. Some Plain Directions How to Dispute with Romish Priests. II. Shewing How Contrary Popery is to the True Ends of the Christian Religion.* London: Brown, Walthoe, Nicholson, Tooke, Pemberton, and Ward, 1714.

Stillingfleet, Edward. *A Discourse Concerning the Idolatry Practiced in the Church of Rome and the Hazard of Salvation in the Communion of It: In Answer to Some Papers of a Revolted Protestant: Wherein a Particular Account is Given of Fanaticism and Divisions in the Church.* 5 vols. London: printed for Henry and George Mortlock, 1709.

———. *The Doctrines and Practices of the Church of Rome Truly Represented.* London: Rogers, 1686.

———. *The Irenicium, or Pacificator Being a Reconciler as to Church Differences.* Philadelphia: Sorin, 1842.

The Story of the Methodist-Lady, or the Injur'd Husband's Revenge, A True History. London: Doughty, [1752].

Tailfer, Pat[rick], et al. *A True and Historical Narrative of the Colony of Georgia in America, from the First Settlement Thereof until This Present Period.* Charles-town: Timothy, 1741.

Tenison, Archbishop of Canterbury Tho[mas]. "20 Anno Christi 1714, Reg. Anglinae Annae 13." In *Concilia Magnae Britanniae et Hiberniae,* edited by David Wilkins. 4 vols. Londini: Gosling, Gyles, Woodward and Davis, 1717.

Thomas, Graham C. G., ed. "George Whitefield and Friends: The Correspondence of Some Early Methodists." *National Library of Wales Journal* 24 (1990) 367–96.

———. "George Whitefield and Friends: The Correspondence of Some Early Methodists." *National Library of Wales Journal* 27.1 (1991) 65–97.

———. "George Whitefield and Friends: The Correspondence of Some Early Methodists." *National Library of Wales Journal* 27.2 (1991) 175–201.

Tillotson, John. *The Hazard of Being Saved in the Church of Rome: A Seasonable Discourse against Popery.* London: Tooke, Tonson, and others, 1722.

"To the Author of Fog's Weekly Journal." *Fog's Weekly Journal* 214, December 9, 1732.

Toplady, Augustus. *A Letter to the Rev. John Wesley Relative to His Pretended Abridgement of Zanchius on Predestination.* London: Gurney, 1770.

[———]. *An Old Fox Tarr'd and Feather'd: Occasioned by What is Called Mr. John Wesley's Calm Address to Our American Colonies. By an Hanoverian.* London: French, 1775.

Venn, Richard. *King George's Title Asserted or a Letter to a Fellow of Cambridge Shewing Lawfulness of Oaths Requir'd for the Present Government.* 2nd ed. London: Morphew, 1715.

Walpole, Horace. *Horace Walpole's Correspondence.* Edited by W. S. Lewis. 48 vols. New Haven: Yale University Press, 1937–83.

———. *Journal of the Reign of George the Third.* 2 vols. London: Bentley, 1845.

Warburton, William. *The Doctrine of Grace: Or The Office and Operations of the Holy Spirit Vindicated from the Insults of Infidelity, and the Abuses of Fanaticism: With Some Thoughts (Humbly Offered to the Consideration of the Established Clergy)*

Regarding the Right Method of Defending Religion against the Attacks of Either Party. In Three Books. London: Miller, 1763.

———. *Letters from a Late Eminent Prelate to One of his Friends.* Kidderminster: Owen, n. d.

Waring, G[eorge]. *A Sermon Occasioned by the Death of the Right Honorable the Countess Dowager of Huntingdon Who Departed this Life 17 June 1791 in the Eighty-fourth Year of Her Age.* Birmingham: Belcher, [1791].

Watson, Robert. *The Life of Lord George Gordon with a Philosophical Review of His Political Conduct.* London: Symonds and Eaton, 1795.

Wesley, Charles. *The Letters of Charles Wesley: A Critical Edition, with Introduction and Notes, Volume 1, 1728–1756.* Edited by Kenneth C. G. Newport and Gareth Lloyd. Oxford: Oxford University Press, 2013.

———. *The Manuscript Journal of the Reverend Charles Wesley, M.A.* Edited by S. T. Kimbrough Jr. and Kenneth C. G. Newport. 2 vols. Nashville: Kingswood, 2007.

———. *The Sermons of Charles Wesley: A Critical Edition with Introduction and Notes.* Edited by Kenneth G. Newport. Oxford: Oxford University Press, 2001.

———. *Short Hymns on Select Passages of the Holy Scriptures.* 2 vols. Bristol: Farley, 1767.

———. *The Unpublished Poetry of Charles Wesley.* Edited by S. T. Kimbrough Jr. and Oliver A. Beckerlegge. 3 vols. Nashville: Kingswood, 1988–92.

Wesley, Charles and John Wesley. *Hymns for Times of Trouble and Persecution.* 2nd ed. Bristol: Farley, 1745.

———. *The Poetical Works of John and Charles Wesley, Reprinted from the Originals, with the Last Corrections of the Authors; Together with the Poems of Charles Wesley Never before Published.* Collected and arranged by G. Osborn. 13 vols. London: Wesleyan-Methodist Conference Office, 1868–72.

———. *A Short View of the Differences between the Moravians Lately in England and the Rev. Mr. John and Charles Wesley.* 2nd ed. Bristol: Farley, 1748.

Wesley, John. "An Account of the Disturbances in My Father's House." *AM,* October 1784.

———. *The Advantage of the Members of the Church of England over Those of the Church of Rome.* Bristol: Farley, 1753.

———. *Advice to the People Called Methodists.* [Newcastle upon Tyne], 1745.

———. *An Answer to the Rev. Mr. Church's Remarks on the Rev. Mr. John Wesley's Last Journal: In a Letter to That Gentleman.* Bristol: Farley, [1745].

———. *A Calm Address to Our American Colonies.* New ed., corrected, and enlarged. London: Hawes, 1775.

———. *Catholick Spirit: A Sermon on 2 Kings x. 15.* London: Cock, 1755; Bristol: Pine, 1770; London: New Chapel, 1789.

———. "Catholick Spirit." In *Sermons on Several Occasions.* 3 vols. London: Strahan, 1750.

———. *The Character of a Methodist.* Bristol: Farley, 1742.

———, ed. *A Christian Library: Consisting of Extracts and Abridgements of the Choicest Pieces of Practical Divinity which Have Been Published in the English Tongue.* 50 vols. Bristol: Farley, 1749–55.

———. *The Christian's Pattern; Or, a Treatise of the Imitation of Christ, Written in Originally in Latin by Thomas á Kempis.* London: Rivington, 1735.

———. *A Collection of Forms of Prayer for Everyday of the Week.* 5th ed. Bristol: Palmer, 1755.

———. *A Compassionate Address to the Inhabitants of Ireland.* Belfast: Magee, 1778.

———. *A Concise History of England, from the Earliest Times to the Death of George II.* 4 vols. London: Hawks, 1775–76.

———. *The Complete English Dictionary, Explaining Most of Those Hard Words, which are Found in the Best English Writers. By a Lover of Good English and Common Sense.* London: Strahan, [1753].

———. "A Disavowal of Persecuting Papists." *AM*, April 1782.

———. *The Doctrine of Original Sin according to Scripture, Reason, and Experience.* Bristol: Farley, 1757.

———. *An Earnest Appeal to Men of Reason and Religion.* 2nd ed. Bristol: Farley, 1743.

———. *Explanatory Notes on the New Testament.* 3 vols. 3rd ed. Bristol: Pine, 1760–62.

———. *Explanatory Notes on the Old Testament.* 3 vols. Bristol: Pine, 1765.

———. *An Extract of the Life of Monsieur De Renty, a Late Nobleman of France.* 4th ed. London: Hawes, 1778, 1786.

———. *A Farther Appeal to Men of Reason and Religion.* London: Strahan, 1745.

———. *Free Grace: A Sermon Preached at Bristol.* Bristol: Farley, 1739.

———. *Free Thoughts on the Present State of Public Affairs in a Letter to a Friend.* London: Oliver, 1770.

———. To John Whittingham. Unpublished letter, July 13, 1780, [broadsheet] MARC MAM JW 5.90.

———. *The Journal of the Rev. John Wesley, A.M.* Edited by Nehemiah Curnock. 8 vols. London: Epworth, 1939.

———. "A Letter from John Wesley." *Gospel Magazine* 7 (1780) 86–89.

———. *Letter to a Roman Catholic.* Dublin: Powell, 1749.

———. "On Popery." *AM*, June, 1781.

———. "On Popery, To the Editors of the *Freeman's Journal*." *AM*, July 4, 1781.

———. *A Practical Treatise on Christian Perfection Extracted from a Late Author* [William Law]. Newcastle: Gooding, 1743.

———. *Predestination Calmly Considered.* London: W. B., 1752.

———. *A Preservative against Unsettled Notions in Religion.* Bristol: Farley, 1758.

———. *Political Writings of John Wesley.* Edited by Graham Maddox. Bristol: Thoemmes, 1998.

———. *Primitive Physick: Or, an Easy Natural Method of Curing Most Diseases.* London: Trye, 1747.

———. *A Sermon on the Death of George Whitefield.* London: Oliver, 1770.

———. *A Short Address to the Inhabitants of Ireland: Occasioned by Some Late Occurrences.* Dublin: Powell, 1749.

———. *A Short History of Methodism.* London: [Bowyer], 1765.

———. *A Short Method of Converting All the Roman Catholicks in the Kingdom of Ireland. Humbly Proposed to the Bishops and Clergy of This Kingdom.* Dublin, 1752.

———. *Some Remarks on Hill's Review of the Doctrines.* 2nd ed. Bristol: Pine, 1772.

———, ed. *A Treatise on Justification Extracted from John Goodwin.* Bristol: Pine, 1765.

———. "Wesley Letters." *PWHS* 8 (1912) 157–84.

———. *A Word to a Protestant.* Bristol: Farley, 1746.

———. *A Word in Season, or, Advice to an Englishman.* n. p., [1744].

———. *A Word in Season: Or, Advice to a Soldier.* Bristol, 1745.

————. *The Works of John Wesley.* Edited by Frank Baker et al. Bicentennial ed. Oxford: Clarendon, 1975–83.

Wesley, Samuel. *The Letters of Samuel Wesley: Professional and Social Correspondence.* Edited by Phillip Olson. Oxford: Oxford University Press, 2001.

Wesley, Samuel, Sr. "A Letter Concerning the Religious Societies." In *The Pious Communicant Rightly Prepar'd; or a Discourse Concerning the Blessed Sacrament.* London, 1700.

————. "On the Death of Her Late Sacred Majesty Queen Mary." In *Elegies of the Queen and Archbishop.* London: Motte, 1695.

Wesley, Susanna. *The Complete Writings of Susanna Wesley.* Edited by Charles Wallace Jr. Oxford: Oxford University Press, 1997.

Whitefield, George. *A Brief Account of the Occasion, Process, and Issue of a Late Trial at the Assize Held at Gloucester, March 3, 1743. Between Some of the People Call'd Methodist, Plaintiffs, and Certain Persons of the Town Minchin-Hampton, in the Said County, Defendants. In a Letter to a Friend.* London: Robinson, 1744.

————. *A Continuation of the Reverend Mr. Whitefield's Journal from His Arrival at Savannah to His Return to London.* London: Hutton, 1739.

————. *Eighteen Sermons Preached by the Late Rev. George Whitefield, A.M., Taken Verbatim in Short-hand and Faithfully Transcribed by Joseph Gurney.* Revised by A. Gifford. London: Gurney, 1771.

————. *A Journal of a Voyage from London to Savannah in Georgia in Two Parts.* London: Hutton, 1738.

————. *Observations on Some Fatal Mistakes, in a Book Lately Published, and Intitled, 'The Doctrine of Grace.'* Edinburgh: Traill, 1763.

————. *A Short Account of God's Dealings with the Reverend Mr. George Whitefield, A.B., Late of Pembroke, College, Oxford, from His Infancy to His Time of Entering Holy Orders.* London: Strahan, 1740.

————. *Some Remarks on a Pamphlet Entitled:* The Enthusiasm of Methodists and Papist Compar'd. London: Strahan, 1749.

Whitehead, John. *The Life of the Rev. John Wesley, M.A.* 2 vols. London: Couchman, 1796.

[Williams, John]. *A Catechism Representing the Doctrines and Practices of the Church of Rome with an Answer Thereunto. By a Protestant of the Church of England.* London: Chiswell, 1686.

[Williams, David]. *A Plan of Association on Constitutional Principles by Which the Outrage of Mobs, and the Necessity of a Military Government Will be Prevented.* London, Kearsley, 1780.

Worrall, Edward Stanislaus, ed. *Returns of Papists.* Reprint, [London]: The Society, 1980–89.

Zwingli, Huldrych. *The Latin Works and the Correspondence of Huldrych Zwingli: Together with Selections from His German Works.* Translated by Samuel Maccauly Jackson and William John Hinke. 3 vols. Philadelphia: Heidelberg, 1922.

Secondary Sources

Abraham, William J. and James Kirby, eds. *The Oxford Handbook of Methodist Studies.* Oxford: Oxford University Press, 2009.

Baker, Frank. "Bishop Lavington and the Methodists." *PWHS* 34 (1963–64) 37–42.

———. *Charles Wesley as Revealed by His Letters*. London: Epworth, 1948.

———. *John Wesley and the Church of England*. 2nd ed. London: Epworth, 2000.

———. "John Wesley and Lord George Gordon." *PWHS* 26 (1947) 45.

———. "Methodism and the '45 Rebellion." *London Quarterly and Holborn Review* 172 (1947) 326–12.

———. *A Union Catalogue of the Publications of John and Charles Wesley*. 2nd ed. Stone Mountain: Zimmerman, 1991.

Barbour, Ruth. "John Whittingham: Coventry Nurseryman, Diarist, Catholic Apologist and Political Activist." *Warwickshire History* 27 (2014) 8–25.

Barnard, Toby. *Irish Protestant Ascents and Descents 1641–1770*. Dublin: Four Courts, 2004.

Bartlett, Thomas. *Ireland: A History*. Cambridge: Cambridge University Press, 2010.

Bebbington, David. *Evangelicalism in Modern Britain from 1730s to the 1980s*. London: Routledge, 2003.

Beebe, Keith Edward, and David Ceri Jones. "Whitefield and the 'Celtic Revivals.'" In *George Whitefield: Life, Context, and Legacy*, edited by Geordan Hammond and David Ceri Jones, 132–49. Oxford: Oxford University Press, 2016.

Bennett, G. V. *The Tory Crisis in the Church and State, 1688–1730: The Career of Francis Atterbury, Bishop of Rochester*. Oxford: Clarendon, 1975.

Best, Gary. *Charles Wesley: A Biography*. London: Epworth, 2006.

Black, Eugene. *The Association: British Extraparliamentary Political Organizations 1769–1793*. Cambridge: Harvard University Press, 1963.

Black, Jeremy. "John Wesley and History." *Wesley and Methodist Studies* 9 (2017) 1–17.

Bocock, Robert, and Kenneth Thompson, eds. *Religion and Ideology: A Reader*. Manchester: Manchester University Press, 1985.

Bossy, John. *The English Catholic Community, 1570–1850*. New York: Oxford University Press, 1976.

Bradshaw, D. B. "William Lunnell, of Dublin." *PWHS* 22 (1939) 73–76.

Brantley, Richard E. *Locke, Wesley and the Method of English Romanticism*. Gainesville: University of Florida Press, 1984.

Breward, Ian. "William Perkins and the Origins of Reformed Casuistry." *Evangelical Quarterly* 40 (1968) 3–18.

Broxap, Henry. *A Biography of Thomas Deacon, the Manchester Non-juror*. Manchester: University of Manchester Press, 1911.

Burrows, Aelred. "Wesley the Catholic." In *John Wesley: Contemporary Perspectives*, edited by John Stacey, 54–66. London: Epworth, 1988.

Burton, Vicki Tolar. *Spiritual Literacy in John Wesley's Methodism: Reading, Writing, and Speaking to Believe*. Waco: Baylor University Press, 2008.

Butler, David. *Methodists and Papists: John Wesley and the Catholic Church in the Eighteenth Century*. London: Darton, Longman, and Todd, 1995.

Byrne, Brendan. "Ignatius Loyola and John Wesley: Experience and Strategies of Conversion." *Colloquium* 19 (1986) 56–66.

Campbell, Kenneth L. *Windows into Men's Souls: Nonconformity in Tudor and Early Stuart England*. Plymouth: Lexington, 2012.

Campbell, Ted A., and Kenneth C. G. Newport, eds. *Charles Wesley: Life, Literature & Legacy*. London: Epworth, 2007.

————. *John Wesley and Christian Antiquity: Religious Vision and Cultural Change.* Nashville: Kingswood, 1991.

————. "The Shape of Wesleyan Thought: The Question of John Wesley's 'Essential Doctrines.'" *Asbury Theological Journal* 59 (2004) 27–48.

Cannon, J. A., ed. *The Oxford Companion to British History.* Revised ed. Oxford: Oxford University Press, 2002.

Canny, Nicholas, ed. *The Oxford History of the British Empire: Volume 1: The Origins of Empire.* Oxford: Oxford University Press, 2001.

Castelo, Daniel, ed. *Embodying Wesley's Catholic Spirit.* Eugene: Pickwick, 2017.

Cell, George Croft. *The Rediscovery of John Wesley.* New York: Holt and Co., 1935.

Chadwick, Harold J., ed. *Madame Jeanne Guyon: Experiencing Union with God through Inner Prayer.* Gainesville: Bridge-Logos, 2001.

Chamberlain, Jeffrey S. *Accommodating High Churchmen: The Clergy of Sussex, 1700–1745.* Chicago: University of Illinois Press, 1997.

Chapman, David M. *In Search of the Catholic Spirit: Wesleyans and Roman Catholics in Dialogue.* London: Epworth, 2004.

Clark, J. C. D. *English Society, 1660–1832.* 2nd ed. Cambridge: Cambridge University Press, 2000.

Clarke, Adam. *Memoirs of the Wesley Family.* London: Kershaw, 1823.

Clifford, Alan C. *Atonement and Justification: English Evangelical Theology 1640–1790: An Evaluation.* Oxford: Oxford University Press, 1990.

Coffey, John. *Persecution and Toleration in Protestant England 1558–1689.* London: Routledge, 2014.

Cobbett, William, and Thomas Cursor Hansard, eds. *The Parliamentary History of England: From the Norman Conquest, in 1066, to the Year 1803.* 36 vols. London: Bagshaw, 1804–14.

Colley, Linda. *Britons: Forging the Nation.* 2nd ed. New Haven: Yale University Press, 2005.

————. *In Defiance of Oligarchy: The Tory Party 1714–60.* Cambridge: Cambridge University Press, 1982.

Collins, Kenneth J. "Assurance." In *The Oxford Handbook of Methodist Studies,* edited by William J. Abraham and James Kirby, 602–17. Oxford: Oxford University Press, 2009.

————. *John Wesley: A Theological Journey.* Nashville: Abingdon, 2003.

————. "Other Thoughts on Aldersgate: Has the Conversionist Paradigm Collapsed?" *Methodist History* 30 (1991) 10–25.

————. "Twentieth Century Interpretations of John Wesley's Aldersgate Experience: Coherence or Confusion." *WTJ* 24 (1989) 18–31.

Collins, Kenneth J., and John R. Tyson, eds. *Conversion in the Wesleyan Tradition.* Nashville: Abingdon, 2001.

Cooke, W. Dennis D. "John Wesley's Anti-Catholic Legacy, True or False?" *Bulletin of the Methodist Historical Society, Ireland Chapter* 6 (2000) 2–11.

Cooney, David Levingstone. *The Methodists in Ireland: A Short History.* Dublin: Columba, 2001.

Coppedge, Allan. *John Wesley in Theological Debate.* Wilmore: Wesley Heritage, 1987.

Cornwall, Robert D. *Visible and Apostolic: The Constitution of the Church in High Church Anglican and Non-Juror Thought.* Newark: University of Delaware Press, 1993.

Culkin, Gerard. "England and the Catholic Church." In vol. 5 of *New Catholic Encyclopedia*, 15 vols., 2nd ed., edited by Berard L. Marthaler. Washington, DC: Catholic University of America, 2003–.

Cunha, Emma Salgard. *John Wesley, Practical Divinity and the Defence of Literature*. New York: Routledge, 2018.

Cunningham, Joseph W. "'Justification by Faith': Richard Baxter's Influence upon John Wesley." *The Asbury Journal* 64 (2009) 55–66.

Cracknell, Kenneth, and Susan J. White. *An Introduction to World Methodism*. Cambridge: Cambridge University Press, 2005.

Crookshank, Charles Henry. *History of Methodism in Ireland*. 3 vols. Belfast: Allen, 1885–88.

Cruickshanks, Eveline. *Political Untouchables: The Tories and the '45*. New York: Holmes & Meier, 1979.

Cruickshanks, Eveline, and Edward Corp, eds. *The Stuart Court in Exile and the Jacobites*. London: Hambledon, 1995.

Cruickshanks, Eveline, and Jeremy Black, eds. *The Jacobite Challenge*. Edinburgh: Donald, 1988.

Cruickshanks, Eveline, et al., eds. *The House of Commons 1690–1715*. 12 vols. Cambridge: Cambridge University Press, 2002.

Cruickshank, Joanna. "Were Early Methodists Masochists? Suffering, Submission, and Sanctification in the Hymns of Charles Wesley." *Bulletin of the John Rylands Library* 88 (2006) 81–100.

Crutcher, Timothy J. *The Crucible of Life: The Role of Experience in John Wesley's Theological Method*. Lexington: Emeth, 2010.

———. *John Wesley: His Life and Thought*. Kansas City: Nazarene, 2015.

Cubie, David L. "Early Methodism: A Paradigm for Non-violence." *WTJ* 37 (2002) 86–105.

Danker, Ryan Nicholas. *Wesley and the Anglicans: Political Division in Early Evangelicalism*. Downers Grove: IVP Academic, 2016.

Davies, R., and G. Rupp, eds. *A History of the Methodist Church in Great Britain*. 4 vols. London: Epworth, 1965.

Dean, Jonathan, ed. *A Heart Strangely Warmed: John and Charles Wesley and Their Writings*. Norwich: Canterbury, 2014.

de Castro, J. P. *The Gordon Riots*. Oxford: Oxford University Press, 1926.

Dickinson, H. T. *The Politics of the People in Eighteenth-Century Britain*. London: Macmillan, 1994.

Dickson, David. "Jacobitism in Eighteenth-century Ireland: A Munster Perspective." *Éire-Ireland* 39 (2004) 38–99.

Donovan, Robert Kent. *No Popery and Radicalism: Opposition to Roman Catholic Relief in Scotland (1778–1792)*. New York: Garland, 1987.

Duffy, Eamon. "Wesley and the Counter Reformation." In *Revival and Religion since 1700: Essays for John Walsh*, edited by Jane Garnett and Colin Matthew, 1–20. London: Hambledon, 1993.

Dussinger, John A. "*The Oxford Methodists* (1733; 1738): The Purloined Letter of John Wesley at Samuel Richardson's Press." In *Theology and Literature in the Age of Johnson: Resisting Secularism*, edited by Melvyn New and Gerard Reedy, S. J., 27–48. Newark: University of Delaware Press, 2012.

Edward, Norman. *Roman Catholicism in England from the Elizabethan Council to the Second Vatican Council.* Oxford: Oxford University Press, 1985.

Edwards, Maldwyn. *Family Circle: A Study of the Epworth Household in Relation to John and Charles Wesley.* London: Epworth, 1961.

Elton, Geoffrey Rudolph, ed. *The Tudor Constitution: Documents and Commentary.* Cambridge: Cambridge University Press, 1982.

England, Thomas R. *The Life of Arthur O'Leary.* London: Longman, Hurst, Rees, Orme, and Brown, 1822.

English, John C. "John Wesley and Francis Rous." *Methodist History* 6 (1968) 28–35.

———. "John Wesley and the Rights of Conscience." *Journal of Church and State* 37 (1995) 351–63.

Evenden, Elizabeth. *Patents, Pictures, and Patronage: John Day and the Tudor Book Trade.* Aldershot: Ashgate, 2008.

Evenden, Elizabeth, and Thomas S. Freeman. "Print, Profit, and Propaganda: The Elizabethan Privy Council and the 1570 Edition of Foxe's 'Book of Martyrs.'" *English Historical Review* 119 (2004) 1288–1307.

Field, David N. *Bid Our Jarring Conflicts Cease: A Wesleyan Theology and Praxis of Church Unity.* Nashville: Foundery, 2017.

"A Five-Minute Introduction." *The Unabridged Acts and Monuments Online or TAMO.* Sheffield: HRI Online Publications, 2011. www.johnfoxe.org.

Fremont-Barnes, Gregory. *The Jacobite Rebellion, 1745–46.* Oxford: Osprey, 2011.

Fudge, Thomas A. *Jan Hus: Religious Reform and Social Revolution in Bohemia.* London: Tauris, 2010.

Gibson, William. *James II and The Trial of the Seven Bishops.* New York: Palgrave Macmillan, 2009.

Greenburg, Devorah. "Eighteenth-century 'Foxe': History, Historiography, and Historical Consequences." *John Foxe's Acts and Monuments Online or TAMO.* Sheffield: HRI Online Publications, 2011. http://www.johnfoxe.org/index.php?realm=more&gototype=modern&type=essay&book=essay8.

———. "In a Tradition of Learned Ministry: Wesley's Foxe." *Journal of Ecclesiastical History* 59 (2008) 227–58.

———. "Reflective Foxe: The Book of Martyrs Transformed, 'Fox' Reinterpreted–Sixteenth through Twenty-First Centuries." PhD diss., Simon Fraser University, 2002.

Gregory, Jeremy. "The Making of a Protestant Nation." In *England's Long Reformation 1500–1800,* edited by Nicholas Tyacke, 314–23. London: UCL, 1998.

Gregory, Jeremy, and John Stevenson, eds. *The Routledge Companion to Britain in the Eighteenth Century, 1688–1820.* London: Routledge, 2007.

Green, V. H. H. *The Young Mr. Wesley.* London: Arnold, 1961.

Griffin, Martin Ignatius Joseph. *Latitudinarianism in the Seventeenth-Century Church of England.* Leiden: Brill, 1992.

Gunter, W. Stephen. *The Limits of Love Divine: John Wesley's Response to Enthusiasm and Antinomianism.* Nashville: Kingswood, 1989.

Haire, Robert. *Wesley's One-and-Twenty Visits to Ireland: A Short Survey.* London: Epworth, 1947.

Halévy, Elie. *The Birth of Methodism in England.* Translated by Bernard Semmel. Chicago: University of Chicago Press, 1971.

Hammond, Geordan. *John Wesley in America: Restoring Primitive Christianity*. Oxford: Oxford University Press, 2014.

———. "John Wesley and 'Imitating Christ.'" *WTJ* 45 (2010) 197–212.

Hammond, Geordan, and David Ceri Jones, eds. *George Whitefield: Life, Context, and Legacy*. Oxford: Oxford University Press, 2016.

Hanham, Andrew. "'So Few Facts': Jacobites, Tories, and the Pretender." *Parliamentary History* 19 (2000) 233–57.

Harris, Tim. *The Politics of the Excluded, c. 1500–1850*. New York: Palgrave MacMillan, 2001.

Hawkins, Jonathan. "Imperial '45: The Jacobite Rebellion in Transatlantic Context." *The Journal of Imperial and Commonwealth History* 24 (1996) 24–47.

Haydon, Colin. "Anti-Catholicism and Obscene Literature: The Case of Mrs. Mary Catherine Cadiere and its Context." In *The Church and Literature*, edited by Peter Clarke and Charlotte Methuen, 202–18. Studies in Church History 48. Woodbridge: Boydell, 2012.

———. *Anti-Catholicism in Eighteenth-Century England, c. 1714–80*. Manchester: Manchester University Press, 1993.

———. "Bishop George Lavington of Exeter (1684–1762) and the *Enthusiasm of Methodists and Papists, Compar'd*." *Southern History* 37 (2015) 60–85.

———. "Eighteenth-Century English Anti-Catholicism: Contexts, Continuity, and Diminution." In *Protestant-Catholic Conflict from the Reformation to the Twenty-first Century*, edited by John Wolffe, 46–70. London: Palgrave Macmillan, 2013.

———. "Parliament and Popery in England 1700–1780." *Parliamentary History* 43 (2000) 49–63.

Haywood, Ian, and John Seed, eds. *The Gordon Riots: Politics, Culture, and Insurrection in Late Eighteenth-Century England*. Cambridge: Cambridge University Press, 2012.

Headly, Anthony J. *Family Crucible: The Influence of Family Dynamics in the Life and Ministry of John Wesley*. Eugene: Wipf & Stock, 2010.

Heitzenrater, Richard P. *The Elusive Mr. Wesley: John Wesley His Own Biographer*. 2 vols. Nashville: Abingdon, 1985.

———. "John Wesley and the Oxford Methodists." PhD diss., Duke University, 1972.

———. "John Wesley's Early Sermons." *PWHS* 37 (1970) 110–28.

———. "John Wesley's Principles and Practice of Preaching." *Methodist History* 37 (1999) 89–106.

———, ed. *The Poor and the People Called Methodists*. Nashville: Abingdon, 2002.

———. *Wesley and the People Called Methodists*. 2nd ed. Nashville: Abingdon, 2013.

Hempton, David. *The Church in the Long Eighteenth Century*. London: Tauris, 2011.

———. "The Methodist Crusade in Ireland 1795–1845." *Irish Historical Studies* 22 (1980) 33–48.

———. *Methodism and Politics in British Society, 1750–1850*. London: Routledge, 2013.

———. *Methodism: Empire of Spirit*. New Haven: Yale University Press, 2006.

———. *Religion and Political Culture in Britain and Ireland: From the Glorious Revolution to the Decline of Empire*. Cambridge: Cambridge University Press, 1996.

———. *The Religion of the People: Methodism and Popular Religion, c. 1750–1900*. London: Routledge, 1996.

Herbermann, Charles G., ed. *Catholic Encyclopedia*. 15 vols. New York: Appleton, 1908.

Hibbert, Christopher. *King Mob*. New York: World, 1958.

Hindmarsh, D. Bruce. *Evangelical Conversion Narrative: Spiritual Autobiography in Early Modern England*. Oxford: Oxford University Press, 2005.

[Holden, H. W.]. *John Wesley in Company with Highchurchmen*. 5th ed. London: Hodges, 1872.

The Homes, Haunts, and Friends of John Wesley: Being the Centenary Number of "The Methodist Recorder." London: Kelly, 1891.

Honderich, Ted, ed. *The Oxford Companion to Philosophy*. 2nd ed. Oxford: Oxford University Press, 2005.

Holt, Geoffrey, SJ. *The English Jesuits in the Age of Reason*. Tunbridge Wells: Burns & Oates, 1993.

Houston, Joel. *Wesley, Whitefield, and the "Free Grace" Controversy: The Crucible of Methodism*. New York: Routledge, 2019.

Hostettler, John. *Thomas Erskine and Trial by Jury*. Hook: Waterside, 2010.

Hughes, Philip. "Catholicism in the South of England: A Survey and Some Figures." *The Tablet: International Catholic News Weekly*, October 16, 1937.

Husenbeth, Frederick. *The Life of the Right Reverend John Milner, D.D., Bishop of Castabala: Vicar Apostolic of the Midland District of England, F.S.A. London, and Cath. Acad. Rome*. Dublin: Duffy, 1862.

Hurley, Michael, ed. *John Wesley's Letter to a Roman Catholic*. Belfast: Epworth, 1967.

Hunter, Frederick. *John Wesley and the Coming Comprehensive Church*. London: Epworth, 1968.

Hynson, Leon. "Human Liberty as Divine Right: A Study in the Political Maturation of John Wesley." *Journal of Church and State* 25 (1983) 57–85.

———. "John Wesley and Political Reality." *Methodist History* 12 (1973) 37–42.

Ingle, Stephen. *The British Party System: An Introduction*. 4th ed. London: Routledge, 2008.

Jackson, Thomas. *The Life of the Rev. Charles Wesley, M.A., Sometime Student of Christ-Church, Oxford: Comprising A Review of His Poetry; Sketches of the Rise and Progress of Methodism; with Notices of Contemporary Events and Characters*. 2 vols. London: Mason, 1841.

Jacob, E. F. "Wilkins's *Concilia* and the Fifteenth Century." *Transactions of the Royal Historical Society* 15 (1932) 91–131.

James, Nancy, ed. *The Complete Madam Guyon*. Brewster: Paraclete, 2007.

Jeffrey, F. *Irish Methodism: An Historical Account of the Traditions, Theology, and Influence*. Belfast: Epworth, 1964.

Jenkinson, Matthew. *Culture and Politics at the Court of Charles II, 1660–1685*. Woodbridge: Boydell & Brewer, 2010.

Jennings, Theodore W., Jr. "John Wesley." In *Empire and the Christian Tradition: New Readings of Classical Theologians*, edited by K. Puilan et al., 256–69. Minneapolis: Fortress, 2007.

———. "John Wesley against Aldersgate." *Quarterly Review* 8 (1988) 3–22.

Jones, David Ceri, et al. *The Elect Methodists: Calvinistic Methodism in England and Wales, 1735–1811*. Cardiff: University of Wales Press, 2012.

Jonsen, Albert R., and Stephen Toulmin. *The Abuse of Casuistry: A History of Moral Reasoning*. Oakland: University of California Press, 1988.

Johnson, Lionel. *The Gordon Riots*. London: Catholic Truth Society, n. d.

Keeble, G. H. *Richard Baxter: Puritan Man of Letters*. Oxford: Clarendon, 1982.

Kent, John. *Wesley and the Wesleyans: Religion in Eighteenth-Century Britain.* Cambridge: Cambridge University Press, 2002.

Kerr, Aaron K. "John and Charles Wesley's Hymns on the Lord's Supper (1745): Their Meaning for Methodist Ecclesial Identity and Ecumenical Dialogue." PhD diss., Duquesne University, 2007.

Khoo, Lorna Lock-Nah, *Wesleyan Eucharistic Spirituality: Its Nature, Sources and Future.* Hindmarsh: ATF, 2005.

King, John N. *Foxe's "Book of Martyrs" and Early Modern Print Culture.* Cambridge: Cambridge University Press, 2006.

Kirkham, Donald Henry. "John Wesley's 'Calm Address': The Response of the Critics." *Methodist History* 14 (1975) 13–23.

————. "Pamphlet Opposition to Methodism: The Eighteenth-Century Evangelical Revival Under Attack." PhD diss., Duke University, 1973.

Langford, P. "Tories and Jacobites 1714–1751." In *The History of the University of Oxford: The Eighteenth Century,* edited by L. S. Sutherland and L. G. Mitchell, 99–128, vol. 5 in *The History of the University of Oxford,* 8 vols., edited by T. H. Aston. Oxford: Clarendon, 1986.

Lee, Philip H. "Thomas Maxfield." *PWHS* 21 (1938) 161–63.

Leites, Edmund, ed. *Conscience and Casuistry in Early Modern Europe.* Cambridge: Cambridge University Press, 1988.

Lehemerg, Stanford E. *The Reformation Parliament 1529–1536.* Cambridge: Cambridge University Press, 1970.

Lenton, John H. "British Preachers in Ireland and Irish Preachers in Britain: The Importance of the Irish Dimension in the 18th Century." *Bulletin of the Methodist Historical Society of Ireland* 16 (2011) 5–38.

————. *John Wesley's Preachers: A Social and Statistical Analysis of the British and Irish Preachers Who Entered the Methodist Itinerancy before 1791.* Milton Keynes: Paternoster, 2009.

Lewis, Simon. "The Mock Preacher: More than Just an Anti-Methodist Play?" *PWHS* 59 (2014) 178–85.

————. "A 'Papal Emissary?' George Whitefield and Anti-Methodist Allegations of Popery, C.1738–C.1750." *Journal of Religious History, Literature and Culture* 1 (2015) 16–34.

Lim, Paul Chang-Ha. *In Pursuit of Purity: Unity, and Liberty: Richard Baxter's Puritan Ecclesiology in Its Seventeenth-Century Context.* Leiden: Brill Academic, 2004.

Livingstone, E. A., ed. *The Concise Oxford Dictionary of the Christian Church.* 3rd ed. Oxford: Oxford University Press, 2006.

Locke, Kenneth A. The *Church in Anglican Theology: An Historical, Theological, and Ecumenical Exploration.* Aldershot: Ashgate, 2009.

Lowery, Kevin Twain. *Salvaging Wesley's Agenda: A New Paradigm for Wesleyan Virtue Ethics.* Eugene: Pickwick, 2008.

Lunn, Julie Ann. "'Simply Resign'd and Lost in God': Resignation and Sanctification in the Hymns of Charles Wesley." PhD diss., 2 vols., University of Durham, 2016.

Lyles, Albert M. "The Hostile Reaction to the American Views of Johnson and Wesley." *Journal of the Rutgers University Library* 24 (1960) 1–14.

————. *Methodism Mocked: The Satiric Reaction to Methodism in the Eighteenth Century.* London: Epworth, 1960.

Mack, Phyllis. *Heart Religion in the Enlightenment: Gender and Emotion in Early Methodism*. Cambridge: Cambridge University Press, 2008.

Massa, Mark, SJ. "The Catholic Wesley: A Revisionist Prolegomenon." *Methodist History* 22 (1983) 38–53.

Maddox, Randy, ed. *Aldersgate Reconsidered*. Nashville: Kingswood, 1990.

———. "John Wesley's Earliest Defence of the Emerging Revival in Bristol." *Wesley and Methodist Studies* 6 (2014) 124–53.

———. "John Wesley's Reading Evidence in the Kingswood School Archives." *Methodist History* 41 (2003) 49–67.

———. "John Wesley's Reading Evidenced in the Book Collection at Wesley's House, London." *Methodist History* 41 (2003) 118–33.

———. "Opinion, Religion, and 'Catholic Spirit': John Wesley on Theological Integrity." *Asbury Theological Journal* 47 (1992) 63–88.

———. *Responsible Grace: John Wesley's Practical Theology*. Nashville: Kingswood, 1994.

Maltby, Judith. *Prayer Book and People in Elizabethan and Stuart England*. Cambridge: Cambridge University Press, 2000.

Marotti, Arthur F., ed. *Catholicism and Anti-Catholicism in Early Modern English Texts*. London: Macmillan, 1999.

McCalman, Ian, et al., eds. *The Oxford Companion to the Romantic Age*. Oxford: Oxford University Press, 1999.

McLynn, Frank. *Bonnie Prince Charlie: Charles Edward Stuart*. 2nd ed. New York: Random House, 2011.

McGonigle, Herbert B. "John Wesley: Exemplar of Catholic Spirit." In *Ecumenism and History: Studies in Honour of John H. Y. Briggs*, edited by Anthony R. Cross, 50–68. Cambria: Paternoster, 2002.

McLoughlin, T. O. *Contesting Ireland: Irish Voices against England in the Eighteenth Century*. Dublin: Four Courts, 1999.

MacKnight, Thomas. *The Life of Henry St. John, Viscount Bolingbroke*. London: Chapman and Hall, 1863.

Macquiban, Timothy, ed. *Pure Universal Love: Reflections on the Wesleys and Inter-Faith Dialogue*. Oxford: Applied Theology, 1995.

McCormack, Matthew. "Supporting Civil Power: Citizen Soldiers and the Gordon Riots." *London Journal* 37 (2012) 27–41.

McInelly, Brett C. *Textual Warfare and the Making of Methodism*. Oxford: Oxford University Press, 2014.

Marshall, John. *John Locke, Toleration and Early Enlightenment Culture*. Cambridge: Cambridge University Press, 2006.

Matthew, H. C. G., and Brian Harrison, eds. *Oxford Dictionary of National Biography*, 60 vols. Online ed. Oxford: Oxford University Press, 2004–.

Middleton, Paul. *Martyrs: A Guide for the Perplexed*. London: Bloomsbury, 2011.

Monk, Robert C. *John Wesley: His Puritan Heritage*. 2nd ed. Lantham: Scarecrow, 1999.

Monod, Paul Kléber. *Jacobitism and the English People, 1688–1788*. Cambridge: Cambridge University Press, 1989.

Morgan, James. *The Life of Thomas Walsh, Composed in Great Part from His Own Accounts*. Ottawa: Holiness Movement, 1906.

New, Alfred H. *Memoir of Selina, Countess of Huntingdon*. Revised ed. New York: Protestant Episcopal Society for the Promotion of Evangelical Knowledge, 1858.

Newport, Kenneth C. G. "Charles Wesley in Ireland." *Proceedings of the Charles Wesley Society* 19 (2015) 15–27.

———. "Revelation 13 and the Papal Antichrist in Eighteenth-Century England: A Study in New Testament *Eisegesis*." *Bulletin of the John Rylands Library* 79 (1997) 143–60.

Newton, John A. *Methodism and Puritans*. London: Williams's Trust, 1964.

———. "Samuel Annesley (1620–1696)." *PWHS* 25 (1985) 29–44.

Nockles, Peter. "The Changing Legacy and Reception of John Foxe's Book of Martyrs in the Long Eighteenth Century: Varies of Anglican, Protestant, and Catholic Response c. 1760 – c. 1850." In *Religion, Politics, and Dissent 1660–1832, Essays in Honour of James E. Bradley*, edited by Robert D. Cornwall and William Gibson, 219–50. Aldershot: Ashgate, 2010.

———. "Charles Wesley, Catholicism, and Anti-Catholicism." In *Charles Wesley: Life, Literature, & Legacy*, edited by Ted A. Campbell and Kenneth C. G. Newport, 141–65. London: Epworth, 2007.

———. "Church Parties in the Pre-Tractarian Church of England, 1750–1833: The 'Orthodox': Some Problems of Definition and Identity." In *The Church of England, c. 1689 – c. 1833: From Toleration to Tractarianism*, edited by John Walsh et al., 334–59. Cambridge: Cambridge University Press, 1993.

———. "'Emissaries of Babylon' or 'Brothers in Christ,' Charles Wesley and Anti-Catholicism." *Wesley and Methodist Studies* 2 (2010) 3–23.

———. *The Oxford Movement in Context: Anglican High Churchmanship, 1760–1857*. Cambridge: Cambridge University Press, 1994.

———. "Reactions to Robert Southey's *Life of Wesley* (1820) Reconsidered." *Journal of Ecclesiastical History* 63 (2012) 61–80.

Noll, Mark A., et al., eds. *Evangelicalism: Comparative Studies of Popular Protestantism in North America, the British Isles and Beyond, 1700–1799*. Oxford: Oxford University Press, 1994.

Norris, Clive Henry. *The Financing of John Wesley's Methodism c.1740–1800*. Oxford: Oxford University Press, 2017.

Norman, Edward. *Roman Catholicism in England from the Elizabethan Settlement to the Second Vatican Council*. Oxford: Oxford University Press, 1985.

Ó Ciardha, Eamon. *Ireland and the Jacobite Cause, 1685–1766: A Fatal Attachment*. Dublin: Four Courts, 2002.

Oliver, Leslie M. "The Seventh Edition of John Foxe's *Acts and Monuments*." *The Papers of the Bibliographical Society of America* 37 (1943) 245–47.

Ollard, S. L., and Gordon Crosse, eds. *A Dictionary of English Church History*. London: Mowbry and Co., 1912.

Olson, Mark. "Exegeting Aldersgate: John Wesley's Interpretation of 24 May 1738." PhD diss., University of Manchester/Nazarene Theological College, 2015.

O'Malley, John, ed. *The First Jesuits*. Cambridge: Harvard University Press, 1995.

Padberg, John W., SJ. "Ignatius, the Popes, and Realistic Reverence." *Studies in the Spirituality of Jesuits* 25 (1993) 1–38.

Palgrave, Reginald F. D. "A Slander upon John Wesley." *The Leisure Hour* (1899) 383–86.

Patterson, W. B. *William Perkins and the Making of a Protestant England*. Oxford: Oxford University Press, 2014.

Piette, Maxim. *John Wesley in the Evolution of Protestantism*. Translated by J. B. Howard. London: Sheed & Ward, 1937.

Podmore, Colin. "The Fetter Lane Society 1739–1740." *PWHS* 47 (1990) 156–85.

———. *The Moravian Church in England, 1728–1760.* Oxford: Clarendon, 1998.

Priest, Stephen. *The British Empiricists.* 2nd ed. New York: Routledge, 2007.

Puilan, K., D. Compier, and J. Rieger, eds. *Empire and the Christian Tradition.* Minneapolis: Fortress, 2007.

Rack, Henry D. "Between Church and Sect: The Origins of Methodism in Manchester." *Bulletin of the John Rylands Library* 80 (1998) 65–88.

———. "A Man of Reason and Religion? Wesley and the Enlightenment." *Wesley and Methodist Studies* 1 (2009) 1–17.

———. "Methodism and Romanticism." *PWHS* 45 (1985) 64–65.

———. *Reasonable Enthusiast: John Wesley and the Rise of Methodism.* 3rd ed. London: Epworth, 2002.

Reed, Ralph. "From Riots to Revivalism: The Gordon Riots of 1780, Methodist Hymnody and the Halevy Thesis revisited." *Methodist History* 26 (1988) 172–87.

Rivers, Isabel. "John Wesley as Editor and Publisher." In *The Cambridge Companion to John Wesley*, edited by Randy Maddox and Jason Vickers, 144–59. Cambridge: Cambridge University Press, 2009.

———. *Reason, Grace, and Sentiment: A Study of the Language of Religion and Ethics in England, 1660–1780, Volume 1: Whichcote to Wesley.* Cambridge: Cambridge University Press, 1991.

———. *Vanity Fair and the Celestial City: Dissenting, Methodist, and Evangelical Literary Culture in England 1720–1800.* Oxford: Oxford University Press, 2018.

Roberts, Griffith T. "John Acourt." *PWHS* 27 (1949) 70–72.

Ronneburg, David. *The Effects of Historical and Economic Changes from 1746 to 1886 on Gaelic Society.* Munich: Grin, 1999.

Rogal, Samuel J. *John Wesley in Ireland 1747–89.* 2 vols. Lampeter: Mellen, 1993.

Ross, Ian Campbell. "Was Berkeley a Jacobite? Passive Obedience Revisited." *Eighteenth-Century Ireland* 20 (2005) 17–30.

Rudé, Gordon F. E. "The Gordon Riots: A Study of the Rioters and their Victims." *Transactions of the Royal Historical Society* 6 (1956) 93–112.

Rupp, Ernest Gordon. *Religion in England, 1688–1791.* Oxford: Clarendon, 1986.

Schlenther, Boyd Stanley. *Queen of the Methodists: The Countess of Huntingdon and the Eighteenth-Century Crisis of Faith and Society.* Durham: Durham Academic, 1997.

Schwenk, James L. *Catholic Spirit: Wesley, Whitefield, and the Quest for Evangelical Unity in Eighteenth-Century British Methodism.* Lanham: Scarecrow, 2008.

Scudi, Abbi Turner. *The Sacheverell Affair.* New York: Columbia, 1939.

Selén, Mats. *The Oxford Movement and Wesleyan Methodism in England, 1833–1882.* Lund: Lund University Press, 1992.

Semmel, Bernard. *The Methodist Revolution.* New York: Basic, 1973.

Seymour, A. C. H. *The Life and Times of Selina, Countess of Huntingdon.* 2 vols. London: Painter, 1840.

Simon, John S. *John Wesley and the Advance of Methodism.* London: Epworth, [1925].

———. *John Wesley: The Last Phase.* London: Epworth, 1934.

Snape, Michael. *Redcoats and Religion: The Forgotten History of the British Soldier from the Age of Marlborough to the Eve of the First World War.* New York: Routledge, 2005.

Smith, Bonnie, ed. *The Oxford Encyclopedia of Women in World History.* 4 vols. Oxford: Oxford University Press, 2008.

Smith, William. *A Consecutive History of the Rise, Progress, and Present State of Wesleyan Methodism in Ireland*. Dublin: Dootlittle, 1830.

Sorabji, Richard. *Moral Conscience through the Ages: Fifth Century B.C.E. to the Present*. Oxford: Oxford University Press, 2014.

South, Malcolm H. *The Jesuits and the Joint Mission to England during 1580–1581*. Lewiston: Mellen, 1999.

Southey, Robert. *The Life of Wesley and the Rise and Progress of Methodism*. 2 vols. London: Longman, Hurst, Rees, Orme, and Brown, 1820.

Sowerby, Scott. *Making Toleration: The Repealers and the Glorious Revolution*. Cambridge: Harvard University Press, 2013.

Stark, David Thomas. "'The Peculiar Doctrine Committed to Our Trust': Ideal and Identity in the First Wesleyan Holiness Revival, 1758–1763." PhD diss., University of Manchester/Nazarene Theological College, 2011.

Stevens, Abel. *The History of the Religious Movement of the Eighteenth Century Called Methodism*. 2 vols. New York: Carlton and Porter, 1860.

Stevenson, John. *Popular Disturbances in England, 1700–1832*. New York: Longman, 1992.

Stone, Ronald H. *John Wesley's Life and Ethics*. Nashville: Abingdon, 2001.

Strong, Rowan. *Anglicanism and the British Empire, c. 1700–1850*. Oxford: Oxford University Press, 2007.

Sutherland, L. S., et al., eds. *The History of the University of Oxford: The Eighteenth Century*. Vol. 5 in *The History of the University of Oxford*, 8 vols., edited by T. H. Aston. Oxford: Clarendon, 1986.

Szechi, Daniel. *1715: The Great Jacobite Rebellion*. New Haven: Yale University Press, 2006.

———. *The Jacobites: Britain and Europe, 1688–1788*. Manchester: University of Manchester Press, 1994.

———. "Retrieving Captain Le Cocq's Plunder." In *Loyalty and Identity: Jacobites at Home and Abroad*, edited by Paul Monod et al., 98–119. New York: Palgrave Macmillan, 2010.

Taggart, Norman W. "Methodists and Roman Catholics: Irish Methodist Perspectives in the Nineteenth Century." *Bulletin of the Wesley Historical Society of Ireland* 8 (2002) 4–19.

Taunton, Ethelred Luke. *The History of the Jesuits in England, 1580–1773*. London: Methuen & Co., 1901.

Thomas, Keith. *Religion and the Decline of Magic*. London: Weidenfield and Nicolson, 1971.

Thompson, E. P. *The Making of the English Working Class*. New York: Random House, 1963.

Truesdale, Al. "John Wesley: Inspiration for an Anti-Catholic Mob?" In *Via Media Philosophy: Holiness unto Truth: Intersections between Wesleyan and Roman Catholic Voices*, edited by Bryan L. Williams, 28–42. Cambridge: Cambridge Scholars, 2005.

Tucker, Karen Westerfield. "Polemic against Stillness in the Hymns of the Lord's Supper." *Bulletin of the John Rylands Library* 88 (2006) 101–19.

Turner, John Munsey. *Conflict and Reconciliation: Studies in Methodism and Ecumenism in England 1740–1982*. London: Epworth, 1985.

Tyerman, Luke. *The Life of the Rev. George Whitefield, B.A., of Pembroke College*. 2 vols. New York: Anson D. F. Randolph & Co., 1877.

———. *The Life and Times of the Rev. John Wesley, M.A., Founder of the Methodists*. 3 vols. New York: Harper & Brothers, 1870.

———. *The Life and Times of the Rev. Samuel Wesley, M.A., Rector of Epworth and Father of John and Charles Wesley, the Founders of Methodism*. London: Simpkin, 1866.

———. *The Oxford Methodists: Memoirs of the Messrs. Clayton, Ingham, Gambold, Hervey and Broughton, with Biographical Notices of Others*. London: Hodder and Stoughton, 1872.

Tyson, John R., and Boyd S. Schlenther. *In the Midst of Early Methodism: Lady Huntingdon and Her Correspondence*. Latham: Scarecrow, 2006.

———. *The Way of the Wesleys: A Short Introduction*. Grand Rapids: Eerdmans, 2014.

Vaudry, Richard W. *Anglicans and the Atlantic World: High Churchmen, Evangelicals, and the Quebec Connection*. Montreal: McGill-Queen's University Press, 2003.

Vickers, Jason E. *Wesley: A Guide for the Perplexed*. London: T&T Clark, 2009.

Vickers, John A. Review of *Methodists and Papists*, by David Butler. *PWHS* 50 (1995) 118–20.

Wakefield, Gordon. *Puritan Devotion: Its Place in the Development of Christian Piety*. Eugene: Wipf and Stock, 2015.

Walmsley, Robert. "John Wesley's Parents: Quarrel and Reconciliation." *PWHS* 29 (1953) 50–7.

Wallace, Charles, Jr. "'Some Stated Employment of Your Mind': Reading, Writing, and Religion in the Life of Susanna Wesley." *Church History* 58 (1989) 354–66.

Walsh, John. "Methodism and the Mob." In *Popular Belief and Practice*, edited by G. J. Cuming and Derek Baker, 213–27. Studies in Church History 8. Cambridge: Cambridge University Press, 1972.

Walsh, John, et al., eds. *The Church of England c. 1689 – c. 1833, From Toleration to Tractarianism*. Cambridge: Cambridge University Press, 1993.

Watson, Douglas. *Fallacies Arising from Ambiguity*. New York: Springer Science and Math Media, 2013.

Watson, Richard. *Life of John Wesley: Founder of the Methodist Societies*. 1st American ed. with translations and notes by John Emory. New York: Carlton & Phillips, 1853.

Ward, W. R. *Georgian Oxford: University Politics in the Eighteenth Century*. Oxford: Clarendon, 1958.

———. *The Protestant Evangelical Awakening*. Cambridge: Cambridge University Press, 2002.

———. "Was There a Methodist Evangelistic Strategy in the Eighteenth Century?" In *England's Long Reformation 1500–1800*, edited by Nicholas Tyacke, 285–306. London: UCL, 1998.

Weber, Theodore. *Politics in the Order of Salvation: Transforming Wesleyan Political Ethics*. Nashville: Kingswood, 2001.

Wilson, Kathleen. *The Sense of the People: Politics, Culture, and Imperialism in England, 1715–1785*. Cambridge: Cambridge University Press, 1998.

Winter, Sean, ed. *Immense, Unfathomed, Unconfined: The Grace of God in Creation, Church and Community: Essays in Honor of Norman Young*. Melbourne: Uniting Academic, 2013.

Wolderstorff, Nicholas. *John Locke and the Ethics of Belief.* Cambridge: Cambridge University Press, 1996.

Wood, Darren Cushman. "John Wesley's Use of the Atonement." *Asbury Theological Journal* 62 (2007) 55–70.

Wood, Joseph Allen. "Tensions between Evangelical Theology and the Established Church: John Wesley's Ecclesiology." PhD diss., University of Manchester/Nazarene Theological College, 2012.

Wright, Robert. *A Memoir of General James Oglethorpe: One of the Earliest Reformers of Prison Discipline in England and the Founder of Georgia, in America.* London: Chapman and Hall, 1867.

Wynkoop, Mildred Bangs. "John Wesley–Mentor or Guru?" *WTJ* 10 (1975) 5–14.

Yates, Kelly Diehl. "Jeffrey the Jacobite Poltergeist: The Politics of the Ghost that Haunted the Epworth Rectory in 1716–17." *WTJ* 50 (2015) 68–79.

———. "'Perhaps He Cannot Know': John Wesley's Use of Doubt as a Principle of His Catholic Spirit." In *Doubting Christianity: The Church and Doubt*, edited by Frances Andrews et al., 331–37. Studies in Church History 52. Cambridge: Cambridge University Press, 2016.

Yates, Nigel. *Eighteenth-Century Britain: Religion and Politics, 1714–1815.* London: Routledge, 2014.

Index